Everyday Nationalism

THE ETHNOGRAPHY OF POLITICAL VIOLENCE

Cynthia Keppley Mahmood, Series Editor

A complete list of books in the series is available from the publisher.

Everyday Nationalism

Women of the Hindu Right in India

Kalyani Devaki Menon

PENN

University of Pennsylvania Press

Philadelphia

Published by
University of Pennsylvania Press
Philadelphia, Pennsylvania 19104-4112

Printed in the United States of America on acid-free paper
10 9 8 7 6 5 4 3 2 1

Library of Congress Cataloging-in-Publication Data
Menon, Kalyani Devaki.
    Everyday nationalism : women of the Hindu right in India / Kalyani Devaki Menon.
        p.   cm.—(The ethnography of political violence)
    Includes bibliographical references and index.
    ISBN 978-0-8122-4196-9 (alk. paper)
    1. Hindu women—India—Delhi—Social conditions.   2. Hindu women—
India—Delhi—Political activity.   3. Nationalism—India—Delhi.   4. Rashtra Sevika
Samiti (Organization)   5. Hinduism and politics—India—Delhi.   6. Muslims—
India—Delhi.   7. India—politics and government—1977—   I. Title.
HQ1173.M46   2009
305.48′6970954—dc22   2009018798

Contents

Note on Transliteration   vii

Introduction   1

Chapter One: Everyday Histories   26

Chapter Two: National Insecurities   54

Chapter Three: Violent Dharma   80

Chapter Four: Benevolent Hindus   105

Chapter Five: Fun, Games, and Deadly Politics   131

Chapter Six: Acceptable Transgressions   157

Notes   183

Glossary   193

Bibliography   195

Index   213

Acknowledgments   221

Note on Transliteration

In order to make this book accessible to a wide audience, I have chosen to use common spellings for Hindi words used in the text. Diacritical transliterations are available in the glossary. I have italicized all the Hindi and Urdu words used in the text. While the names of most books have been italicized, the names of sacred texts like the Bhagavad Gita have not been italicized. Quotations from sacred texts are cited by chapter and verse. The particular translation has only been identified on the first reference by translator's name and date; however, all subsequent uses of the text are from the same translation.

Introduction

"What is the point of building a Ram temple on the blood of so many Indians? It is meaningless." Ela Dube, a member of the Hindu nationalist organization Sewa Bharati, raised this rhetorical question in October 1999.[1] Although she did not know me, like many other Hindu nationalist women I met while conducting fieldwork in Delhi in 1999, Ela did not hesitate to meet me and generously invited me into her home in a Delhi Development Authority Middle Income Group colony to talk to her. It was Navaratri, the Hindu festival that marks the slaying of the buffalo demon Mahisasura by the goddess. Auspiciously dressed in a red blouse and a bright yellow sari, Ela had spent the morning doing *puja* (worship). As a pious Hindu woman, she was fasting but insisted on serving me tea and biscuits as she told me of her involvement with the movement, her own political views, and the work that she does as a member of Sewa Bharati.

Like many of the women I worked with, Ela came from a family with strong connections to the Rashtriya Swayamsevak Sangh (RSS), the all male paramilitary organization that is the ideological core of the Hindu nationalist movement. Born and raised in Banaras, Ela informed me that her father had gone against her grandfather's wishes to insist that his three daughters attend university. After completing her degree at Banaras Hindu University, Ela became a teacher in Faridabad, where she lived with her husband and sons until 1993 when they moved to Delhi. In Delhi she started her own school in a *jhuggi* (makeshift hut) in the slums near her housing colony that, by 1999, had blossomed into a 140-student school in a permanent building. It was here that she was approached by Sewa Bharati and asked to join the organization. Given her long association with the RSS, and her belief that its members are true *desh bhakts* (patriots) committed to Vedic values, she readily agreed. She is now in charge of one of the zonal subdivisions of the Delhi wing of the organization.

I was surprised to hear her say that it was meaningless to build a temple to the Hindu god Ram "on the blood of so many Indians," because during our conversation that afternoon Ela had spoken in the most glowing terms of the RSS and the Vishwa Hindu Parishad (VHP). The

VHP spearheaded the Ramjanmabhumi movement to build the Ramjan-mabhumi temple in Ayodhya at the spot that they claimed marked Ram's birthplace.[2] Contending that the Mughal Emperor Babur (1483–1530) had destroyed a Ram temple to build his mosque, the Babri Masjid, the VHP rallied Hindu nationalists in the eighties to destroy the mosque and build a temple in its place. Amid the violent conflagrations that flared up between Hindus and Muslims, the Ramjanmabhumi movement enabled the VHP to consolidate a base of support, particularly among middle-/upper-caste north Indian Hindus. While violence played an integral role not only in consolidating community, but also in catapulting Hindu nationalists from the margins of Indian politics in the early 1980s to leading the national government in the late nineties (1998–2004), Ela questions these tactics in her conversation with me.

Uttered seven years after Hindu nationalists destroyed the mosque on December 6, 1992, and a little over a year after they came into power at the national level, Ela's words transgress Hindu nationalist politics and, in so doing, constitute a dissonant act within the movement. These acts, inflected by and evocative of other norms and discourses, transgress the ideological norms of the movement and consequently fail to provide a seamless reproduction of its ideology. While most Hindu nationalists believe that the violent politics of the Ramjanmabhumi movement constitute the first necessary steps toward reclaiming India as a Hindu nation, Ela is a dissonant subject who is committed to Hindu nationalism, but cannot condone the violence and bloodshed instigated by the destruction of the mosque. Transgressing the normative constructions of Hindu nationalist ideology, Ela told me that it was more fitting to build a hospital on this desecrated site than to give in to the demands of the extremists within the Hindu nationalist movement who had allowed, and even encouraged, the blood-drenched politics of the Ramjanmabhumi temple.

Here I identify Ela as a dissonant subject to draw attention to her transgression of a Hindu nationalist norm. However, it is important to note that in other ways she resembled many of the women I worked with in Delhi and diligently reproduced the normative constructions of the movement in her work for Sewa Bharati. Like other Hindu nationalist women, she was worried that Hindu "Vedic" values were being lost to "westernization" (*paschimi sabhyata*). In our conversation that afternoon she also expressed her suspicion of the morality and motives of Muslims and Christians in India. Thus, while Ela challenges a central item on their political agenda—the building of the Ramjanmabhumi temple "on the blood of so many Indians"—she clearly embraces views that are fundamental to the Hindu nationalist movement's ideology and politics in India. By calling Ela a dissonant subject, I am not suggesting that she is consciously subverting the movement's goals or resisting its larger ideological agenda. Rather, I am drawing attention to the everyday acts that complicate our analysis of Hindu nationalist subjects who may strive to reproduce the movement's norms, but occasionally transgress them to become, however temporarily, dissonant subjects. Making sense of their dissonant moments—when Hindu nationalist subjects fail to perform Hindu nationalist norms—and the ways the movement deals with such failed performances of prescribed subjectivities is critical to understanding the fraught and complex reproduction and expansion of Hindu nationalism.

Ela is one of many women involved in the Hindu nationalist movement, a family of organizations linked to the RSS (Sangh Parivar), which is committed to establishing India as a Hindu nation.[3] Since the 1980s the movement has shifted from the margins to the center of Indian politics, with its electoral wing the Bharatiya Janata Party (BJP) leading the national government in coalition with other parties from 1998 until 2004. Most Hindu nationalists claim a primordial connection between religion and territory, arguing that India is both their motherland and their sacred land (Map 1). They not only see Islam and Christianity as religions foreign to India, but also suggest that these religions have oppressed Hindus and defiled the sacred soil of the nation. Hindu nationalists have engaged in extreme violence against Muslims and Christians in India, most notably in 2002 when thousands of Muslims were killed by Hindu mobs on a rampage in Gujarat. They justify their violent engagement with religious minorities in India by portraying themselves as victims of religious persecution and political aggression. While they accuse Christian missionaries of engaging in antinational activities and tricking Hindus into converting out of the fold, they accuse Muslims of having persecuted Hindus for centuries and, increasingly in the present, of their alleged connections to Islamic militants in Kashmir and elsewhere. Yet, although most of those I worked with mobilized these constructions of the past and the present to legitimize Hindu nationalist violence against Indian Muslims and Christians, a few like Ela disagreed. Indeed, Ela's dissonant voice defies any attempt to homogenize a movement that while presenting multiple fronts as it reaches out to the diverse groups that mark the plural landscapes of modern India, also has to struggle to keep dissonance in check.

Ela is one of several Hindu nationalist women I worked with while conducting fieldwork in Delhi from January 1999 until January 2000. These women belonged to multiple wings of the Hindu nationalist movement, each affiliated with one of three well-recognized Hindu nationalist organizations—the Rashtriya Swayamsevak Sangh (RSS), the Bharatiya Janata Party (BJP), and the Vishwa Hindu Parishad (VHP).[4]

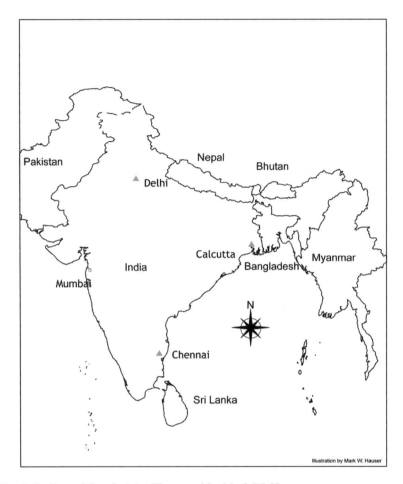

Map 1. India and South Asia. Illustrated by Mark W. Hauser.

For the women I worked with, the RSS formed the ideological core of Hindu nationalism from which the other organizations branched out in different directions.[5] Indeed, many came from RSS families and were encouraged by them to join women's wings of the Hindu nationalist movement. The women's wing explicitly linked to the exclusively male RSS is the Rashtra Sevika Samiti (Samiti). Like the RSS that runs daily *shakhas* (branches) for the ideological and physical training of male youth, the Samiti runs weekly *shakhas* for girls and young women. Additionally, many of my interlocutors belonged to Durga Vahini or Matri Shakti, women's groups associated with the VHP. These VHP women, along with female ascetics belonging to another VHP affiliate, the Sadhvi Shakti Parishad, were extremely active and visible in the Ramjanmab-humi movement spearheaded by the VHP. I also worked with women in Mahila Morcha, the women's group affiliated with the BJP, the electoral wing of the Hindu nationalist movement that has been a major player on the Indian political scene.[6] Finally, several of the women I worked with belonged to Sewa Bharati, an organization whose Delhi wing focuses primarily on the uplift of the urban poor through, for instance, providing education and vocational training to impoverished communi-ties.[7] While women are rooted in one of these organizations, they fre-quently affiliate with others either simultaneously or successively. These different organizations provide varying façades for the Hindu nationalist movement, which enable its expansionary politics.

I am interested in the expansionary strategies through which women in different wings of the movement recruit support in the plural land-scapes of modern India. These expansionary strategies include the proc-esses through which activists articulate the needs, desires, fears, agendas, and interests of diverse audiences with the goals of the movement in order to craft a mass base that enables the dominance of Hindu nation-alism in India. While others have examined the varied interventions of organizations within the Hindu nationalist movement,[8] I want to enrich our understanding of the Hindu right in contemporary India ethno-graphically by focusing on the everyday constructions of ideology and politics through which activists garner support at the grassroots level. I look at how they use history, religion, politics, and social work to articu-late the everyday fears, desires, needs, and interests of diverse groups with the movement's goals.

As a result of these expansionary strategies, those recruited into the movement joined for multiple reasons and did not embrace an identical politics or vision. It is the ability to absorb these different positions and encompass different agendas that has enabled the Hindu nationalist movement's swift ascendance on the sociopolitical landscape of India. However, while the movement might bring diverse individuals into its embrace, this does not necessarily mean that all perspectives are equally valued. Indeed, there are normative constructions within the Hindu nationalist movement that are diligently reproduced by activists in their everyday work for the movement. Much of the pluralism in Hindu nationalism is consonant with these normative constructions. However, sometimes women like Ela engage in acts that clearly transgress them in particular contexts, even though they may strive to meet these expecta-tions at other times, in other aspects of their lives, and in their work for the movement. I call these women dissonant subjects when they trans-gress Hindu nationalism—by failing to perform Hindu nationalist norms and evoking other ways of being and knowing—to draw attention to their moments of dissonance, which, I contend, are analytically important. While several scholars have examined the normative constructions of Hindu nationalism, I believe that we must also look at moments of dissonance when Hindu nationalists become dissonant subjects, for what they reveal about the everyday compromises the movement must make to continue its expansion across the sociopolitical landscape of the country.

Centering Women in Hindu Nationalism

Hindu nationalist women are extremely visible in the movement. The women I worked with were participants in rallies and protests, ran schools and training camps, conducted social work at hospitals and in low-income areas, and organized and participated in religious events throughout Delhi. While men in Hindu nationalist groups engage in similar activities, it is important to pay attention to the highly gendered ways in which women participate in the movement, disseminate its ideology, and, most critically, use their gendered positions to recruit other women into the movement. Indeed, a gendered analysis of Hindu nationalism reveals that women play a central role in building support for the movement as they deploy strategies and networks that may be beyond the reach of men. This ability to use gender-based resources to recruit support for Hindu nationalism underlies their importance, and indeed their visibility, in the movement.

Women's roles in the movement are modeled on their primary role in much of Hindu society, as mothers, wives, and caretakers of their families. While some have resisted the marital norm, in general women are actively discouraged from remaining unmarried. At a Samiti *shakha* in Saket, Meera Saxena, a prominent figure in the BJP, told a room full of young women that it upsets her when girls say to her "Aunty, I don't want to become a mother. I don't have time." In her lecture, she insisted that all women must be mothers even if they are also engineers or doctors. She asked those gathered: how can we expect our culture to survive unless we have children and ensure its passing to the next generation? Meera's words echo a key theme in Hindu nationalist discourse—that women as mothers are responsible for reproducing the Hindu nation and are therefore absolutely central to the movement.

Indeed, it is motherhood that structures the role they are to play in the movement and that grounds their claims to agency and citizenship. As mothers in their families they are responsible for teaching their children Hindu nationalist values and culture. As members of the movement, they are expected to disseminate these values and culture to their larger family of the Hindu nation (see T. Sarkar 1995, 1998; Bacchetta

1996, 2004). As mothers within the patrilineal kinship structures that most belong to, they must be self-sacrificing, virtuous, and subservient to the authority of their husbands. Similarly, as Hindu nationalist women they must privilege the needs of the nation, while always remaining subservient to male authority (A. Basu 1995; Banerjee 1995). The metonymy of family and nation (Mankekar 1999) in Hindu nationalism ensures that women's roles within their biological families are expanded to include the role they play within the wider network of the Hindu nation.

The imaging of women as mothers of the nation enables Hindu nationalist women, many of whom come from very conservative social backgrounds, to be active outside the immediate confines of their biological families. While their participation in the public sphere might not have been tolerated otherwise, their activism in what has been carefully constructed as a moral/religious movement is deemed not only acceptable but necessary, given their roles as cultural reproducers of the nation. It has been suggested that women use traditional sources of female power and religious activities to define a place for themselves in public life in contexts where they are subject to greater controls over their movements because they are viewed as reproducers of the nation and symbols of community honor (Yuval-Davis 1997: 62–67). Pnina Werbner asserts, "women's active citizenship starts from pre-established cultural domains of female power and rightful ownership or responsibility. These culturally defined domains . . . create the conditions of possibility for women's civic activism" (Werbner 1999: 221). Motherhood provides the most dominant "condition of possibility" for Hindu nationalist women's activism in the public sphere.

Women's gender-based roles and responsibilities also open up avenues for the Hindu nationalist movement to intervene in arenas that are traditionally not the sphere of male action. Indeed, as scholars have noted in other contexts, it is because of their gendered roles, and the cultural assumptions embedded in them, that women are sought after and recruited by right-wing movements that may appear, at first glance, to be male-dominated.[9] The pivotal role that Hindu nationalist women play because of their gendered identities became apparent to me when I went to visit Vasanti in her room in the compound of a temple in northwest Delhi that the VHP had arranged for her. As a single woman, living in the temple's compound under the watchful eye of an elderly priest and his family not only gave her security, but also forestalled questions about her moral character that many women from her social background residing outside the protection of their fathers'/husbands' families might have faced. Although she is single, a position available if not encouraged for Hindu nationalist women, Vasanti's activism continues to be informed by gender-based roles and responsibilities and to uphold the norms of female behavior and morality. A member of Durga Vahini, Vasanti was overseeing a VHP project on tribal women. When I visited her, there were five of these women residing in the adjoining room. Vasanti informed me that they were only there temporarily until she found jobs for them as servants in homes in Delhi. In the meantime, Vasanti was training them, teaching them how to cook and clean. We both benefited from this "training," since these women cooked and served lunch and tea as I spent time with Vasanti that day.

Vasanti told me that the VHP helps tribal women find work and keeps them safe when they could be wandering around Delhi for months looking for a job. Yet the VHP also clearly benefits from the services they provide the women. These women enable VHP activists like Vasanti to get in contact with people throughout Delhi and then provide a reason to continue their relationship with these families. Ostensibly checking up on these women and the work they are doing, VHP activists like Vasanti can make multiple visits to these homes, disseminate Hindu nationalist ideas at these venues, and perhaps recruit new members into the movement.

In most middle- and upper-class families in India, women would be primarily responsible for hiring maids and dealing with women like Vasanti who are performing the role of employment agents for the VHP. It is unlikely that a male member of the VHP could make repeated visits to a home to check up on a female servant without raising the suspicions of the employer (male or female). And he certainly would not be able to build the kind of rapport with a female employer that could enable him to disseminate the movement's message and perhaps recruit women into the movement. Thus women like Vasanti play a key role, not only in recruiting other women into the movement, but also in disseminating Hindu nationalist ideas to women they encounter who are primarily responsible for shaping their children's outlook. According to the movement, women, in their roles as mothers can fashion the next generation in ways that further the politics of Hindu nationalism.

Many of the roles performed by women in the movement follow these normative constructions of gender. When I visited a variety of different types of schools for boys and girls run by Sewa Bharati in South Delhi, all the teachers I met were women. Women teachers also ran the day care centers, which take care of preschool children. This is not to say that there are no male teachers in Hindu nationalist schools. Men do teach in these schools, particularly in the rural one-teacher schools, *ekal vidyalayas*, run by the RSS or its affiliates. Yet my experience in the urban context suggests a predominance of women teachers in these Sewa Bharati schools, partly because these jobs are poorly paid and undervalued, and also because teaching is seen as an acceptable vocation for women, blending as it does with their gendered roles in the family. These schools are important sites at which Hindu nationalists produce and reproduce the movement's ideas to others, making women central to the expansionary tactics of the movement.

Although circumscribed within Hindu nationalist constructions of gender, women are empowered by these "gender essentialisms" (Fox 1996: 40), since their participation in the movement gives them a level of independence and authority they might not have otherwise had. Within Hindu nationalism, while women are expected to be subservient to male authority, they are nevertheless understood to be very powerful. As mothers, they have authority over their children, and Hindu nationalist women's organizations seek to teach women to understand this power and use it to further the movement's goals. As members of Hindu nationalist women's groups, they are taught that Hindu women need to be strong and actively engage in Hindu nationalist politics. Clearly distinguishing their engagement from feminist politics, Sneha, an eighteen-year-old college student in charge of one of the zonal divisions of Delhi's Durga Vahini told me, "Girls today want to be free. We ask them, do you want to be free or strong" (*mukti ya shakti*)? The various women's wings of the Hindu nationalist movement did in fact train women to be strong and assertive, skills that were critical to their ability to disseminate Hindu nationalist ideology successfully. As a relatively nonconfrontational person, I was often struck by their willingness to enter into arguments with and challenge those with opposing views. These were women who demanded visibility and voice in public arenas as they vocally participated in Hindu nationalist protests, courted arrest, and, on occasion, violence, to get their messages heard.

For instance, as I accompanied Urvashi Aggarwal, a member of the VHP's Matri Shakti as well as the BJP's Mahila Morcha, on a major public protest in Delhi, I noticed how she and her colleague Jamuna Sinha tried to catch the attention of one of the reporters because they wanted to be interviewed about the protest. Earlier that day, as we were traveling to the site of the protest, Urvashi had told me that she had purposely chosen to wear an old sari because there were always police at these events who not only arrested people, but also used water hoses to disperse crowds. Immediately apprehensive, I said nervously that I had no desire to be arrested. Urvashi laughed at my discomfort and said this was all part of the ritual—the police would simply tell everyone they had been arrested and then set them free shortly thereafter. Urvashi clearly relished the idea of a confrontation with the police, as indeed she desired the visibility that would come from being interviewed by the media. As I watched Urvashi and Jamuna courting the media, and heard the barely suppressed excitement in Urvashi's voice as she talked about the possibility of arrest and water cannons, it became clear to me how much Hindu nationalist women, unlike many in their social worlds, wanted to be seen and heard publicly. Through their assertive presence, women effectively reproduce Hindu nationalist ideology to new audiences that they encounter in their everyday work for the movement.

Women and Everyday Hindu Nationalism

As I followed women around Delhi or engaged in casual conversations with them in their homes or en route to schools, hospitals, programs, meetings, *shakhas*, and protests, I learned a great deal about everyday Hindu nationalism. These everyday articulations of Hindu nationalist ideology by women activists, while sharing much in common with messages promulgated by others in the movement, were necessarily shaped by the daily contingencies faced by women as they conducted their work. They were shaped by particular political events, oppositional individuals, and diverse audiences, the particular trajectory of arguments or conversations, as indeed the fears, insecurities, and exigencies of life in modern India. These articulations should not be understood as adulterated versions of Hindu nationalist ideology. Rather, if we can accept that ideologies are produced in multiple sites—whether in publications, speeches of the movement's leaders, or the narratives of Hindu nationalist women working at the grassroots—then these articulations are important and potentially transformative sites for the production of Hindu nationalist ideologies.

Of central importance in women's everyday narratives is the imaging of self and "other" that provides the axis around which Hindu nationalist ideologies are configured. Women activists used constructions of history, politics, and religion to craft a Hindu nationalist self primordially linked to the nation, as well as a Muslim and sometimes Christian, "other" that posed a threat to the cultural, religious, and political actualization of Hindu nationhood. This concern with constructing self and "other" is similar to other right-wing movements, which Paola Bacchetta and Margaret Power define as those that "differentially draw on, produce, and mobilize naturalized or culturalized self/Other criteria to reify or forge hierarchical differences" (2002: 4). The women I worked with actively circulated such self/other distinctions that not only gave Hindus a privileged claim to the nation, but also fashioned an "other" that Hindus needed to mobilize against.

Like other Hindu nationalists, the women I worked with in Delhi represented the territorial bounds of India as sacred soil, as the very body of the goddess Bharat Mata (Mother India). They conceptualized Hindus as the children of Bharat Mata, an image that implies a primordial link not only between Hindus and the goddess, but also with the geographical boundaries of India. Operating in India's plural religious worlds, women activists utilized the image of Bharat Mata, along with various Hindu rituals, prayers, and discourses, to unify Hindus by crafting a homogeneous "self" for the nation. In so doing, they depicted Hindu nationalism not just as a political but also as a religious movement and appealed to all Hindus regardless of caste, regional, or sectarian affiliation. In their everyday work for the movement, Hindu nationalist women were able to produce and disseminate a new nationalist Hinduism in which Hindu nationalist politics and religious ideas were inextricably linked. Demonstrating how religious imagery gains meaning from social and political fields (see Asad 1983), the women I worked with suggested that it was the *dharma* (sacred duty) of all Hindus to participate in the Hindu nationalist movement to honor Bharat Mata by establishing India as a Hindu nation.

While the image of India as Bharat Mata enabled my interlocutors to construct a Hindu self primordially linked to the nation by blood, culture, religion, and territory, it also allowed them to portray Muslims as cultural, political, and religious "others." Although the earliest Indian Muslim communities were established in the seventh century C.E., well before the modern nation of India was "imagined" (Anderson 1983), for most Hindu nationalists Muslims are either Hindus who have been forcibly converted and corrupted, or foreigners who may be tolerated, but do not belong. In their everyday work for the movement, Hindu nationalist women constructed a historical trajectory that traced Muslim presence in India to a series of invasions from central Asia beginning in the eleventh century, and portrayed a besieged Hindu nation struggling for centuries under the yoke of foreign rule and religious humiliation. This construction of the past is central to the movement's imagination of both Hindu self and Muslim "other," and is vital to the cultural politics of Hindu nationalists today who suggest that Hindus must avenge this past.

While women were adept at fashioning compelling narratives about the Hindu nation and its "others," it is essential to acknowledge that their ability to circulate these ideas successfully was aided by the familiarity of these narratives to the listeners. Indeed, Hindu nationalist constructions of "self" and "other" are entrenched in an earlier politics of difference that saturated the discourses of anticolonial Indian nationalists struggling for independence from British colonial rule. These discourses, which drew liberally on the writings of Orientalist historians, not only influenced British imaginings of India, but also colored Indian nationalist constructions of the nation. In these discourses the nation was essentially a Hindu one that had struggled for centuries under the yoke of foreign tyranny—first Muslim, then British—setting the stage for religious conflict between Hindus and Muslims in colonial and postcolonial India (Eqbal Ahmad in Barsamian 2000: 2–4; P. Chatterjee 1993).[10] Bred in the cradle of colonial rule, this politics of difference not only has generated violence between Hindus and Muslims in the country, but also bolsters Hindu nationalist claims to indigeneity in contemporary India.

Gender and sexuality were pivotal to the narratives of self and "other" produced by the women I worked with, as they were to the politics of difference that emerged in the colonial context (see, e.g., Baber 2000; Gupta 2002). In their everyday work for the movement, women often told stories about the atrocities Muslim rulers had allegedly committed against the Hindu nation, particularly against Hindu women. In their stories, the specter of the Muslim male who has engaged in sexual violence against Hindu women in the past or the present, provides the primary justification for Hindu nationalist violence against the Muslim minority in India today. This imaging of Muslims has been central to Hindu nationalist discourse, most notably in the writings of V. D. Savarkar, an important Hindu nationalist ideologue (Savarkar 1971). Building on Orientalist histories, Savarkar portrayed a glorious Hindu culture made weak and effeminate by centuries of Muslim rule. Savarkar's incendiary writings are imbued with references to sexuality that represent Muslims as "naturally" lascivious, lustful invaders who dishonored Hindu women,[11] while Hindu men are portrayed as feminine— lacking the will and the vigor to put an end to Muslim carnage. Savarkar calls upon Hindu youth to avenge violently an alleged history of violence against Hindu women in order to reclaim their (Hindu men's) masculinity and the vitality of the nation (Savarkar 1971; Agarwal 1995). This gendered construction of history, that perpetuates the logic of revenge, is widely promulgated to young female recruits, and remains central to mobilizing support for the politics and actions of the movement today.

This logic of revenge and concern with reclaiming Hindu masculinity is also crucial to the violence associated with Hindu nationalism today (Bhatt 2001; Bacchetta 2004; Banerjee 2005; Jaffrelot 2007).[12] The Gujarat pogrom of 2002, when over two thousand Muslims were killed by Hindus engaging in extreme forms of violence, particularly sexual violence against women, is a chilling reminder of the deadly power of violent assertions of masculinity. The specter of Muslim violence, and the concomitant concern with Hindu masculinity, also creates a place for women's activism in the public arena, since it suggests that women must develop the strength and skills to defend themselves against attack (Bacchetta 2004).[13] Building on Savarkar's ideas above, women activists argued that Hindu men had become too weak to protect women, and so women needed to develop the strength and skills to defend themselves against attack. In their view, women are not just hapless victims of male aggression, but rather must become agents in the public sphere who claim their rights and space and actively participate in the construction of the nation (Tharu and Niranjana 1999: 513; Banerjee 1995: 218).

While the women I worked with did not directly engage in Hindu nationalist violence against Muslims and Christians, their words and deeds shape and mark this violence in palpable ways.[14] They were actively involved in rousing Hindus to embrace the violent worldview of the movement and participate in its violent politics against religious minorities. Their narratives skillfully draw on the insecurities of the current global moment to create what Arjun Appadurai has called "a fear of small numbers," and generate violence against religious minorities (2006: 6–7).[15] Indeed, it is their everyday images and stories, and the fears and desires they mobilize, that fuel violent conflagrations. It is therefore imperative to understand, as Veena Das has argued, not only that the violent event is "attached to the everyday," but also that the everyday is "eventful" (2007: 8). When we situate violence in the context of everyday life (Robben and Nordstrom 1995), it becomes clear that violent actors are not only those who actively engage in rioting and killing, but also those whose words and deeds inform violent events in less tangible but extremely critical ways.

In constructing their narratives women drew not only on reservoirs of knowledge built over their years of involvement with the Hindu nationalist movement, but also on pamphlets and publications published by different organizations in the movement. For instance, Payal Aggarwal, a *pracharika*, or unmarried, celibate woman who has devoted her life to the Samiti, read pamphlets and publications printed by both her own organization and the RSS as part of her ongoing training. As the person in charge of Samiti *shakhas* throughout Delhi, she used her knowledge to train women and girls who ran individual *shakhas*, who in turn taught members of their own *shakhas*. Thus, many of the ideas that are taught in these *shakhas* are similar to those promulgated in other wings of the movement and are shaped by the writings and ideas of some of the most prominent, and male, ideologues of Hindu nationalism. While other scholars have examined the productions of Hindu nationalist ideologues, I focus on how this ideology takes shape on the ground in the everyday words and deeds of Hindu nationalist women conducting their work for the movement.

Ethnography enabled me to see how individual women understood the movement's ideology, and how their own particular locations, politics, and ideas led them to reshape this ideology in their conversations with me or others they encountered. Sometimes, as with Ela whom I introduced earlier, this was because they did not necessarily agree with their leaders. At other times, women activists were responding to the particularities of the communities or individuals they were working with. Since their primary goal is to draw diverse individuals toward the goals of the movement, it is imperative that they tailor messages in ways that appeal to and resonate with those they encounter. Most importantly, the women themselves live in worlds that are influenced by multiple and often competing ideological systems. These are social worlds that are marked by what Robert Hefner has called the "deep pluralism" that characterizes the modern world, that results from the increasing proximity of groups who necessarily share each other's "lifeworlds" (Hefner 2005, 2004: 26; see also Hefner 1998: 98; Habermas 1991). Thus, although deeply committed to Hindu nationalism, women were also influenced by and drawn to other discourses that vied for dominance within their social worlds, and had to balance their nationalist commitments against other desires and allegiances and the contingencies of everyday life.

Focusing on how Hindu nationalist ideology is produced, reproduced, and transformed on the ground illuminates some of these complexities. I analyze the varied processes through which the movement recruits support among women and the diverse motivations that draw them to Hindu nationalism, even as their lives are shaped by competing ideologies and infused by complex and often transgressive desires. Seduced by other ways of being and knowing or compelled by the exigencies of daily life, occasionally women like Ela were dissonant subjects who transgressed the normative constructions of Hindu nationalism. I pay attention to these dissonant subjects because they provide a lens through which to analyze the movement and grasp the complexities of allegiance and belonging in the modern world.

Ideology and Dissonance in Hindu Nationalism

I refer to Ela as a dissonant subject because in my conversation with her she contravened the normative constructions of Hindu nationalist ideology. While in other respects she is the ideal Hindu nationalist subject, on the topic of religious violence she radically rejects the movement's views. I met several women like Ela, who were committed to the Hindu nationalist movement, and yet consciously transgressed its normative expectations in one way or another. On the one hand, one can argue that it is simply common sense that all members of a movement will not follow its ideological messages in every respect. I have no argument with those who make this contention. Indeed, as most ethnographers are well aware, individuals are not cultural automata who always say and do what they are expected to. On the other hand, most analyses of Hindu nationalism have focused on normative ideological constructions and models of behavior. Undoubtedly these are invaluable interventions that have shaped our understanding of Hindu nationalism. However, I also draw attention to the moments when individuals transgress norms and become dissonant subjects because I believe they reveal the everyday compromises this violent movement must make in the process of producing hegemony.

Several scholars have examined the varied interventions of organizations in the Hindu nationalist movement to demonstrate that its malleable countenance is precisely what has enabled its reach in India. Thomas Hansen suggests that "diversification" was a conscious RSS strategy after 1949 and resulted in the multiple organizations of the Sangh Parivar (1999: 96–97). While their particular interventions may vary, each of these organizations recognizes the authority of the RSS over them. However, to reach the broadest audience, they have effectively branded themselves in different ways. For instance, the VHP was created to bring religious authorities and organizations into the movement (see Hansen 1999: 101; Katju 2003: 2). Yet not only the façade but also the substance of the interventions varies. Thus, for example, in order to recruit women into the movement the Rashtra Sevika Samiti clearly espouses constructions of nation and subject that diverge in some ways from those promulgated by the RSS (Bacchetta 1996). Such diverging perspectives exist within Hindu nationalist organizations as well, as Amrita Basu has noted in the case of the BJP (1998: 174, 1995). These diverging tendencies remind us that Hindu nationalism, like any cultural system, is not a seamless totality but contains multiple possibilities, ambiguities, and inconsistencies.[16] However, while these diverging tendencies illustrate the pluralism within Hindu nationalism enabled by its multiple façades, such tendencies, as these scholars have noted, are kept in check by certain normative presumptions scripted by the RSS.

The imaging of India as a Hindu nation, the commitment to a unified Hindu identity that transcends regional, sectarian, and caste affiliations, the construction of religious "others" who have persecuted this nation throughout history, the need for violent reclamations of Hindu masculinity, and the construction of women as virtuous guardians of culture are all normative constructions that provide the very raison d'être for the Hindu nationalist movement. Women reproduce these normative constructions as they perform their everyday tasks for the movement. In fact, these constructions are central to their ability to produce the "imagined community" (Anderson 1983) of the Hindu nation amid the pluralism that characterizes Indian modernity, a central task of postcolonial nationalisms struggling for hegemony in their plural social and political worlds (P. Chatterjee 1986).[17] Whether at lectures delivered in training camps or in casual conversations with those they encountered, women activists articulated norms in ways that resonated with people's constructions of the past, appealed to their fears and insecurities in the present, and represented the movement as the protector of the nation and its citizens. They skillfully reconfigured Hindu nationalist politics as a sacred obligation, and used religious texts, discourses, symbols, and rituals to construct the nation, Hindu subjectivity, and indeed Hinduism itself, in ways that furthered the movement's agenda.

Through these everyday acts, women activists attempt to make Hindu nationalist norms hegemonic in India. Here I understand hegemony to be "that order of signs and practices, relations and distinctions, images and epistemologies—drawn from a historically situated cultural field— that come to be taken-for-granted as the natural and received shape of the world and everything that inhabits it" (Comaroff and Comaroff 1991: 23). I focus on the processes through which women attempted to "naturalize" the ideology of Hindu nationalism to give it hegemonic power on the sociopolitical landscape of the country. Indeed, Hindu nationalist constructions of subjectivity, particularly of gender and religion, have increasingly become naturalized in the political sphere, and, in that sense, are hegemonic.[18] Yet hegemony is a process that, as Raymond Williams has asserted, "has continually to be renewed, recreated, defended and modified" because it is constantly "resisted, limited, altered, challenged by pressures not at all its own" (1977: 112). Women must therefore constantly renew the hegemony of Hindu nationalist ideas in India, through the lessons they teach in schools, the songs and prayers they teach new recruits, the religious events they organize in neighborhoods, the speeches they deliver in *shakhas*, the conversations they engage in with those who are not members of the movement, and indeed in their own actions and commitments. They must consistently neutralize or appropriate contradictory positions and conflicts in order to ensure that the movement gains and maintains its hegemonic position.

To appeal to diverse audiences and compel them toward the hegemonic narrative of Hindu nationalism, women tailored their messages in various ways enabling an ideological pluralism that embraced diverging tendencies, while continuing to reproduce Hindu nationalist norms. For instance, women's historical tales, discussed in the next chapter, diverge from men's stories of the past to construct women as historical agents. However, they continue to renew normative Hindu nationalist narratives about Muslims and about Hindu history that bolster the movement's claims to nation in contemporary India. Women's roles within the movement are also indicative of the pluralism embraced by Hindu nationalists. Vasanti, who is single, and Payal, who is a celibate *pracharika*, represent the plural roles available to women within the movement despite the privileging of motherhood. Yet, by living in a temple compound under the gaze of a priest and his family (Vasanti), and committing to celibacy (Payal), these women continue to renew the normative expectation that Hindu women's sexuality be contained within the sanctified space of marriage and motherhood. Indeed, it is clear in these instances that by continuing to reproduce normative constructions in Hindu nationalist ideology, pluralism can enable hegemony.

However, women's narratives, statements, and acts did not always renew ideological norms. On occasion, they transgressed the normative constructions of Hindu nationalism by failing to perform them and citing instead other norms embedded in different ideological systems. It is these words and deeds that I call dissonant acts. When we view Hindu nationalism through the lens of ethnography, we become privy to the daily production of ideology made complex by the exigencies of the everyday, by the complexities of the individual, and by the ambiguities of circumstance. I saw that while women strove to reproduce the normative constructions of the movement in their everyday work, due to the circumstances of their lives, competing expectations, or because they were compelled by other ways of being, they occasionally transgressed them. As a feminist ethnographer, I was interested in examining not only dominant ideological constructions, but also the ways in which women variously inhabited, reshaped, challenged, or transgressed them in everyday life.[19] It became clear to me that women not only contend with multiple and often competing ideologies as they disseminate Hindu nationalist ideas to diverse audiences, but are also influenced and shaped by them. For instance, despite ideological constructions that require women to be chaste and pure and keep their sexuality within the sanctified space of marriage, I heard women talk about boyfriends and extramarital affairs. Although the movement is committed to creating a Hindu identity that transcends caste divisions to mobilize a base, one of the first questions I was asked when I met women was about my caste background. These transgressions may seem small, but they are indicative of the way women's subjectivities are formed at the interstices of multiple ideological systems. When women transgress the norm by engaging in such dissonant acts, they fail to inhabit Hindu nationalist subjectivity and become, however temporarily, dissonant subjects.

The subject—by which I mean discursive positions like man, woman, Hindu, Muslim—is never fixed, but rather is made meaningful in particular discursive fields (Laclau and Mouffe 1985: 115; see also Butler 2004: 45). These fields may include plural and indeed competing ideological systems, which can result in struggles to determine the meaning of subject positions (see Hall 1985: 104, 112). Therefore, while Hindu nationalists might attempt to define what it means to be a "Hindu" or a "woman," in the plural context of modern India many other ideological systems in the same discursive field might provide contesting and alternative understandings of these very subject positions. Indeed, as Laclau and Mouffe have made clear, the nature of the subject is contingent and dependent on the extent to which a discourse can fix its meaning in a plural discursive field, a process that is never complete and always open to contestation (Laclau and Mouffe 1985: 116, 111–12).[20] As individuals traversing the plural landscapes of modern India, the women I worked with may have identified as Hindu nationalists, but other ways of being and knowing also operated in their worlds and influenced their everyday acts.

The hegemonic power of Hindu nationalism is jeopardized when women's acts are informed by other ideologies, since its own constructions of subject and nation must be constantly reiterated for it to maintain its position. Speaking of ideologies of gender, Judith Butler argues that while the gendered subject has no ontological reality, we perceive gender to be real because of a "reiterated enactment of norms" that produce "the appearance of gender as an abiding interior depth" (1997:14; 1999:173). She contends that the illusion of gender is sustained by performative acts which are "ritualized productions" that continuously "cite" the discursive norms that create them and, in so doing, sustain their regulatory power and their existence (Butler 1993: 13).[21] Butler is very clear that this repetition is not a matter of choice but rather is often coerced by the regulatory regimes within which the acts are performed.[22] She asserts, "This iterability implies that "performance" is not a singular "act" or event, but a ritualized production, a ritual reiterated under and through constraint, under and through the force of prohibition and taboo, with the threat of ostracism and even death controlling and compelling the shape of the production, but not, I will insist, determining it fully in advance" (1993: 95).

It is evident that powerful regulatory regimes operate within the Hindu nationalist movement to compel its members to act in ways that reiterate its ideological norms and to discipline dissonant subjects. This became abundantly clear in June 2005, when L. K. Advani, then president of the BJP and leader of the opposition in the Indian Parliament, visited Pakistan. During his visit, Advani made several public statements that transgressed Hindu nationalist norms.[23] For instance, in an interview with Hamid Mir on Geo TV, Advani claimed that the day the Babri Masjid was demolished "was the saddest day of my life," a statement that directly contradicted the RSS construction of the event as "an achievement."[24] While Advani's statements are best understood as an attempt to reposition himself as a BJP moderate, they were viewed by the RSS as a betrayal, transgressing the very core of Hindu nationalist understandings of self and "other." Advani was forced to step down as BJP president in December 2005. Yet the fact that he continues to be leader of the opposition and a powerful voice in the BJP is indicative of the Hindu nationalist movement's ability to embrace dissonant subjects even as its regulatory regimes discipline their acts. This ability is key to understanding its expansionary power.

Hindu nationalist women also operate within the regulatory regimes of the movement and are compelled to "cite" its normative constructions to sustain Hindu nationalist ideology in the world. On occasion, however, they are drawn to other ideologies and fail to "cite" Hindu nationalist norms in their everyday acts. For instance, when they spoke of their own love affairs or gossiped about those of others, they not only failed to reproduce the normative construction of the chaste female subject, but transgressed it by citing other possibilities. In these instances, I label these women dissonant subjects not to imply a permanent state, but to illuminate the moments of dissonance when they transgress Hindu nationalist norms. Indeed, as I have already suggested, women wholly inhabit Hindu nationalist subjectivity at other moments. My point in highlighting dissonant subjectivity is simply to show the movement's willingness to embrace such dissonance within its ranks.

It is critical to reiterate here that dissonant acts are simply a transgression of the norm. While they can include a conscious subversion of or resistance to the norm, they should not be reduced to either. Rather than analyze women's acts as simply resistance/compliance, subversion/collusion, or hypocrisy/sincerity, looking at dissonance allows us to examine the complexities of subject formation in the modern world. It allows us to analyze the complex reasons why women, or men like Advani, choose to act in the ways that they do. In Advani's case, his acts are better understood as attempts to reinvent his public persona with a view to positioning himself as an acceptable candidate for prime minister in the future than as a conscious subversion of or resistance to the RSS diktat. Women discussing affairs are not merely being hypocritical, but demonstrating how their subjectivities are informed by multiple ideologies. Indeed, focusing on dissonance enables us to see how individuals are imbricated in and compelled by multiple ideological systems in contemporary India.

Although the expansionary strategies of Hindu nationalism have created a plurality of perspectives within the movement, this does not mean that all positions are equally valued. While acts that reproduce normative constructions are embraced as plural tendencies within Hindu

nationalism, dissonant acts, which transgress the norm and are therefore not consonant with any of these tendencies, are disciplined by its
regulatory regimes. Indeed, given the efforts taken to institute the
norms, it is not surprising that positions that transgress and/or challenge normative constructions are understood to be problematic and
are disciplined, marginalized, or silenced. What interests me here, and
the reason that I draw attention to women like Ela who become dissonant subjects, is that despite their transgressive acts, they continue to be
valued members of the movement.

Of course, as Advani's example indicates, both men and women can
become dissonant subjects in the Hindu nationalist movement. However, since my primary concern is to examine the centrality of women in
the Hindu nationalist movement, I look at women who have transgressed the norm. Whether male or female, I think we need to pay attention to dissonant subjects, not because they are unique, but for what they
reveal about the expansionary tactics of Hindu nationalism. It is my contention that the expansionary successes of Hindu nationalism may be
due not only to the ability of its members to resonate with diverse audiences, but also critically to their willingness to eschew ideological purity
and embrace dissonant subjects within the ranks of the movement, even
as they signal the fissures within.

On Locations and Dislocations: Conducting Research on Hindu Nationalist Women

I began this project on women in the Hindu nationalist movement to
understand what motivated individuals to engage in extreme violence
against those they labeled as "enemies." As a secular Indian feminist, I
was deeply disturbed by the escalation of religious conflict and violence
against religious minorities in India, as indeed by the high visibility of
women in the Hindu right. Heeding the call for a more politically
engaged anthropology,[25] and believing that dialogue and transformation require studying the cultural logics of those we might disagree with,
I sought to engage with Hindu nationalist women to understand what
motivated them to join this violent and exclusionary religious movement.[26]

Fieldwork on a movement with multiple wings spread throughout
India's capital city required a multisited ethnographic strategy. I conducted research in multiple "locations," not only because I engaged
with women in multiple wings of the movement, but also because their
homes and work sites drew me into different parts of the city (Map 2).
Since I was simultaneously working with women in many different wings
of the movement who did not necessarily know each other, I did not

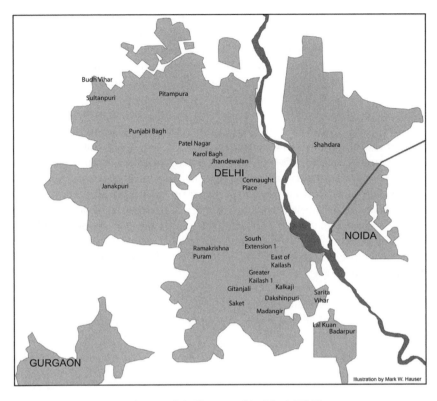

Map 2. Sites of fieldwork in Delhi. Illustrated by Mark W. Hauser.

have a "community" with whom I could live and immerse myself. This created a research experience that had its advantages and disadvantages. On the one hand, I had the freedom to make my own decisions about where and with whom I would spend any given day. And, at the end of long, often emotionally grueling days, I had the luxury of coming home to unwind. On the other hand, it also meant I spent hours stuck in Delhi traffic inhaling the bus exhaust enveloping my autorickshaw, only to find at the end of a ninety minute journey that the women I was supposed to meet had changed their plans at the last minute. I therefore had to be not only organized enough to have a back up plan, but also patient enough to reenter the traffic jam, get over my irritation, and emerge smiling, though wind-blown and dusty, at another location.

While this could be terribly frustrating, it is also part of conducting fieldwork with extremely busy women who are juggling multiple obligations at home and at work. Despite how busy they were, the women I worked with were extremely generous with their time, allowing me to tag along with them as they conducted their work for the movement, and fielding questions about who I was and why I was there in a good-natured manner. Knowing that I was a researcher and not a member of the movement did not stop them from talking to me. In part this was because as a young, [then] unmarried woman who was still "studying," I was not seen as a threat. However, I also believe that women, and men, spoke to me because I was writing about them,[27] and because of my connections with an American university. If Urvashi's efforts to be interviewed by the media described above are any indication, it is also the case that women talked to me—at least in part—because they wanted to be part of my project and to shape my representation of women in the Hindu nationalist movement. Indeed, I had to be wary not only of my own ethnographic authority (Clifford 1988), but also of how my highly trained interlocutors could use me to further their own agendas.[28]

Their willingness to talk to me also had to do with the fact that I was usually introduced through their superiors. Hindu nationalism is a deeply hierarchical movement, and I followed the proper channels to make contact with women working at the grassroots level so as not to jeopardize my own access to members of the movement, or create problems for the women I spoke to. Yet this too, as I was made horribly aware in a conversation with Kalpana Saxena, came with its own perilous politics. Kalpana, a supervisor of Sewa Bharati schools in one Delhi zone, agreed to meet me when I called saying that Ela, her superior, had given me her number and asked if I could talk to her about her work. She spent several days showing me schools run by the organization. She was generous to a fault, insisting on plying me with tea and food at her home, paying my bus fare despite my attempts to prevent this, and providing valuable information on the workings of the organization and her own trajectory within it. She also questioned me about whom I planned to vote for, why I would not vote for the BJP, and, when I indicated that I had a problem with Hindu nationalist violence, angrily asked what I would do if someone came and took my house from me.

Nevertheless, she was kind to me, so I was stunned when she said one day that she had done all this against her better judgment because her superiors had told her to. She asserted that people like me destroy Indian culture by telling the west about India and providing them with knowledge that they could use to convert people and bring cultural ruin. She said that she disapproved of what I was doing and consequently had never been sure how much to show me. Distressed, I responded that had I known about this, I would never have imposed on her or said anything to her superiors. Thoroughly shaken after this encounter, and uncomfortable with the vast differentials in power between us, I never contacted her again. Having obtained her consent to talk to her after explaining that her participation in my project was entirely voluntary and confidential, I had assumed that she was talking to me because she wanted to, despite her awareness of who I was and where I was coming from. I was dismayed that she had spoken to me because she felt powerless given who I was and where I was coming from. This conversation with Kalpana taught me first hand about the politics of working in such a hierarchical setting, and indeed about the limits of "consent."[29]

Unlike Kalpana, most of the women I worked most closely with were happy to have me as a participant observer and began to trust and confide in me. While I conducted both semi-structured and unstructured interviews, the most valuable information often came in the form of casual conversations, particularly as we got more comfortable with one another. Although I did use a tape recorder for some of my interviews and to record speeches, it proved to be a hindrance in the field, since women would adopt the official positions of the movement when the tape recorder was turned on. These were often in stark contrast with things they may have told me immediately before I turned on the tape recorder, or that I already knew about them. Clearly, despite my promise of confidentiality, they feared the consequences of articulating views on tape that opposed those promulgated by their leaders in this violent and hierarchical movement. Also, casual conversations, which often yielded the most valuable information about everyday Hindu nationalism and dissonant subjects, immediately became stilted in the presence of a tape recorder. Consequently, I found it much more productive to very quickly paraphrase the gist of conversations in a notebook, carefully transcribing key phrases or sentences as we were conversing, and incorporating these into my fieldnotes at the end of the day.

Not counting those participants I observed and casually met at various programs and events, I worked with forty-five women and ten men in various wings of the Hindu nationalist movement in Delhi. With few exceptions, most were North Indian and belonged to castes associated with the first three *varna* (social class) categories of priests (*brahmins*), warriors (*kshatriyas*), and commoners (*vaishyas*).[30] While some women like Ela were highly educated and clearly middle to upper-middle class, with Delhi Development Authority (DDA) homes for middle-income groups or houses in private upper-middle-class colonies, the majority were not so wealthy or educated. Most, like Urvashi and Kalpana, were lower-middle-class women who lived in DDA low-income housing, or like Vasanti and Payal, in rooms paid for by the movement. Most of these women had been to school, although many had not attended college. Almost all of them were deeply religious, and claimed an intrinsic link between their religious identity and their politics. Contrary to the sepa-ration of religion and politics that has marked the intellectual legacies of the west (Asad 1983), and similar to women involved in religious poli-tics in other parts of the world (Deeb 2006: 35), for many of these women religious ideas, discourses, and obligations were inextricably intertwined with their political agendas.[31]

As an upper-middle-class South Indian feminist raised in a staunchly secular and not particularly religious family, educated at elite English-medium schools in India and, at the time, working toward a doctorate in the United States, I was extremely different from those I worked with. Yet they benevolently accepted my presence among them, patiently answered my questions, and, at times, protected me. I was particularly grateful to Urvashi on one occasion when we had to travel from one part of the city to another to participate in a Hindu nationalist rally. All the women were traveling in tempos (open back flatbed trucks) rented for the occasion. As Urvashi and I were deciding on which of the already crowded tempos to climb into, one sleazy man, who had been trying to engage both of us in conversation earlier, sidled up to Urvashi and offered to take me on the back of his scooter. I was really worried that Urvashi would agree, but, instead, she turned around, pinned him with a look, and said, with all the authority of a grandmother who recognizes a shady operator when she sees one, that I was coming with her in the tempo and would not go with him on the scooter. It was a dramatic moment, and the man quickly slunk away leaving me with an over-whelming sense of gratitude to Urvashi for rescuing me from an uncom-fortable, and potentially dangerous, situation.

From incidents such as this one, it became clear to me that, despite our many differences, several of the women I worked with were fond of me. As a feminist ethnographer committed to doing "homework" rather than "fieldwork" (Visweswaran 1994: 113), to focusing not just on difference, but also on points of identification (Narayan 1993: 673), I was able to develop fairly close relationships with many of my interlocu-tors. Yet, while there were many points of intersection and understand-ing between my interlocutors and myself, there were also profound differences that we were both aware of and that need to be acknowl-edged. These women supported a movement that I opposed, and expressed views about the nation and its minorities that I found highly objectionable. Although I became fairly close to some of the women I worked with, the disagreements between us were those of principle that struck at the very basis of our constructions of morality, of right and wrong, of worldview. They were the kind of disagreements that upset me greatly because they challenged the legitimacy of people who were part of my world and sustained my existence within it. These differences of politics and worldview have unquestionably influenced how I made sense of what was being said and represented my ethnographic encounter in this book (see Clifford and Marcus 1986; Robben and Nordstrom 1995: 3).

Ultimately, this book is an attempt to make sense of women with whom I profoundly disagree. It is driven by a desire to understand what draws thousands upon thousands of women, and men, to a movement that is xenophobic, exclusionary, and tremendously violent, and to explain its meteoric rise on the sociopolitical landscape of the country in the late eighties and the nineties. I focus on the myriad ways Hindu nationalist women reach out to diverse audiences to mobilize a mass base. I examine the way they use religion, constructions of history, discourses of national insecurity, narratives of religious persecution, and ideas and practices of social responsibility to reach out to different groups of people and articulate with their everyday needs, desires, fears, and interests. This, I argue, is at the root of their expansionary power. But it is also what limits their ideological control over their membership. As the movement expands, drawing in diverse groups of people from different social, political, and cultural locations in modern India, it must also contend with dissonant subjects who transgress the ideal subjectivities created for them by Hindu nationalism. My goal is to examine how the acts of Hindu nationalist women, whether compliant or dissonant, are central to understanding the Hindu nationalist movement in modern India.

Chapter 1
Everyday Histories

"Who lit the fire?" Atal Behari Vajpayee, prime minister of India, asked this question at a speech delivered in April 2002 while Hindu nationalists orchestrated a violent pogrom against the Muslim community in Gujarat.[1] Asserting that Muslims in Godhra had set fire to a section of the Sabarmati Express transporting Hindu nationalists, Hindu mobs killed, tortured, and raped Muslim men and women to avenge the deaths of fifty-seven individuals killed in the fire. Conservatively, about two thousand Muslims were killed in this violence and several thousands were displaced. Subsequent forensic reports indicate that the fire began inside the train, belying the story that Muslims outside the train attacked the Sabarmati Express. More troubling has been the mounting evidence that Hindu violence against Muslims in Gujarat was not spontaneous but pre-planned with apparent state complicity.[2] Yet, months after this violent pogrom against Muslims, the Hindu nationalist chief minister of Gujarat, Narendra Modi, went to the polls and won a resounding victory that reveals how violence is centrally implicated in the construction of political communities[3] and ingrained into the very workings of democracy in India (see Basu and Roy 2007). Even as these details emerged in 2002, in his speech Vajpayee boldly asserted that, while the carnage in Gujarat was regrettable, "we should not forget how the tragedy of Gujarat started. The subsequent developments were no doubt condemnable, but who lit the fire?" As one reads the full text of his speech, it becomes clear that the attack on the train was not the only incident that "lit the fire" of Hindu wrath. Rather, a past (forcible conversions to Islam and the destruction of Hindu temples) and a present (al Qaeda and Muslim militancy in Kashmir) of perceived Muslim injustices against Hindus are summoned to justify Hindu violence against Muslim communities in Gujarat.

Vajpayee's historical trajectory skillfully gathers isolated cases from India's past and present and weaves them into a tale already crystallized in Hindu nationalist historiography and instantly recognizable to many. Indeed, it is this very historiography, built around the specter of a Muslim male "other" who has inflicted violence against Hindus, particularly

Hindu women, for centuries, that imbues meaning into Vajpayee's words. More important, as evident in Hindu nationalist documents distributed at the time (Jaffrelot 2007: 185–86), this deeply gendered and highly sexualized construction of a violent past is centrally implicated in the Gujarat pogrom when Hindu nationalists sought to redress this revisionist history by unleashing unspeakable acts of violence against Muslim women and men.

In this chapter I locate these violent acts in the context of the everyday (Das 2007:8), by illustrating how the historiography that inspired them is central to the everyday Hindu nationalism disseminated by women to diverse audiences. These histories are in fact key to the expansionary tactics of activists who articulate these constructions of the past with women's fears about male violence, their understandings of motherhood, and their sense of patriotic duty. Focusing on the everyday, I show how women use these histories not only to recruit women into the movement to expand its base, but also to reiterate normative Hindu nationalist constructions of the past and "naturalize" them in their social worlds. I believe that their successful dissemination of these histories enabled the worldview that validated Vajpayee's words for many Hindus and mobilized thousands to engage in anti-Muslim violence in Gujarat.

While reiterating Hindu nationalist norms, women construct a gendered history that is specifically used to recruit women into the movement's politics and violence. Whereas most Hindu nationalist histories image women as victims of Muslim aggression, I focus on a series of historical tales related by women belonging to the Delhi wing of the Rashtra Sevika Samiti (henceforth Samiti), which position them as agents in the gendered history of the Hindu nation. Using data collected from participant observation, interviews, and conversations with members of the movement, as well as pamphlets and volumes published by them, I examine how women use these historical tales not only to disseminate Hindu nationalist histories but also to redefine the female subject in ways that explain their own roles and activism in the movement today. Specifically analyzing the use of stories about Jijabai, mother of the seventeenth-century Hindu king Shivaji, I suggest that Samiti women present a gendered vision of the past in which women play a role in the nation's destiny. Positioning motherhood as a site for female agency, Samiti women portray Jijabai as an "enlightened mother," worthy of emulation, who fought for the Hindu nation through her son Shivaji by inculcating in him the values, ideology, strength, and patriotism the Hindu nation lacked. New recruits are taught that they must aspire to become like Jijabai, facilitating the cultural and political renaissance of the Hindu nation in India by molding the new generation.

While many of these ideas resonate with narratives produced by other wings of the movement, the stories about Jijabai also provide an alternative to dominant constructions of both male and female subjectivity in the movement. Since many of the constructions of history and culture embraced by Hindu nationalists were first imagined by ideologues in the all-male Rashtriya Swayamsevak Sangh (RSS), I focus here on the discrepancies between RSS and Samiti constructions of Jijabai's story. Samiti stories about Jijabai suggest that she was responsible for birthing and envisioning the nation through her son Shivaji, and so diverge from the RSS narrative of Shivaji as the founder of the Hindu nation. In so doing, they provide an alternate reading of the past and present: one in which women are the primary agents in the creation and reproduction of the Hindu nation. These divergent images of the female subject reveal the expansionary tactics of Hindu nationalist activists as they variously frame the message of the movement to reach out to different constituencies.

To me, these images illustrate the divergent tendencies within Hindu nationalist ideology. Although they may inspire dissonant acts, they are not in themselves dissonant, since they do not transgress the norm by invoking other ideological systems. Rather they cite, recall, or reiterate the normative constructions that have been used to recruit support for the volatile politics of the movement. By embracing diversity while still citing the normative constructions of the movement, the stories about Jijabai illustrate the pluralism within Hindu nationalism. This pluralism is precisely what enables it to appeal to different constituencies, in this case, women. These stories therefore are best understood as an integral part of the expansionary tactics of Samiti members who, while providing an alternative to RSS constructions of female subjectivity in some ways and thereby recruiting women into their ranks, also at times entirely endorse its constructions of the past, of Muslims, of the relationship between Hindus and "others" throughout history, and indeed of women. In fact, while the stories might testify to the multiplicity of perspectives within Hindu nationalist ideology, it is also critical to see how this very plurality is woven into a more "singular vision" (Gold and Gujar 2002: 83).[4] My goal is to examine the normative vision contained in these stories and to show how women activists use them to disseminate the ideology of the movement, to recruit new members, and to mobilize them toward the violent politics of Hindu nationalism.

Rashtra Sevika Samiti

Ever since the Muslim invaders came to India there have been atrocities committed against women and, consequently, society was no longer a safe place for them. In ancient India Hindu society gave women a lot of freedom and there was no *parda* (veiling) and women could wander around alone with no fear. All this has changed with Muslim invasions and now women have to stay at home, maintain *parda*. Because in those days if the Muslims saw women and liked the way they looked they would just pick them up and force them to become part of the harem. Ever since these times, women have been unsafe and even today a woman out of doors is not safe. This is why the Samiti teaches women to defend themselves and also gives them mental strength to overcome their fear. To this end, weekly *shakhas* are held in various parts of Delhi. (Usha Chati, Speech at Dharam Bhavan, November 25, 1999)

The Rashtra Sevika Samiti is often identified as the women's wing of the Rashtriya Swayamsevak Sangh. When I inquired into the relationship between the RSS and the Samiti, Aparna Pandit, a leader of the Delhi Samiti, referred to it as a "parallel organization" of the RSS, appropriating a greater degree of independence from the vision of the RSS than would be afforded to its women's wing. While I focus on the members of the Samiti who were based in Delhi, the Samiti has a broad network of activists throughout India, some of whom I had occasion to meet during their visits to Delhi. The organization of the Samiti is around a centralized command structure headed by a Pramukh Sanchalika based in Nagpur, Maharashtra, who supervises the work of the different regional branches.[5] I met Usha Chati, then Pramukh Sanchalika of the Samiti, on one of her visits to Delhi, when she came to address a gathering of women and girls at Dharam Bhavan in South Extension I, an upper-middle-class colony in South Delhi. Apart from Usha and a few other Samiti women whom I already knew, most of the approximately twenty-five women and girls gathered in the room were not Samiti members. Most were enrolled in one of the Sewa Bharati sewing classes in the nearby, less wealthy Kotla colony, and had been brought by their instructor to listen to Usha. One woman leaned over and asked me who Usha was. When I explained that she was the leader of the Samiti, she asked me what the Samiti was. Clearly, despite being enrolled in a Sewa Bharati class, she had little connection with or knowledge about the other organizations in the Hindu nationalist movement.

Usha, apparently aware that most of those in the audience knew little about her organization, began to tell those gathered about the Samiti. The above excerpt, in which she articulates Hindu nationalist history about Muslims in India with women's everyday fears about safety, was her response to a rhetorical question she had just posed, "Why have women become so scared?" She told the women and girls present that Lakshmibai Kelkar had established the Samiti, fearing that centuries of Muslim atrocities against Hindu women had made them weak and frightened. Usha asserted that Kelkar had founded the Samiti to give Hindu women the mental strength to overcome their fear and to teach them to defend themselves. Whereas the Samiti was indeed founded in 1936 by Kelkar along with Dr. Keshav Baliram Hedgewar, the founder of the RSS, there are multiple versions of Kelkar's motivation to create an organization for women that illustrate how the past is tailored to appeal to diverse audiences (see Bacchetta 2004: 7–9). Usha's narrative indexes a normative construction in Hindu nationalist ideology about Muslim aggression against Hindus/nation, while also resonating with the movement's construction of the present marked by the Kargil War between India and Pakistan just months earlier. Clearly Samiti women used this narrative in their everyday work to draw new recruits, since, at the end of the meeting, those gathered were informed that Samiti workers would contact them about forming a *shakha* (branch).

Of all the Hindu nationalist women's groups I worked with, the Samiti, mirroring the Sangh in this respect, was by far the most organized, holding weekly *shakhas* in different parts of the city. Neera Gupta, an elderly leader of the Delhi Samiti, told me that the organization runs about fifty *shakhas* in the city. Bemoaning this small number in a city the size of Delhi, she explained that young women and girls aren't joining *shakhas* in the same numbers these days, because people no longer see the importance of creating community and think only in terms of the nuclear family. Samiti *shakhas* create a hierarchically organized community of women and inculcate discipline and obedience in its ranks (see Alter 1994). At every Samiti event I attended, leaders expended energy arranging participants in rigid lines and rows and ensuring that nobody spoke out of turn, activities that not only disciplined the audience but also reinforced organizational hierarchies. For an anthropologist among Hindu nationalists, the Samiti also provided some of the deepest challenges of fieldwork. While women in other organizations were content to have me follow them on their daily rounds, watch from the sidelines as they performed their various tasks, and participate when I desired to, Samiti women would tolerate my presence only as a full participant in their activities. Thus, although they knew I was a researcher, I was required to participate in the *shakhas* I attended, learning the physical and intellectual exercises the other women and girls were learning.

While participant-observation is the cornerstone of ethnographic fieldwork, it is, as many fieldwork memoirs have illustrated, not only a process fraught with political agendas of which one might be only partially aware, but also one that often uncomfortably forces one to confront one's politics and social location.[6] Being a participant gave me a unique vantage point on Samiti activities, but it could also be quite challenging at a personal level. I was made painfully aware of this when I was invited to attend a *shakha* held to observe a Samiti (and RSS) festival called Gurudakshina Utsav. At this event, when Samiti members honor their *gurus* (teachers), I was expected not only to give a token payment to the *guru* (*gurudakshina*), but also to salute the saffron flag of the RSS.

I found the latter particularly distressing. I was sitting next to Neera Gupta, as one by one Samiti members got up from their rows at the command of the *shakha* leader, walked to the front of the room, offered rose petals to the pictures of Lakshmibai Kelkar and the goddess Bharat Mata, turned to face the saffron flag hoisted to the right, and smartly performed the distinctive RSS salute before returning to their places. Neera leaned over and whispered in my ear, "It's military style." I nodded, only to see her lean over again and say, "Kalyani, you will also have to do this." My heart sank at the thought of paying homage to a flag that represented a politics that I found reprehensible. When my turn came, I unhappily rose to my feet, meekly placed flower petals in front of the portraits, and then tried to get away with simply putting my hands together in a common greeting (*namaste*). The *shakha* leader immediately walked up to me and showed me how to do the RSS salute, standing by patiently as I gritted my teeth and did the needful.

When I met Neera at her home in a posh upper-middle-class colony in South Delhi five days later, I asked her why she had made me salute the flag when I was not a member of the Samiti. She explained that the flag represented all the *gurus* who have taught us along with their values and *dharma*. It also symbolized an undivided India, apparently represented in the shape of the flag, and the unity of all Hindus.[7] She asserted that I was saluting my nation (*rashtra*) and these ideas, and that it was very important I do so. While her explanation only made me more uncomfortable, I also recognized the value of being a participant in the Samiti's activities. Indeed, saluting the Hindu nationalist flag and, at other moments, being compelled to sing songs that contained lyrics promoting a Hindu chauvinism that went against my own secular and pluralist vision of India was deeply problematic to me. At the same time, my subject position as a researcher who was not a Hindu nationalist was productive since it instigated Samiti women to direct their individual attention and their powers of persuasion—along with their historical tales and cultural and political ideology—toward me. Participating in Samiti *shakhas* and listening to women activists disseminating historical tales like those described here enabled me to see how the everyday acts of women were indeed "eventful" (Das 2007: 8). I saw how they articulated these histories in ways that appealed to women's everyday fears, interests, and desires. These acts not only recruited new members into the embrace of the movement, but also reiterated normative constructions of the past that justified Hindu nationalist violence in the present.

Jijabai: The Visionary

"We will become Jijabai," Aparna Pandit said to a group of women and girls gathered on the roof of a low building in Sultanpuri that housed the BJP office (*karyalaya*) and was also the home of a member of the BJP. Illustrating the close cooperation between the different women's organizations in the movement, the head of the local chapter of the BHP, Mahila Morcha, had invited women and girls living in Sultanpuri on the outskirts of northwest Delhi to come and learn more about Samiti activities. This *shakha* was the first attempt of the Samiti to assert a presence in this community of Balmikis, a Dalit[8] group who had been resettled from slums in central Delhi in one of the various attempts to "clean up" the city during the Asian games in the early 1980s. The first attempt to discipline those gathered had gotten off to a rocky start when it became clear that despite the best efforts of Payal and Ramani, a Malayali member of the Samiti who runs a *shakha* on Sundays in Sultanpuri, they were simply not going to sit in straight lines equidistant from one another. Finally, tired of watching their exasperated attempts to explain what they wanted, Aparna began the *shakha* by asking for someone to lead the group in a devotional song. After three young girls obliged her with a song, Payal introduced the Samiti women to the group. Then Aparna addressed the group, saying that she wanted the women to initiate and attend a *shakha* in Sultanpuri. To emphasize the need for *shakhas* to organize women so that they could be "aware" and "active" in the public arena, she began to talk about Jijabai, telling the women, in the words above, that they should model their own activism on this historical figure.

Claiming that Jijabai's story would teach them the importance of being "active" and "aware," Aparna began to relate the following vignette, which I have paraphrased from my notes. One day when Shivaji was a boy, he was sitting with his mother. From where they were sitting they could see a hill upon which was flying a green flag. His mother said to Shivaji that when he grew up he would have to fight so that the flag on top of the hill would be our saffron flag and not the green flag of the foreigner's *raj*.[9] The story was familiar to me, since I had already encountered it in the Rashtra Sevika Samiti *shakha* guide (*boudhik pustak*) for January–March 1999, but it was clearly still relevant that day in mid-September when Aparna recounted it.[10] In the printed version of the vignette Shivaji asks Jijabai, while playing an Indian dice game called *chauser*, "What are the terms for victory" (Rashtra Sevika Samiti 1999a: 8)? In response she points to a green flag on top of the nearby Kondana Fort and asks that it be replaced by a different color when she wins the game. The next sentence states that Shivaji satisfied these "inspiring terms for victory." Most important, while in the printed version this vignette is part of a longer narrative in which the antagonists are explicitly identified as Muslim, in Aparna's version the communities are coded by color (saffron for Hindu and green for Muslim). Uncertain of the political affiliations of those gathered, Aparna does not explicitly name Muslims as the antagonists. Although the vignette is about the establishment of Hindu unity under Shivaji and overcoming the subjugation of Hindus under Muslim rule, Aparna also chooses not to emphasize these points to the women present. Instead, in keeping with her goals that day, she asks them to model themselves on Jijabai and uses this vignette to convey how they, under the guidance of the Samiti, can participate in the construction of the nation.

Most of those gathered listened quietly to what Aparna had to say. One woman, however, loudly questioned her, saying that while it was all very well to talk about educating women, what about the difficulty of getting girls into schools? Aparna responded that this was precisely why they needed a *shakha*, a place where they could come together to discuss these issues. The protester did not buy Aparna's reasoning and continued to voice her concerns. Rather than allow her authority to be challenged by getting into an argument, Aparna called the meeting to a close. However, before she dismissed the group, they discussed the possibility of a *shakha* in Sultanpuri. After some discussion, Aparna announced that Ramani would lead a *shakha* for the group the following Sunday at a wedding hall that belonged, ironically, to the family of the protesting woman. Clearly, the concerns she voiced did not preclude her from offering her family's space to the Samiti. On this occasion, Aparna demonstrated her organizing skills by attempting to articulate the woman's concern toward the Samiti's goals and, when that seemed to fail, to call the meeting to a close while she still had the group's support. Yet, since she was able to create consensus around a time for the *shakha* among those gathered and recruit the protester into offering a location for them to meet, clearly Aparna had succeeded in meeting her goals that day. The story about Jijabai was critical not only for recruiting women to organize the *shakha*, but also for bringing a lower-caste group into the embrace of an organization and a movement dominated by upper-caste men and women.[11]

Stories about Jijabai are used by members of the Samiti in Delhi not only to recruit women into the Hindu nationalist movement, but also to transmit cultural ideals, their understandings of the past and women's roles in it.[12] Related during *shakhas*, or sometimes in casual conversations, the stories are integral to the process by which Samiti women reproduce and disseminate Hindu nationalist historiography and reiterate the normative constructions of Hindus and Muslims that configure it. Not only do these everyday histories fashion the filters through which people understand their lives and provide the framework within which communities are "imagined" (Anderson 1983), but also, as Vajpayee's statements at the beginning of this chapter demonstrate, they can

become important justifications for nationalist action today. The historical tales recounted by women also provide an arena to construct both
male and female subjectivity in the Hindu nation, through the insertion
of individuals within larger historical trajectories, or "mythico-histories"
(Malkki 1995).[13] Liisa Malkki defines mythico-history as "a process of
world making" concerned with "the ordering and reordering of social
and political categories, with the defining of self in distinction to the
other, with good and evil" in order to constitute "a *moral order* of the
world" (1995: 55–56, original emphasis). The stories I discuss are integral to the process of world making engaged in by Samiti women as they
reiterate Hindu nationalist norms and create a place for themselves in
the past and the present of Hindu nationalism. As they construct a historical agency for women in the Samiti, Jijabai emerges as the visionary
who led both men and women in the fight for the Hindu nation through
her son Shivaji.

Shivaji was a seventeenth-century king and leader of the Marathas, a
peasant community in western India. Shivaji is deeply revered by many
Hindu nationalists, particularly those belonging to the RSS. His importance is clearly signaled in a meeting room in the RSS office in Ramakrishna Puram in Delhi, where a picture of Shivaji decorates the wall
alongside pictures of successive Sarsanghchalaks (Supreme Leaders) of
the RSS, Keshavrao Baliram Hedgewar, Madhava Sadashivrao Golwalkar,
Madhukar Dattatreya Devaras, and Rajendra Singh,[14] a picture of the sixteenth-century Rajput ruler Maharana Pratap, and one of goddess
Bharat Mata. The symbolic power of Shivaji for members of the RSS
today in part builds on his iconic status in multiple popular and nationalist movements throughout history that have used him to mobilize support for divergent and even contradictory interests (Hansen 2001;
O'Hanlon 1985). As Rosalind O'Hanlon (1985) has shown, Shivaji has
been used to mobilize support for the anti-colonial nationalist movement, as a leader and protector of the lower castes, as a visionary who
fought for a common Maratha culture that transcended religious divisions, and also as a protector of the Hindu religion, Brahmins, and cows
(symbolizing religious orthodoxy), from Muslims. It is this last image of
Shivaji that is key to RSS portrayals of him today.

For Samiti women, Shivaji's achievements were enabled by the exemplary behavior of his mother Jijabai. There has been very little scholarship on Jijabai, and most references to her are contained in larger
histories about Shivaji. Jijabai is sometimes alluded to in the histories of
these movements (see O'Hanlon 1985: 170) as an ideal mother who
taught Shivaji the right values that later guided him in his fight for
Hindu sovereignty. However, she does not achieve the kind of centrality
that is conferred upon her in Samiti versions of the past. While building

upon an existing Maratha idealization of motherhood through the figure of Jijabai, Samiti stories project Jijabai as a visionary who played an integral role in shaping the Hindu nation. Importantly, in contrast to the construction of women as victims of Muslim aggression in most Hindu nationalist histories produced by the RSS, Samiti stories reconstruct the female subject as a historical agent who confronts and challenges the atrocities supposedly committed against Hindus and their nation. This fact not only affects Samiti constructions of the past, but also enables women like Usha to urge new recruits to actively prevent their own victimization by joining the Samiti and learning to defend themselves. Jijabai therefore becomes a key symbol through which the Samiti mobilizes women to become active in the Hindu nationalist movement by modeling themselves on women who played a role in constructing the Hindu nation.

Jijabai is one of three women who are exalted by Samiti women and believed to provide important role models for Hindu womanhood. Payal Aggarwal conveyed the centrality of these women at a three-day training camp (*shivir*) I attended along with Samiti initiates in December 1999. Payal is a twenty-nine-year-old *pracharika*, one of thirty-three Samiti women in 1999 who had chosen to remain celibate in order to devote their lives to the organization. Born into an RSS family, Payal now lives with an older woman in rooms organized by the Samiti in the compound of a temple in Delhi. It had not been easy for her to become a *pracharika* because, while her mother was more supportive, her father had been very keen for her to get married. But she managed to convince them that this was how she wanted to spend her life, and she is now entirely dependent on the Samiti for her needs. In charge of *shakhas* throughout Delhi, it was also Payal's job to organize the *shivir* we were attending. Leading the "discussion" session, which was really a lecture about the Samiti, she began to talk about three female historical figures—Ahilyabai Holkar, Rani Lakshmibhai, and Jijabai—who epitomized three virtues lauded by Samiti women. Payal explained that Ahilyabai Holkar, a queen of Indore, exemplified *kartritva*, providing a model for responsible administration, and Rani Lakshmibai, the legendary queen of Jhansi, epitomized *netritva* or leadership. Jijabai embodied the ideal of *matritva*, enlightened motherhood, for inculcating Hindu values in her son Shivaji and inspiring him to fight against the oppression of Hindus. It was Jijabai, she emphasized, who taught Shivaji, who subsequently fought to establish a free Hindu nation.

It is perhaps worth mentioning that during my year in the field, it was Jijabai who cropped up in conversations and lectures rather than the other two women. Many women in the Samiti told me proudly about how they had managed to convince the government to put out a postage stamp featuring Jijabai holding a young Shivaji in her arms. During my interview with Aparna at her home in Karol Bagh, as she was explaining the Samiti's activities she told me, quite spontaneously and with pride in her voice, that Vajpayee himself had attended the function organized by the Samiti to launch the stamp. When I met Payal in her room in west Delhi, which also functions as a Samiti office, I noticed that a picture of the stamp had been placed on a shelf on the wall near the entrance alongside a picture of Lakshmibai Kelkar, the Samiti's founder, and various deities. To me this privileged positioning illustrated the significance Samiti women attached to Jijabai over the other historical figures mentioned by Payal. This positioning, along with the concerted effort to garner official recognition of Jijabai's historical significance in the form of a postage stamp, also exemplified the importance placed on motherhood over the other two virtues Payal mentioned, privileging this role as the site for female activism in everyday life.

This favoring of Jijabai by the Samiti must be juxtaposed against the supremacy accorded to Shivaji by the RSS and in almost all Hindu nationalist accounts of history. Jijabai's importance rests in her centrality to Samiti women's constructions of their own subjectivity. In the story below, which I have translated from the original Hindi, it is clear that they see her as a visionary who challenged others to participate in shaping Hindu destiny:

Jijabai was Chatrapati Maharaj Shivaji's mother. She was born in 1597. Since childhood Jijabai saw the atrocities committed by Mughals against Hindus, their temples, and Hindu women. She saw screaming women being abducted during the day. One day during her childhood she was standing on the terrace with a friend (*saheli*). She saw a man urinating on the wall of the Shiva temple. She became very angry. She complained about this to her family. But everyone remained silent. An elderly person said: "Daughter, he is a Muslim. He is a government worker. We cannot say anything to him." Her soft heart was filled with distress seeing all this and [she wondered] whose victory are these Hindus struggling for? Why couldn't this event show them the way to independence? Who would motivate them? Nobody was prepared to give her the answers to her questions. (Rashtra Sevika Samiti 1999a: 7)

In this story Jijabai stands alone as the visionary who must teach others to respect themselves and fight against Muslim rule. The Hindus in the story are presented as weak and cowardly because of their silence, while Jijabai is the self-conscious agent who must take matters into her own hands, a theme that is critical to the Samiti's own construction of self. Several Samiti members told me that the existence of violence against women today testifies to the fact that men cannot defend women effectively and that women must learn to defend themselves not only by increasing their physical strength but also by ensuring that they help promote the right values in their families and social worlds. For example, an elderly Samiti woman who resides in Nagpur and has devoted her entire life to the organization told me on a brief visit to Delhi that only women could resolve the problems in society by starting with what was happening in their own homes. Yet women's roles do not end with the domestic realm but also include participating in shaping the culture of the Hindu nation and protecting it against cultural and political threats from beyond the borders.

Jijabai is a visionary in this story precisely because she is able to fathom the threats to Hindu culture, values, and nationhood and is determined to bring an end to this situation. In fact, in the version related to me by Neera Gupta, Jijabai was angered rather than distressed by the passivity of Hindu men who averted their eyes from the urinating man instead of confronting him. According to Neera, Jijabai shouted at the Hindu men, asking them: "Have you no shame? This Muslim is urinating on the wall of your temple and you are too scared to stop him?" Neera contended that on that day Jijabai swore that when she had a son she would make sure that he was not a coward and would be strong enough to fight those who showed disrespect to his country and his religion.

What I find particularly interesting about this tale is the way it projects Jijabai as the agent who will change the social situation rather than suggesting, as most Hindu nationalist accounts would, that it is the task of Hindu men to reclaim their masculinity. For instance, in his book *Six Glorious Epochs of Indian History*, Hindu nationalist ideologue V. D. Savarkar applauds those Hindu kings who committed atrocities against Muslims, forcibly converted Muslim women to Hinduism, married them off to Hindu men, or made them into concubines "like the Hindu women by the Muslims before them" (Savarkar 1971: 203).[15] Suggesting that the effeminacy of Hindu men had permitted Muslim atrocities against Hindu women, Sarvarkar equates such acts with masculinity (Agarwal 1995). As I suggested earlier, this construction of Hindu effeminacy predates Savarkar and is apparent in the work of British Orientalist historians like Robert Orme, who contends that the Indian [Hindu] must be "the most effeminate inhabitant of the globe" (Orme 1974 [1782]: 306).[16] Such images of Hindu effeminacy prompt Savarkar and other members of the Hindu elite in colonial India, to participate in reforming Hindu society and the Hindu male (Gupta 2002). It is during this period that we see novels about the valor of various Hindu historical figures like Shivaji emerging to counter British allegations of Hindu effeminacy (Gupta 2002: 231).[17]

The image of a hypersexual Muslim fanatic preying on effeminate Hindus was also not simply a Hindu nationalist invention. It builds on earlier constructions of Muslim sexuality and communal relations dating back to the colonial period. Orientalist historian James Mill compares the "eunuch"-like qualities of the Hindu to the character of the "Mahomedan," whom he describes as being "more manly, more vigorous" (Mill 1972 [1817]: 721).[18] Zaheer Baber asserts that, while communal identities may have existed in different forms in various regional contexts, "the process of institutionalizing specific communities was intimately associated with the administrative imperatives of the colonial state" in which the alleged "oriental despotism" of Muslims justified the protective presence of the colonizers (Baber 2000: 64–65). In fact, the Hindu elite actively contributed to the Orientalist fantasy by widely disseminating this image of a predatory Muslim male through pamphlets and publications that sought to rouse Hindus to reclaim their nation and save their women from Muslims (Gupta 2002).

Returning to our tale, the alleged barbarity of Muslims is codified in the act of urinating on a temple wall, and in the claim that they committed atrocities not only against Hindus in general, but against women in particular. This image articulates with normative Hindu nationalist constructions already entrenched in historical memory of the relationship between Hindus and Muslims.[19] An important part of this historical narrative is the projection of Muslims as sexual predators, a theme that is recurrent in the stories about Jijabai, as well as other Hindu nationalist stories discussed below about historical figures such as Akbar and the Nizam of Hyderabad. This image of the predatory Muslim male is not only central to mobilizing Hindu men to engage in the extreme acts of violence we saw in Gujarat, but also critical to justifying women's activism in the movement today. At the Dharam Bhavan event, Usha uses this image to urge women to join the Samiti and learn to defend themselves. As Paola Bacchetta contends, this image of a predatory "other" embodied in the Muslim male allows Samiti women to construct their activism as "self-defense" and thereby enables them to occupy spaces and learn skills that would have been considered part of the male domain (2004: 80–81). I would add here that the suggestion that Hindu men do not or cannot defend women effectively also enables Samiti women's activism and is crucial to their construction of female subjectivity.

Neera Gupta told me the above story about Jijabai in the context of a larger statement about what she saw as the humiliation of Hindus at the hands of Muslims throughout history, a juxtaposition that makes the connection between these historical tales and Hindu nationalist historiography abundantly clear. These stories both reflect and reiterate a normative Hindu nationalist construction of the past in which Hindu women have suffered at the hands of lustful Muslim rulers throughout history. Indeed, it is this normative construction, consistently recalled and cited in women's everyday narratives, which imbues these stories

with significance. Below I examine this and other normative constructions of the past that are embedded in these stories and provide the context within which they are performed and understood.

Narrating the Hindu Nationalist Past

Cultural symbols are not meaningful in and of themselves, but rather
gain their salience from becoming meaningful in the everyday lives and
struggles of people.[20] In the case of nationalist symbols, such resonance
is critical to the process through which individuals come to imagine
themselves as subjects of the nation. Following Stathis Gourgouris,
nationalist subjectivity is not simply imposed on individuals; rather, "one
'becomes' a nationalist subject insofar as one *believes* oneself to be a witness to this mysterious process or ritual called 'a national community,'
insofar as one participates in (imagines, constructs, *dreams*) the fantasy
of belonging to a national community" (Gourgouris 1996: 34, original
emphasis). The national fantasy is sustained by the desire of the nationalist subject to give the nation ontological status (1996: 35). The historical tales discussed here enabled women to appeal to and resonate with
the everyday fears and stereotypes of those they encountered, instigating
their desire to participate in, and become subjects of, the Hindu nationalist fantasy. Each retelling reiterated the ideology that grounds the fantasy on which the Hindu nation is constructed. Such stories therefore
are integral not only to grasping Hindu national constructions of the
past, but also to understanding how the nation itself is given the appearance of the real (see for instance Butler 1997: 14; 1999: 173). Below I
examine the intricate weaving of nationalist and personal histories by
members of the movement to construct a "nationalist fantasy" that both
establishes the ontology of the Hindu nation and compels its subjects
toward a Hindu nationalist vision of the past, present, and future.

The image of a Hindu nation struggling for actualization against the
tyranny of Muslim rule is a key trajectory of the nationalist fantasy that
grounds the Hindu nation. Indeed, it is a normative construction that is
consistently recalled in the everyday narratives of Hindu nationalist
women. I was told several stories that vividly described how Hindus, particularly Hindu women, had been victimized by Muslim rule. Neera told
me the following tales in the context of a conversation about why veiling
is more prevalent among Muslim and Hindu women in North India than
in the South. Her stated reason—which echoes Usha's speech at Dharam
Bhavan in interesting ways—was that North India was always at battle
against Muslims, and veiling had to be strictly maintained because Muslim men would just take off with "whatever pretty woman they saw wandering around."

To illustrate her point, she related a story about a childhood visit she had made with her mother to Hyderabad in the 1940s, when it was still a princely state in pre-independence India. Neera told me that she and her mother were at the market when they suddenly noticed that people had begun rushing around and closing all the shop windows. They asked someone why this was happening, and he said, "the Nizam is coming."[21] Then a person told them to get off the streets, saying that if the Nizam passed by and took a fancy to either of them, they would be whisked off to the harem where he already had a hundred other women with whom he was now bored. Neera told me that she and her mother immediately went and hid. To end her story, Neera said, when the Nizam was "chased . . . out of there [Hyderabad] in 1953 they found about 400 women in the harem."[22]

For Neera, the Nizam fitted into a larger stereotype of Muslim rulers in India. She insisted that the Nizam was not an exception, but similar to others like the Mughal emperor Akbar. In the secular imagination, Akbar, a sixteenth-century Mughal emperor, is admired for his efforts to bridge the gap between his Hindu and Muslim subjects through, for instance, political and marital alliances with Hindus, and for attempting a composite cultural style in architecture, religion, and language (see Spear 1978: 34, 36, 49). Most Hindu nationalist constructions of Akbar seem to directly contradict this image of the emperor. Asserting that Akbar too had several women in his harem, Neera claimed that he held a *mina bazaar* (market)[23] exclusively for women and could pick anyone he wanted there. This story about Akbar's *mina bazaar* was elaborated in much greater detail by Aditya Trivedi, a senior member of the Delhi Vishwa Hindu Parishad, illustrating the permeation of these images throughout the various wings of the movement. During an interview in his office in an upper-middle-class housing colony in Delhi, Aditya informed me that all Muslim kings had engaged in forcible conversions and committed atrocities against Hindu women. He said that even Akbar, who is considered "broadminded," organized a monthly *mina bazaar*. When I asked him what this was, he said (in English):

A sort of monthly market. So every month all beautiful Hindu ladies were made to visit that market. And Akbar used to choose out of them. And those most beautiful ladies were made to enter the harem. One Rajputani, Akbar tried to molest her. He in some veiled way took her into a corner. And when she came to know that it is Akbar she attacked him, pinned him down, took her dagger out, and she was going to kill him when he begged her mercy and told her "you are my mother." That is the story. Well known one. The poet Dinkar[24] has drafted it into a long poem. So none of them was at all tolerant. It was only a difference of degree.

Aditya Trivedi's words illustrate Hindu nationalist constructions of history that are part of the broader trajectory of cultural memory in which the stories about Jijabai must be situated. The story itself is not a recent invention. Charu Gupta (2002: 244) documents a similar story about Akbar during the colonial period, when the Hindu elite was concerned with constructing a foundation for a Hindu nation. In the version of this story she discusses, Akbar is said to have dressed as a veiled woman in order to gaze on Hindu women's bodies—and here I think the attempt to challenge Muslim masculinity is clear. Over time the reference to Akbar having adopted women's clothing has become a reference to Akbar's deception—"in some veiled way"—revealing the different agendas of the movement. In Aditya's story, the purpose is not to challenge Akbar's masculinity by claiming that he put on women's clothing, but rather to symbolize how *all* Muslim rulers were untrustworthy and threatened the honor of Hindu women.

Aditya's intention in this story—similar to Neera's—is to reiterate the Hindu nationalist construction of the predatory nature of Muslims and to suggest that they are unjust and cruel rulers. At particular risk are Hindu women, whose honor and virtue must be defended. Recalling a normative image that configures Hindu nationalist historiography, Akbar's immorality is conveyed through the construction of him as a Muslim ruler who cannot contain his lust and the suggestion that he, like the Nizam in Neera's story, abuses his power by victimizing Hindu women. Yet a year in the field taught me that Hindu nationalist men are not immune to showering inappropriate attentions on young unmarried women. Indeed, while Aditya—a middle-aged man—was always a ready source of information, I often felt uncomfortable in innuendo-laden conversations with him, as also by his frequent attempts at physical contact, which would have been deemed inappropriate by the gender codes of the movement. On one occasion, as I was leaving his office, he put an arm around my shoulder to say goodbye, a gesture that made me extremely uneasy. Additionally, if gossip can be believed, a complaint had been registered with his superiors after he made a pass at a member of the movement. Yet, despite his own inappropriate behavior, Aditya projects the burden of male exploitation of women to Muslim men and shifts the focus away from Hindu men who may have engaged in similar acts. In fact almost all my interlocutors, with a couple of notable exceptions, projected such actions onto the specter of a Muslim man, past or present. As Paola Bacchetta has argued, this transference of sexual violence away from Hindu men onto Muslims is critical for the continued production of the Hindu nation (2004: 81).

Although victimized by Muslim men in these stories, women often play an active role either by defending themselves or inspiring others to avenge their dishonor. In Aditya's tale the Rajput woman overpowers Akbar and threatens to kill him. Here it is no accident that the woman who challenges Akbar's advances is a Rajput, a North Indian caste legendary for its bravery and courage. However, even as she breaks with convention with her display of strength, aggression, and potential violence, the Rajput woman reaffirms traditional Hindu nationalist stereotypes by forgiving Akbar when he calls her "mother." As Neera explained to me, echoing an image that is integral to Hindu nationalist constructions of womanhood, forgiveness is intrinsic to motherhood. Unlike the Rajput woman in this tale, Jijabai does not engage in violent acts herself but instead inspires her son Shivaji to avenge the honor of Hindu women.

Gender is a crucial dynamic in these stories since, as is clear in the vignette below, it is because women have allegedly borne the brunt of Muslim aggression that Jijabai is able to goad her son into action.

One day a singer was telling the brave story of Rani Padmini through his songs. In the middle of the story Shivaji got up to leave so his mother asked him the reason why he was leaving. Shivaji said that he found himself incapable of listening to the horror of the event. Then his mother said that the Muslims carried away your own aunt (*chachi*). She said that in this country mothers and sisters are constantly bearing these atrocities and you can't even listen to them? In this way his mother inspired Shivaji to free mothers and sisters from these atrocities and take revenge. (Rashtra Sevika Samiti 1999a: 8)

As in those above, in this story the conflict between Hindus and Muslims is constructed upon the territory of the female body, signaling a trend seen in India and other parts of the world wherein nationalist discourses are articulated through gendered imagery in which women become the pre-eminent symbols of nationalist identity and honor.[25] In fact, the Samiti makes this connection between woman and nation quite explicitly in one Jijabai story proclaiming, "a woman is like a mother, to dishonor her is to dishonor the nation" (Rashtra Sevika Samiti 1999a: 8). Indeed, both the violations of national honor and the need to avenge that honor are articulated through gendered imagery. Ritu Menon and Kamla Bhasin (1998) have argued that it is because the honor of men and their communities is located in women's bodies that women become the targets of violence at the hands of both their own and the rival community. Menon and Bhasin suggest that communal violence against women must be understood as part of a larger, more everyday "patriarchal consensus" on violence against women (1998: 58, 60; see also Cockburn 2004: 43–44). In the story above, what precisely "revenge" consists of remains unarticulated. Yet, regardless of how Shivaji may have acted in these circumstances, if the violence against women in Gujarat in 2002 is any indication, in contemporary Hindu nationalism revenge entails sexual violation, humiliation, and torture (see, e.g., Jaffrelot 2007: 184–86).

The tale above refers to a well-known piece of folklore in which the Rajput queen of Mewar, Rani Padmini, along with the other women of Chittor in Rajasthan, committed *jauhar* (mass immolation) when it became apparent that her husband was going to lose in battle to his Muslim enemy Ala-ud-Din Khilji (Harlan 1995: 209). Lindsey Harlan (1995) discusses this story in the context of Rajput women's current projection of Rani Padmini as the ultimate *pativrata* (one who worships her husband) who follows her husband even to his death. The Hindu nationalist versions focus on another theme that already exists in folklore and cultural memory of Padmini's sacrifice, signifying her refusal to be captured by Muslims to be put in their harem. In this tale, in the context of this historical trajectory Shivaji is presented as lacking the courage even to listen to these stories about the plight of Hindu women. Again it is Jijabai who, through her ability to bear the pain and burden of these stories, must guide her son to rightful action.

Also key is the idea that these women were family. It is Shivaji's aunt who is carried off by the Muslims. The horror of the event is personal, not simply part of a more anonymous historical record. This personalization of history, also clearly visible in Neera's tale, is something I heard time and again in different contexts from different people when I asked what motivated them or others to join this movement. Urvashi Aggarwal, a woman in her fifties who is a member of Matri Shakti and Mahila Morcha, told me in a passionate tone:

During the partition of India [in 1947] the atrocities committed against Hindus were terrible. Husbands and fathers were forced to watch as their wives, daughters, and mothers were raped in front of them and the pretty ones were just carried off. Women were maimed and their breasts were cut off in front of their husbands, brothers, fathers, and sons. *It is people who remember this history who have become members of the VHP.* There are many people who have joined the VHP because their families were directly affected by this history. (my emphasis)

The personalization of historical narrative becomes a powerful tool through which constructions of the past are both legitimized and shrouded with an aura of factuality. The stories are powerful because they reinterpret events, experiences, and figures that already lurk in the pools of collective memory, as part of Hindu nationalist "mythico-histories" (Malkki 1995: 55). Peter van der Veer argues that the use of "historical referentiality" by nationalist discourses to establish the ontology of the nation suggests that modernist realism, the "worship of facts," is a cornerstone of nationalist discourses (van der Veer 1999: 150). Discursive devices that endow "historical referentiality," such as providing the exact dates of Shivaji's battles or the year of his and Jijabai's birth, well-known events like the partition or the mass immolation of Queen Pad-mini and her female subjects, or famous historical figures such as Akbar or Shivaji, contribute to the aura of factuality that is conveyed through these stories. For many in the movement, these stories become a convincing vision of the past and of the relationship between Hindus and Muslims through history, and, as Urvashi suggests, motivate them to participate in the politics of Hindu nationalism.

Jijabai: Brave Wife and Enlightened Mother

Historical tales such as these are central to crafting, disseminating, and reiterating Hindu nationalist constructions of the subject. Related by Hindu nationalist women in their daily work for the movement, the stories not only reproduce Hindu nationalist constructions of a Muslim "other," but also image Hindu male and female subjectivity in ways that enable women's activism in the public sphere. Women like Jijabai are envisioned as having the courage and strength that Hindu men, even cultural icons like Shivaji, are seen to lack. Indeed, the image of Hindu men as ineffective or cowardly is as central to justifying women's claim to political agency in the movement as the construction of Muslims as sexual predators discussed above. However, while drawing women into the public sphere, this agency is usually enabled through their existing roles within the family. In these stories, Jijabai represents the model wife whose loyalty is to her husband's patrilineage and the values it upholds. This is eloquently conveyed in the following tale describing an encounter between Jijabai and her father, Sardar Lakhuji Jadhavrao.

Lakhuji Jadhavrao Sardar was the first army commander to receive a post in the Nizam's empire. Jijabai was married to Shahji, the son of Maloji. Shahji and Jad-havrao did not get along. Jadhavrao was aligned with the Mughals, while Shahji was aligned with the Marathas. One day Jijabai was captured by the Mughals. Now she was in her father's captivity. Jijabai was about to become a mother. Upon seeing his daughter's condition Jadhavrao said: "Daughter, why are you putting yourself through so much suffering? Let us immediately go to my house in Sindhkhed and I will make arrangements for a nursemaid." Jijabai was a brave wife. How could she accept such a solution? She fearlessly replied to her father: "You want to take revenge on the Bhonsle family. I am standing here before you, why don't you take revenge on me? Since the day of my marriage when I became a part of the Bhonsle family, since that day my ties with your family have been broken. I am a brave wife of the Bhonsle family. I love the bread (*roti*) that I receive at my husband's house more than that cooked in your house as well as more than all the diamonds and pearls at your house. I will not go to your house." When Jijabai was voicing her defiance (*hunkar*) she looked like a vision of mother Durga. Jadhavrao saw no reason to remain there and moved on from there. (Rashtra Sevika Samiti 1999b: 13–14)

This story invokes the patrilineal ideology that is central to Hindu nationalist constructions of the national community (e.g., A. Basu 1995; Sarkar 1995), in which a woman's connection to her natal home is severed on marriage. Calling on patrilineal discourses of kinship,[26] Jijabai's rejection of Muslim rule is metaphorically conveyed through her assertion that all ties with her father's house, and the values therein, were broken on the day that she was married. Now she belongs to her husband's family and has adopted their values, particularly their vision of Maratha sovereignty, which, as a good wife and virtuous daughter-in-law, she too must share. This is an interesting reading of history, since it suggests that Jijabai's affinal family did not ally with Muslim rulers. In fact, at the time, five Muslim rulers were battling to control the Deccan, and while Jijabai's husband Shahji allied with one of these—the Nizam Shah of Ahmednagar—her father shifted allegiance from the Nizam to Shah Jahan of the Mughal Empire (Laine 2003: 4). Significantly, in this version of the story, Jijabai's valor is conveyed through her staunch defense of her husband's family and her rejection of the comforts of her father's home for the austerities required by her commitment to the values and struggles of her husband's home. Her father's immorality is expressed by his commitment to the Muslim ruler, which enables him to walk away from his daughter and allow her to experience the hardships of prison despite the fact that she is pregnant. Her pregnancy makes Jijabai's rejection of her natal family all the more intense since in many patrilineal communities in India women are expected to go back to their parents' home to give birth.

It is Jijabai's courage and righteous defiance in these circumstances that underlies her identification with the goddess Durga, the embodiment of *shakti*, the female principle, often called on to uphold the moral order and defeat immorality. This association of Jijabai with the goddess resonates with Hindu nationalist constructions of Hindu womanhood—expressed by both men and women—that virtuous Hindu women are like goddesses. In the Devi Mahatmaya, the goddess in the form of Durga is created to destroy the Buffalo Demon and thereby uphold the moral order of the world.[27] In this ancient sacred Hindu text, the goddess is created from the combined *shakti* of the male gods, who are not able to destroy the demon themselves. Therefore, in this vignette Jijabai's connection with the goddess Durga not only signals her fight for morality against the assumed immoralities of Muslim rule, but also implies that, as a woman, she is uniquely positioned to do so. The story suggests that, like Jijabai, it is absolutely critical for Hindu nationalist women to harness their energies and *shakti* for the production and reproduction of the Hindu nation.

Jijabai embodies what the Samiti calls enlightened motherhood, a trait that is fundamental to the organization's constructions of ideal female subjectivity. Explaining this concept to me, Neera Gupta said that the Samiti's goal was to organize Hindu women and teach them the values of their own culture so that they could pass these on to their children. Several women told me that women must model their lives on Jijabai, and, just as Jijabai taught her son the values and courage to fight for Hindu sovereignty, they too must teach their children these values. One Jijabai story explicitly states that these are values embodied in the ancient Hindu epics, the Ramayana and the Mahabharata.[28] According to these narratives, Jijabai went to great lengths to ensure that Shivaji grew up in an environment conducive to building character. In the Samiti version, although Jijabai's husband Shahji lived in Bangalore, with his permission she moved to Pune and lived under the guardianship of Dadoji Khond Dev,[29] feeling that the luxurious lifestyle in Bangalore would not be conducive to building Shivaji's moral and physical strength. The story contends that Jijabai began to shape Shivaji's character while he was still in her womb:

The pregnant Jijabai prayed to the eternal Bhavani ma to give her a good son. On the 10 of April 1627 in Shivneri fort, the protector of cows and Brahmins, the founder of the Hindu nation, the great king Shivaji was born. Even when he was in her womb Jijamata taught Shivaji. Her objective was that this boy become the protector of cows and Brahmins and the motivating force of the Hindu nation. For this reason she made sure that there was a proper cultural environment in the house that would promote young Shivaji's character formation even while he was still in her womb. (Rashtra Sevika Samiti 1999a: 7)

The stories about Jijabai construct motherhood as the site through which Hindu nationalist women can insert themselves as historical agents in the mythico-history of the Hindu nation. Tanika Sarkar (1995, 1999) has argued that women's roles in the movement are clearly situated within the family as the guardians of Hindu nationalist traditions, values, morals, and ideology, whose primary responsibility is to cultivate these ideas in their children. The strategic use of motherhood to construct a subjectivity for Hindu nationalist women resonates with the way motherhood has been deployed in various political contexts to create a legitimate political place for women even as it limits access to other places (see Taussig 1992; Gonzalez and Kampwirth 2001; Kampwirth 2001). Karen Kampwirth has argued that it is precisely because of the negative, even immoral, connotations of women's participation in the political sphere that women strategically deploy the "language of maternalism" to launch their political agendas (Kampwirth 2001: 96). Indeed, women often claim their place in the nation through equating citizenship with the responsibilities of motherhood, thus redefining an already existing avenue of female power (Werbner 1999). In Hindu nationalist constructions of womanhood, as much as motherhood limits women's roles and agency, it is also a subjectivity that does give women a great deal of power.

Samiti stories depict Jijabai as straddling the divide between respecting patriarchal authority and the hierarchies of orthodox Hinduism and challenging some of the boundaries of women's roles established by the other wings of the movement. For instance, she gets her husband's permission before embarking on the radical step of establishing a separate residence in Pune. While leading men and women in the fight for the Hindu nation, she still upholds Hindu orthodoxy. For example, she is described as wanting a son who will be "the protector of cows and Brahmins." This suggests that these stories endorse an upper-caste vision of Shivaji in which he protects the pillars of religious orthodoxy: Brahmins and cows. This sentiment resonates with the predominantly upper-/middle-caste composition of the movement. While recently the movement has made a concerted effort to recruit members from lower-caste groups, almost all the women I worked with, and all those mentioned here, belong to upper-/middle-caste groups.[30]

Jijabai: The Architect of the Hindu Nation

In these stories, Jijabai emerges as a woman with vision, whose deep devotion to the Hindu nation leads her to foster feelings of patriotism and a commitment to fighting for its actualization in her son, Shivaji. In Samiti accounts, it is because of Jijabai's "enlightened motherhood" that Shivaji is inspired to engage in the struggle to establish a Hindu nation. This construction of female subjectivity is in keeping with images of womanhood in other wings of the Hindu nationalist movement, of women as mothers of the family/nation whose primary responsibility is to inculcate the right values in their children. Yet the stories about Jijabai also reveal significant moments of departure from the narratives produced by the RSS to which the Samiti is most closely aligned, which indicate an alternative construction of female subjectivity. This alternative construction is nicely captured in the following vignette that describes a famous encounter between Shivaji and his Muslim rival Afzal Khan:

Jijabai not only inspired Shivaji but she also gave him lessons about strategy. When Afzal Khan attacked Shivaji with a large army then Jijabai advised him that Afzal Khan would not fight by the rules because Jijabai could not forget that Afzal Khan had killed Sambha Ji by cheating.[31] It is by following the advice of mother Jija that Shivaji killed a powerful enemy like Afzal Khan. In this way many moments of trial occurred but Jijamata did not allow any of these moments to put out the coals of self-rule. (Rashtra Sevika Samiti 1999a: 8–9)

In this vignette, Shivaji defeats Afzal Khan because of Jijabai's timely advice. It is because Jijabai understands Khan's tactics that Shivaji is able to overcome him, not because of his own knowledge of his enemy or the wisdom of his own strategy.

This portrait of Shivaji's encounter with Afzal Khan is in stark contrast to the RSS version of the same event, in which there is no mention of Jijabai. Most RSS histories construct Shivaji as the paradigmatic national hero, radiating courage, strength, and righteous commitment to the Hindu nation. In these histories, if Jijabai is mentioned at all, it is only to say that she was a good mother. The RSS men I spoke to also never mentioned Jijabai, suggesting a similar marginalization of her by men in everyday life. It is critical to contrast the silence of men on the subject of Jijabai with the active projection of Jijabai as the mother of the nation by Samiti women.

The various vignettes about Shivaji are found in a pamphlet called *Sangh Utsav* (Rashtriya Swayamsevak Sangh 1999), or festivals celebrated by the RSS. The one in question celebrating the legacy of Shivaji is Hindu Samrajaya Dinotsav, the festival celebrating the establishment of the Hindu empire. The section begins with a description of the sociopolitical context in which Shivaji rose to power, detailing the atrocities of Muslim rule that are the cornerstone of Hindu nationalist histories. The pamphlet claims that Hindus had forgotten their gods, religion, and culture and had accepted foreign (read: Muslim) rule. It then suggests, "even today we are in the same state" (Rashtriya Swayamsevak Sangh 1999: 32). Finally, projecting Shivaji as a role model for Hindu nationalists today, it says: "but in just such terribly hopeless circumstances" Shivaji established his strong and independent nation (32). The next sentence directs Hindus to spend some time thinking about how Shivaji's success was possible. After this the vignettes start.

The first story, about Shivaji's encounter with Afzal Khan, deviates in important ways from Samiti histories of this moment. In the RSS account, Shivaji, realizing the gravity of the social situation when he was only eleven years old, organizes his friends to fight for the Hindu nation. This is different from the Samiti version of this event, where it is Jijabai who realizes that the battle for the Hindu nation cannot be fought alone and therefore trains not only the young Shivaji but also his friends in the values of Hindu sovereignty and the arts of war. The contrasts between the two histories become even more stark when the author of the RSS account describes how Shivaji killed and defeated Afzal Khan:

All of Maharashtra trembled with fear because of Afzal Khan's record of atrocities and the strength of his army. Having taken the vow to capture Shivaji alive, he left Bijapur with a great army. The temples that fell along his path were being destroyed. Even the god of Shivaji's lineage, Tulja Bhavani's temple was demolished by Afzal Khan. There was lamentation from all directions. In that terrible situation Shivaji's foresight came to use. He took his small army and made his base in the impenetrable and impassable fort at Pratap Garh. There he waited for his enemy to come to him because he did not want to fight his enemy's grand army on the battleground with his own small army. Shivaji waited for the appropriate time with great calm and strength. Afzal Khan saw that Shivaji was not coming out of the fort. Was it possible that he was afraid? Afzal Khan brought his great army through the impassable mountainous jungle with a view to surrounding the fort. Shivaji wanted just this, that Afzal Khan would leave the battleground and enter the mountainous jungle.[32] According to his plan Shivaji baited Khan by talking about reconciliation. He suggested I want to come to some compromise with you. I am willing to come with you to your king. I will even be willing to serve your king. With the help of these lures Shivaji was able to get Afzal Khan to agree to a place and time for a meeting. Afzal Khan was very strong and very proud. He thought that he was catching Shivaji in his net. That is why he agreed to all the conditions and came to meet Shivaji. Even then Afzal Khan had some doubts in his mind but Shivaji had complete faith in his own victory. Afzal Khan was killed and his grand army was also destroyed. Shivaji gained an unprecedented victory and at the same time attained great respect. (Rashtriya Swayamsevak Sangh 1999: 33–34)

The author goes on to assert that this incident gave Shivaji international fame and that today many consider him even greater than Napoleon, Julius Caesar, and Hannibal (35).

The meeting between Khan and Shivaji is a well-known piece of folklore in India that describes how Shivaji, pretending to embrace Khan, uses the tiger claws he has secretly worn on his fingers to disembowel him. When one contrasts this version of the story with the historical narrative constructed by M. G. Ranade (1900) about the same event, it becomes clear that Hindu nationalist histories about Shivaji build on an earlier Maratha nationalism. The RSS version, like the other nationalist constructions of Shivaji, build on an already existing body of hagiographical literature (*bakhars*) produced by Maharashtrian Brahmins in the seventeenth and eighteenth centuries and now very much part of popular versions of history in Maharashtra (Gordon 1993: 1; see also Hansen 2001). This literature projects Shivaji as "a near divine figure, regularly inspired by the goddess Bhavani to great deeds, which were primarily important as a Hindu resistance to Muslim domination and as leading to the establishment of a Hindu state" (1).[33] These *bakhars* were widely used by historians particularly during the colonial and nationalist periods (1–3). The similarities between the RSS and Maratha nationalist versions are not surprising, since, although today the RSS has branches all over the country, the organization was founded by Maharashtrian Brahmins.

Yet Samiti accounts, instead of contributing to the Hindu nationalist glorification of Shivaji, suggest that Jijabai (not Shivaji) was responsible for the birth of the Hindu nation. In Samiti narratives, Jijabai not only inspires Shivaji in his struggle, she guides him every step of the way to victory through her brilliant strategizing and unfailing commitment. Indeed, in these stories it is Jijabai, not Shivaji, who is constructed as the cultural icon, in contrast to the Hindu nationalist construction of Shivaji as archetypal cultural hero. Samiti stories almost portray Shivaji as a pawn in Jijabai's strategic victory over Muslims. Men, in general, are portrayed as weak, immoral, or fickle. While Jijabai's father is clearly both weak and immoral, Shivaji is represented as vacillating in his commitment to the fight for the Hindu nation. And in the many "moments of trial" it is Jijabai, not Shivaji, who preserves those vulnerable incipient "coals of self rule" through her cunning strategy and exemplary commitment.

The symbolic power of Jijabai resides in her multivocality, because even as she reinforces gender roles in the movement by situating her activism within her traditional role as a mother, she also embodies a departure from male constructions of gender. The stories represent men as incapable and lost without the guiding force of women like Jijabai, using their roles as mothers to become historical agents. The construction of women as the bearers of the nation's culture and the primary transmitters of this culture to the new generations of nationalist subjects is common throughout the movement (A. Basu 1995; T. Sarkar 1995, 1999; Bacchetta 1996). The construction of men in Samiti stories, even a man as iconic as Shivaji, provides an important alternative to constructions of gender in the movement, and it is one that enables women's activism in the movement.

How should we understand these moments of departure? Paola Bacchetta explains discrepancies between RSS and Samiti constructions by arguing that the ideology of the RSS (or Sangh) "leaves little space for women-actors to exist, and so the Samiti, in order to craft a Hindu nationalism which women can relate to, is obliged to exit the realm of the Sangh's discourse at some points" (Bacchetta 1996: 127). Bacchetta argues that such discrepancies become critical to recruiting women into the Samiti. In this sense, then, these discrepancies are central to understanding the expansionary power of Hindu nationalism since a more active role for women is necessary to create a place for women's activism in the movement. Indeed, these stories illuminate the way different wings of the movement variously frame its ideology to appeal to diverse audiences. As Bacchetta notes, the differences between RSS and Samiti discourses are ways of ensuring "women's complicity" with the larger goals of Hindu nationalism through enabling a specifically female agency (161).

These stories do not constitute what I am calling dissonance in this book, because they do not transgress the normative constructions of the movement. Rather, as I have suggested, they clearly reiterate the normative constructions of Hindu nationalism. As such they are indicative of the pluralism within Hindu nationalism that embraces divergent tendencies in order to appeal to diverse audiences while still citing its norms. This is precisely what enables the production of Hindu nationalist hegemony. Yet, can the image of a woman who shapes the destiny of the nation inspire dissonant acts among women in the movement? It is important to acknowledge here that while divergent ideas do not constitute dissonance, they could potentially lead to dissonant acts that transgress the norm. Ultimately, however, these stories are best understood as part of the expansionary tactics of women who use alternative visions of gender to draw women into the embrace of Hindu nationalism and to reiterate normative Hindu nationalist constructions of the past to diverse audiences in their everyday work for the movement. The constructions of self and "other" and the logic of revenge that are contained in these stories have mobilized thousands of Hindus to engage in violence against Muslims in contemporary India.

Conclusion

What motivated so many men and women to condone and engage in horrific acts of violence against the Muslim community in Gujarat? The Gujarat tragedy is a powerful reminder that stories are never just so, and women are not bystanders in the violence of men. The stories recounted here are everyday articulations of history that illuminate how violent events like the Gujarat pogrom are, in Veena Das's words, "attached to the everyday" (2007: 8). The stories about Jijabai are also not simply tales about a historical figure, but, as I have shown, are used to mobilize women, to call on them to emulate Jijabai by taking part in the historical creation of the nation. The historical trajectory of immoral and lustful Muslim kings fighting honorable Hindu rulers is a key part of Hindu nationalist constructions of the past. By telling these stories in their daily work for the movement, Samiti women produce and reproduce Hindu nationalist histories, reshape collective memories of the past, and reiterate key elements of Hindu nationalist ideology. Indeed women's acts are central to creating a hegemonic narrative of the past since each retelling further "naturalizes" Hindu nationalist historiography in the communities in which they work (see Comaroff and Comaroff 1991: 22–24). It is this very narrative that operationalizes the image of an "other" whose apparent historical misdeeds must be violently, even brutally, avenged today. While these stories focus on the specter of a Muslim "other," similar constructions of the past and present are mobilized to legitimize violence against the Christian minority in India. In each of these cases, history, and the violence it engenders, is central to the imagination of the nation and its subjects in contemporary India.

I have shown how the stories about Jijabai construct a historically rooted subjectivity for women in its ranks. This subjectivity is not simply limited to women's nurturing and procreative roles as mothers but also embraces the possibility that women, as mothers, can be the agents of historical change. In many ways Samiti constructions of female subjectivity reflect existing images of Hindu womanhood upheld by other wings of the movement. For instance, Samiti stories about Jijabai construct motherhood as the primary site for agency and suggest that it is through their sons that their aspirations are most fully realized and their contributions most meaningful. Indeed, the use of "traditional" female roles such as those of mothers (T. Sarkar 1995, 1999), or female ascetics (A. Basu 1995), to carve out a place for women in the movement is key to understanding the successful mobilization of women in the various wings of the Hindu nationalist movement. Yet Samiti stories about Jijabai, more than simply creating a place for women through reinstating "traditional" constructions of womanhood also provide an alternative vision of gender to that propagated by the RSS.

In Samiti representations men are portrayed as weak and lacking commitment, while women, through the figure of Jijabai, are depicted as integral to the historical creation of the Hindu nation. At the very heart of the discrepant viewpoints of men and women is the suggestion that Jijabai, not Shivaji, was responsible for founding the Hindu nation. Jijabai's role in these stories is not simply to teach Shivaji the values, courage, and morality needed to become the leader and defender of the Hindu nation. Although she never takes up arms and only acts through Shivaji, through her counseling and strategizing, she herself becomes this very leader and defender. Jijabai, through her exemplary vision, bravery, and leadership, becomes the agent who takes it upon herself to change the course of history, the fate of Hindus, and the fate of women, by rousing her son to action. She guides Shivaji every step of the way not only through nurturing him emotionally, but also by fostering in him her own abilities as a tactician and strategist. Thus, even as they endorse the revisionist history of the RSS and appear to propagate the ideals of subjectivity upheld by the movement at large, the stories about Jijabai present an alternative to the movement's construction of the role of women in the historical creation of the nation.

Ultimately, however, these diverging perspectives on gender both recall the same historical narrative, one that positions Muslims as the "other" and Hindus as a persecuted nation that must avenge atrocities allegedly committed against them. These are normative constructions in Hindu nationalist discourse that are effectively disseminated to new audiences as these stories are related. However, the views in the stories are persuasive recruiting tools that draw women into the movement by providing them with a role model who is powerful, intelligent, and determined to establish a sovereign Hindu nation. These everyday artic-ulations of the past are compelling calls to action that have mobilized large numbers of women to "become like Jijabai" and enter the violent politics of Hindu nationalism.

Chapter 2

National Insecurities

Australian missionary Graham Staines and his two young sons were murdered in the eastern Indian state of Orissa during the night of January 22–23, 1999, when the station wagon in which they had been sleeping was set on fire. According to the Wadhwa Commission Report (1999), a government investigation undertaken by Supreme Court Justice D. P. Wadhwa, a group led by Dara Singh was responsible for this gruesome murder. Although police records cited in this report clearly point to Dara Singh's connections with the Hindu nationalist group Bajrang Dal and the BJP, the report fails to find any links between these organizations and those involved in the Staines murder. The report suggests that it was the tensions generated by missionary activity and conversions to Christianity in the area that created the conditions for Staines's murder.[1] This was not the first incident of violence against Christians in India. In fact, the fatal attack on Staines and his sons came in the wake of months of attacks on Christians, Christian missionaries, and Christian churches,[2] and only days after Hindu nationalist prime minister Atal Behari Vajpayee had called for a "national debate on conversions" in response to violence in the Dangs district of Gujarat. In each instance, Hindu nationalist leaders claimed that it was missionary activity that engendered violence between Hindus and Christians in these areas, a view unfortunately echoed in the Wadhwa Commission Report and indeed in Vajpayee's call for a "national debate" (see also S. Sarkar 2002: 217). In one instance, after four nuns had been gang-raped by Hindus in Madhya Pradesh in September 1998, B. L. Sharma Prem, a VHP leader and former BJP minister, asserted that these violent acts testified to "the anger of patriotic Hindu youth against the anti-national forces" (cited in Narula 1999: 33). In each of these cases, the politics of Christian conversion, deemed anti-Hindu and anti-national, is held to blame for Hindu violence against Christians.

Anti-Christian mobilization was an expansionary tactic that enabled my interlocutors to represent Hindu nationalism as a movement dedicated to protecting India from moral, cultural, and political threats. Arguing that individuals converted to Christianity only because they had been tricked by missionaries or seduced by the material remuneration offered, Hindu nationalists asserted that Christian proselytizing was part of a conspiracy to destroy "Indian" (Hindu) culture and to destabilize the "Indian" polity. At rallies and protests they tried to recruit new members into the movement's embrace by articulating these narratives with already existing suspicions about Christian missionaries and insecurities about the vulnerability of India's borders. This anti-Christian mobilization not only angered many Hindus, but also, in the cases above, led to violence against Christians that created a "fixed and charged" identity for Hindus (Appadurai 2006: 7). Here I analyze both women's and men's everyday narratives to explore how anti-Christian mobilization creates an arena for Hindu nationalists not only to position themselves as the moral protectors of the nation, but also to define and "fix" national identity. The subtle differences in emphasis in these narratives reveal not only the varying concerns of men and women, but also perhaps the gendered nature of the interventions made by each of them in the Hindu nationalist movement.

Claiming that Hinduism does not engage in conversion, both men and women suggest that missionaries are drawing people away from a group that cannot be replenished (S. Sarkar 2002: 221). Although Hindu nationalists have been actively converting tribal populations to Hinduism, the men and women I spoke to gloss such acts as "reconversion" and argued that they are simply enabling individuals to return to their "original" religious affiliation. Implicit in this argument, is the idea that Hinduism was the original religion of India, primordially linked to the land and its denizens. Anti-Christian mobilization and "reconversion" activities in tribal areas enable Hindu nationalists to recode national territory as Hindu space which must be cleansed of the presumably immoral and antinational presence of Christian interlopers. Conversion, or in this case "reconversion," also places individuals within a new epistemological universe, one that requires, as Robert Hefner claims, a "commitment to a new kind of moral authority and a new or reconceptualized social identity" (Hefner 1993: 17). Thus, reconversion, and the anti-Christian mobilization around conversions, enable Hindu nationalists to create and define nationalist subjectivity and to convert both Hindus and non-Hindus into a new kind of subject.

The effective linking of conversion to Christianity with issues of national security and cultural actualization allows Hindu nationalists to mobilize support for the movement, particularly among those who may not necessarily be seduced by, or even receptive to, the platform of Hindu chauvinism. In order to recruit support among diverse audiences who may not buy their primordial claims or constructions of the past, Hindu nationalist activists capitalize on already existing widely held fears about threats to national security to present the movement as the guardian of the nation. Postcolonial India has been beset by conflicts over territory and borders, whether with Pakistan over the line of control, or from secessionist movements in Punjab, Kashmir, and various parts of the northeast. In their everyday words and deeds, Hindu nationalist activists articulate Christian missionary activity as a threat to national territory with stories of missionary collusion with India's "enemies." Building on an already hegemonic narrative, they also suggest that missionaries present a cultural threat by bringing western ideas and morals to India and threatening the Hindu values that lie at the core of the nation. Thus anti-Christian mobilization is cast as a patriotic challenge to political and cultural threats to India, a move that enables Hindu nationalists to present themselves as the protectors and also the natural representatives of the cultural heritage and political reigns of the nation.

India as a Hindu Land

A long line of tempos slowly made their way from Badarpur on the Delhi-Haryana border to the I. P. Depot in Delhi. I sat in one of these tempos, baking in the hot afternoon sun, with Urvashi, two other women, a little girl, and three men. Apart from the girl and myself, all the others were affiliated with one of the Hindu nationalist organizations that form the Sangh Parivar (RSS family). Two blue riot control vehicles were part of the procession, and there were armed policemen stationed all along the route. Having heard Sewa Bharati women in a passing tempo singing *bhajans* (devotional songs), Urvashi decided it would be a good idea for us to sing too. As I wilted in the afternoon sun, deeply regretting that I had left my bottle of water at home in my rush to meet Urvashi that morning, I weakly joined in. At the I. P Depot, where I recognized several people from all wings of the movement, we were all served generous quantities of *puri-aloo* (fried bread and potatoes). Many of those in our tempo decided that they had had enough and were going to return home. Urvashi and I switched places with women in a Sewa Bharati tempo who also wanted to leave, and I was pleased to see Kalpana seated among the remaining women. Now joined by several other tempos, the procession continued to Karol Bagh in central Delhi.

It was November 4, and we were all participating in a Delhi-wide protest organized by Hindu nationalists in anticipation of the pope's impending arrival in India the next day. Although members of all wings of the Hindu nationalist movement based in Delhi were participating in this event, I discovered that several of those in the Sewa Bharati tempo with me were not affiliated with the organization, but instead worked in one of their schools or were enrolled in one of their vocational programs. While contributing to the masses present at the procession, they were participating at Kalpana's invitation and chose to return home without listening to the speeches delivered by various members of the Hindu nationalist movement in Karol Bagh. I stayed behind, joining a group of VHP women I knew, listening to speeches by religious renouncers and Hindu nationalist leaders decrying missionary activity and conversions to Christianity in India to the huge crowd of Hindu nationalists, spectators, and reporters gathered there. Underlying the speeches, as indeed my conversations with the women I was with, was the basic contention that India was a Hindu land in which Christians could only be interlopers.

This imaging of India as Hindu and the related concern about conversions to Christianity predate Hindu nationalism. While large-scale violence between Hindus and Christians is relatively unprecedented, tensions and debates between the two communities in the modern period date to the arrival of missionaries in British India in the nineteenth century (Jaffrelot 1999: 14; Dirks 1996: 126). In their efforts to gain converts, missionaries depicted India and Hinduism as morally degenerate, a portrayal that also served to legitimize colonial rule.[3] As has been well documented, this portrayal of India prompted several Hindu reform movements—including the Brahmo Samaj movement and the Arya Samaj movement—that sought to reclaim a glorious past for the nation rather than contest colonial representations of India. These Hindu reform movements not only attempted to cleanse Hinduism of practices such as *sati* and child marriage which had been reviled by missionaries and colonial administrators alike, but also focused their efforts on creating a new nationalist Hinduism compatible with modernity and in the image of Christianity.

Picking up on missionary critiques, the leaders of these movements decried polytheism, ritualism, and idolatry and began to project the Vedas and the Upanishads, ancient Hindu sacred texts, as the true essence of Hinduism (Madan 1997: 205).[4] They also became increasingly concerned about conversions to other religions. As technologies of modernity like the census began to lay the groundwork for nationalism based on enumerable differences and majoritarian politics (see Cohn 1988; van der Veer 1995: 13–14), Hindu leaders became even more concerned about conversions to other religions. Thus, it was also during this period that the Arya Samaj movement began to counter conversions to other religions, particularly Sikhism and Islam, with reconversion ceremonies, which they called *shuddhi*, or purification (Madan 1997: 213). Like Hindu nationalist "reconversions" today, *shuddhi* implicitly assumes that the convert was originally Hindu and indeed that religious identities and boundaries in the pre-colonial period were clearly demarcated and relatively stable (S. Sarkar 2002).

This effort to reform Hinduism and fashion it in the image of Christianity as a rational, monotheistic religion fit for a modern world served two functions. By projecting a glorious Hindu past, these movements were able to challenge colonial and missionary critiques of Indian culture, by countering them with a pristine, monotheistic Hinduism inherently suited to the modern world. In so doing, they also attempted to prevent people suffering from caste discrimination or otherwise susceptible to missionary rhetoric, from converting to other religions. The new national Hinduism was presented as a religion superior to Christianity and Islam and, more importantly, as "original" to India. Hinduism became the primordial religion of the nation, imposed upon the political territory of colonial India imaged as the body of goddess Bharat Mata. The missionary presence was therefore an important impetus for reforming Hinduism and central to the process through which India was imagined as Hindu. During this period Christianity, like Islam, began to be viewed as a religion foreign to India, a shift enabled in part by the colonial administration (see Viswanathan 1996: 78, 157–56).

For Hindu nationalists too, the indigeneity of Hindus is not simply imagined, but etched into the sacred cartography of the nation envisioned as the body of Bharat Mata (see also T. Sarkar 2001: 278). Recalling this sacred geography, a Rashtra Sevika Samiti prayer to Bharat Mata says, "In the north, the Himalaya Mountains form your head / The Indian Ocean washes your feet in the south." Like many pictorial representations of Bharat Mata, the goddess's body is literally imposed on the map of India, with the Himalayas forming her head while the Indian Ocean, in a gesture reminiscent of Hindu ritual worship, washes her feet. In fact, Hindu nationalists often use religious images like Bharat Mata, or stories and rituals to claim territory as sacred space. The destruction of the Babri Masjid was justified by precisely such claims based in stories about the birth of Lord Ram on the exact site of the mosque. More pertinent to this chapter are the recent attempts to claim the Dangs district of Gujarat—the site of major Hindu-Christian violence in 1998—as sacred space, to legitimize the violent conflicts with the Christian community there.

Hindu nationalists claim that Dangs was the site where the Hindu god/king Ram met Shabari, a woman of lower status, who tasted a fruit to ensure that it was sweet before offering it to Ram. According to orthodox Hindu rules of purity and pollution, Shabari's acts would have polluted the offering. Yet, according to this well-known story, Ram recognizes the purity of Shabari's purpose and accepts the offering as entirely untainted. This story not only challenges ideas of purity and pollution in orthodox Hinduism, but also is clearly about Ram *bhakti* (devotion), a theme that has become central to Hindu nationalist politics and constructions of religion. Hindu nationalists have built a temple to Shabari in Dangs, and in February 2006 they organized a Shabri Kumbh Mela (religious fair) at this site. According to a report by the Peoples Union for Civil Liberties, a pillar near the temple reads, "Our resolve is to free the world from the ideologies of conversion and jihad."[5] Through the story of Shabari, Dangs is imagined as Hindu territory usurped by Christians who are "foreign" to the boundaries of the nation.

Yet the nation itself is inherently a product of modernity, and many Christian communities in India existed well before India—as a political entity—was ever "imagined" (Anderson 1983). For instance, while Syrian Christians in Kerala, the Indian state with the oldest traditions of Christianity in the country, trace their conversion to St. Thomas himself in 52 C.E., historical evidence establishes the existence of these communities by the fourth century C.E. (Dempsey 2001: 5). The vast majority of Kerala Christians are Syrian Catholics, Orthodox Syrian/Jacobites, or Latin Catholics, all of whom had established communities well before British colonial rule (7–8).[6] More important for the purposes of this chapter is that many of these Christian communities are older than many traditions of Hinduism in India (S. Sarkar 2002: 241) and understand themselves and their religious traditions to be "virtually indigenous" (Dempsey 2001: 28).

Yet, despite the long history of Christianity in India, the women I worked with claimed that these communities are the result of recent forcible attempts to convert low-caste Hindus and "tribals" out of the fold. Insistently referring to indigenous peoples as *vanavasis* (forest dwellers) rather than *adivasis* (indigenous people), the term preferred by individuals belonging to such groups, Hindu nationalists have focused their "reconversion" efforts on them. Rejecting even the term "reconversion" used by other Hindu nationalists, one member of the VHP said, "We don't engage in conversion or reconversion. They are coming back of their own accord to their original religion." *Adivasis*, with their uncontested claims to being the indigenous inhabitants of India, play a central role in bolstering Hindu nationalist assertions of Hindu indigenousness in the face of theories that the Aryan-speaking people responsible for the earliest Hindu texts may have migrated from elsewhere. Fiercely contesting what they call the "myth of the Aryan invasion," Hindu nationalists argue that Hinduism originated in India and therefore that Hindus are the rightful inheritors of the Indian polity.

This articulation of the indigenousness of Hinduism simultaneously

casts Islam and Christianity as not only religiously distinct but also spa-
tially "other." James Ferguson and Akhil Gupta argue, "The distinctive-
ness of societies, nations, and cultures is based on a seemingly
unproblematic division of space, on the fact that they occupy 'naturally'
discontinuous spaces. The premise of discontinuity forms the starting
point from which to theorize contact, conflict, and contradiction
between cultures and societies" (1992: 6; see also Alonso 1994: 395).
This inscription of certain cultures, religions, ethnicities, and races onto
territorial spaces, is a powerful tool in the hands of Hindu nationalists
today, since it simultaneously deems other religious traditions inauthen-
tic and non-indigenous. Moreover, as Ferguson and Gupta assert, the
danger of this kind of objectification of culture in space is also its failure
to "account for cultural differences *within* a locality" (Ferguson and
Gupta 1992: 7, original emphasis). This became clear to me when I
learned that many of my interlocutors suspected that I was a Christian
precisely because I did not fit into their objectified understanding of
what it meant to be Hindu. Indeed, some of the ensuing interactions
and conversations were an object lesson to me on how to be Hindu in a
Hindu nation.

Nowhere was this more apparent than in my interactions with Urvashi.
Although Urvashi was very fond of me, she was exceedingly suspicious
of me throughout the time that I spent working with Hindu nationalists
in Delhi. She did not really seem to care that I did not support Hindu
nationalism. What she did care about was why. And she suspected that
it was because I was Christian. At one of our very first meetings, she
asked me several times if I was Christian. She never quite believed me
when I said I was not. While this was partly because she knew I did not
support Hindu nationalist ideas, it was also because I did not appear to
her to be a Hindu. For instance, I never participated in the *arti* (worship) at the various events she took me to. At one event in Rama Krishna
Puram in Delhi, she told me to go up to the stage and perform *arti*.
When I did not do this, it must have confirmed her worst suspicions,
although she never said so. At the rally mentioned above, when she
noticed my silence she told me that I must join in the slogan shouting
after and during the speeches. She insisted that if I did not do this people would think I was a Christian. After this incident, she told another
woman whom we both knew very well that she was convinced that I was
Christian. What was most interesting to me about Urvashi's comment to
her friend was that she assumed that I was a Christian because I did not
participate in the slogan shouting and because I did not participate in
the *arti*. How could I be a Hindu if I did not agree with the politics of
the movement? My refusal to participate in these rituals of politics and
religion, above all, sealed my identity as Christian in Urvashi's mind. To

be Hindu meant subscribing to the nationalist Hinduism and Hindu nationalist politics of the movement.

Urvashi's suspicions must be understood within a Hindu nationalist cultural lexicon that deems Christianity and missionary activity not only foreign, but also duplicitous, immoral, and antinational. Below I examine how women and men in the movement perceive Christianity in general and the work of missionaries in particular. I begin by examining Hindu nationalist stories about missionaries engaging in fraudulent behavior to convert Hindus. My interlocutors saw a qualitative difference between Christian conversions and their own "reconversion" ceremonies, arguing that the latter simply bring Hindus back to the fold. In this section, I suggest that Hindu nationalists use these ceremonies to create a new kind of Hindu nationalist subject. The next section examines how those I worked with articulated Christian missionary activity as a cultural threat to the nation. Using gendered discourses, Hindu nationalists argue that Christianity threatens the cultural purity of Hindu India by introducing western and immoral practices. The last section focuses on the perceived threat to national security posed by Christian missionaries. Capitalizing on already existing fears of insurgency in India, Hindu nationalists establish Christian missionaries as a threat to the political integrity of the nation.

Converting Innocents: The Politics of Conversion and Reconversion

These missionaries, they go to villages and hoodwink innocent and uneducated villagers. There was a missionary who took three magnets on which he had pasted pictures of Ram, Sita and Ravana. The uneducated villagers knew nothing about magnets. The missionary had cleverly placed the picture of Ram and Sita on magnets with a positive charge while the picture of Ravana was on a negative charge. He then showed it to the villagers and asked them: why is Sita always going toward Ravana and not to Ram, her husband. He said that Hinduism was such a corrupt religion to worship Sita when she was so low as to be attracted to Ravana and to turn away from her husband. (Rajesh Mishra, December 20, 1999)

I first met Rajesh Mishra at his home in an upper-middle-class neighborhood toward the end of fieldwork, although I had met his wife Sita several times at various VHP events. When he learned from his wife, a senior member of the Delhi VHP, that I was from Kerala, he invited me to lunch at their house to discuss the logistics of a trip to the famous Gurvayur Temple that the Mishras were planning later that year. The Mishras were well educated, upper-middle-class Brahmins who, like many I met, were strongly opposed to Muslims and Christians, and whose families were closely involved with the RSS and VHP. They were extremely willing to talk to me and, because they knew that I was working toward a doctorate in the United States, introduced me to their grandson, who was doing his Ph.D. at a prestigious American university and was home for the holidays. After a discussion of places to stay around Gurvayur and other temples worth visiting in the area, the conversation shifted to the large populations of Muslims and Christians in the state and eventually to the subject of conversions. Mishra's statement above plays on a common argument made by my interlocutors, namely that Christian missionaries trick innocent Hindus into converting to Christianity. Mishra's story recalls the popular Hindu epic Ramayana about the god-king Ram. In this epic, Ram's wife Sita is kidnapped by the demon-king Ravana and taken to Lanka, where Ram with his army of monkeys must rescue her. In most versions of the epic, Sita emerges as the embodiment of purity and virtue despite attempts by Ravana to seduce her (see, for instance, Mankekar 1999). Indeed, for many Hindus, Sita is the ideal *pativrata*, a woman who is completely devoted to her husband and serves his every need. In Mishra's story, however, the missionary suggests the contrary.

In Mishra's version of the story, the missionary uses his devious tricks to "hoodwink" innocent villagers and cast aspersions on Sita's chastity in order to denigrate Hinduism. The story embodies many criticisms that Hindu nationalism has against Christian proselytizing: the duplicity of missionaries, their inaccurate and disrespectful denunciations of Hinduism, and the naiveté of the rural Hindus they target. Mishra's portrayal of the ignorance of the rural poor was a representation I encountered among several members of the Hindu nationalist movement in Delhi, many of them lower-middle/middle/upper-middle class and middle-/upper-caste. For example, Urvashi told me a story that, like the one above, suggests the naiveté of the convert while portraying missionaries as devious and calculating. Urvashi had been filling me in on what had transpired at a VHP women's meeting that I had missed the previous week as we walked toward the bus stop with Shashi, a member of Matri Shakti. After informing me that they had discussed various events that the VHP was organizing to protest the Pope's visit over a month later, she started telling me how missionaries convert Hindus. She said, "These Christians mix medicines like aspirin into water and say this is holy water. Then they give this water to sick Hindus and they get cured." Urvashi argued that the missionaries then claim that the recovery was a divine miracle and tell the person that it was the holy water blessed by Christ that cured them. Urvashi asserted that this was how missionaries establish the power of Christianity and Christian holy water and trick unsuspecting and ignorant Hindus into converting from

Hinduism to Christianity. She informed me that missionaries also give money and food to convert people.

These stories reflect the belief held, by both men and women in the movement, that nobody converts of his/her own volition. Converts are innocents who have either been duped, as the above stories demonstrate, or, as Jayant Chandra, a Delhi University lecturer and long-standing member of the RSS, suggests, they have converted because of material inducements offered by missionaries. A couple of weeks after the rally to protest the pope's visit, I met Jayant, one of the three men I had traveled with during the procession, and asked him to tell me more about the event. We were sitting in the living room of his small and scruffy upper-story apartment that was also home to several mice nervously scuttling around, when Jayant remarked, "If someone converts because he wants to that is his outlook. But here . . . there is inducement. Conveniences are offered. If your child does not have a job then one will be given. A person who does not have bread to fill his stomach does not worry too much about his religion. He says, ok, I must fill my stomach." Here Jayant articulates a view shared by many of the women I worked with. For instance, in the conversation above, Urvashi claimed that missionaries give ten thousand rupees to Hindus to convert. At a Samiti training camp in December, a *pracharika* named Rukmini said that a man dressed as Santa Claus was giving thirty-rupee gifts to children in Delhi's Connaught Place in order to warn Samiti initiates about Christian evangelizing. It was also clear to me that many women I worked with believed that the social work programs, schools, and hospitals run by Christian missionaries were schemes to convert Hindus to Christianity. In their narratives, converts are either naïve or desperate for material necessities. They are poor, or they are ignorant enough to be tricked by missionaries. Either way, converts are essentially moral while the missionaries who convert them are immoral.

While the women I worked with were very critical of missionaries offering inducements in order to convert people, they saw no logical contradiction in their own efforts to prevent conversions by similar inducements. Ela Dube told me that one of the main aims of Sewa Bharati is to prevent conversions by starting schools in slums and among *adivasi* populations. Ela said that when people from the slum behind her house complained to her about a missionary school that was teaching children "Jesus *ki kahaniyan*" (stories about Jesus) rather than anything useful, she opened a Sewa Bharati school there. She also told me that Sewa Bharati had started a residential school called Sewa Dham in Mandoli village near Delhi, for boys from *adivasi* areas all over India, where they are protected from missionaries. Indeed, the purpose of the school is not only to prevent the *adivasis* from converting to Christianity but also to teach them that they are Hindus, and that their own religions are simply a local, and therefore corrupt, expression of Hinduism (see Hansen 1999: 104).

Others in the movement, while clearly situating social work as a response to conversions, place the blame on Hindus not missionaries. Sneha, an eighteen-year-old member of Durga Vahini who coordinates activities in the Trans-Jamuna region, informed me that nobody converts of his/her own free will. Involved with Durga Vahini since she was ten, and now working toward a degree in politics at a Delhi college, Sneha was an extremely articulate young woman. While telling me about the activities of her organization, she argued that Durga Vahini needed to unite Hindus across caste lines and help "*vanavasis*" to prevent them from converting to Christianity. She said, "we are teaching girls to do this in the training camp in Gujarat that is taking place right now. We tell our members to work in *harijan bastis* (dalit colonies). If Christians can use this to convert people we have to show them that we think of them as equals."

Similarly, Taiji (elder sister), an elderly *pracharika* who has devoted fifty years of her life to the Rashtra Sevika Samiti, told me, when I met her at Neera's house on her visit to Delhi, "We [Hindus] are the ones who have shunned the poor and the lower castes while the Christian missionaries have embraced them (*gale lagaya hai*). If we do not want people to convert we must make sure that they are well taken care of within our own communities. Otherwise how can you blame them for converting?" Sumit Sarkar (2002) has argued that it is the social uplift and social justice work some strains of Christianity engage in that Hindu nationalists fear, a sentiment that is resonant in Taiji's narrative. Confined to a wheelchair after breaking her hipbone two years ago, Taiji looked frail as she sat on the bed during our conversation. Yet she continues to travel all over the country as part of her work for the Samiti, and was extremely animated that day. She told me that the movement's work is increasingly directed toward the uplift of poor and backward caste communities. This was why, when the cyclone hit Orissa, "our girls went running there." They distributed steel plates, bowls, and glasses because "these people had nothing left." The movement sends its troops to demonstrate to cyclone victims that they are part of a larger, benevolent Hindu community. Neither Taiji nor others I spoke to saw this as duplicity on the part of the movement. More disturbing was the failure to question the ethics of capitalizing on the tragedy of cyclone victims, although missionary activity is considered immoral for doing so.

I also learned from my conversations with women in various wings of the movement that Hindu nationalist organizations offer direct material rewards to establish community and to prevent people from converting.

I was told by women in two different organizations of occasions when they offered to pay a woman's dowry to prevent her from converting to Christianity. Vimla, a member of Durga Vahini in her late twenties, told me that she had prevented an entire family from converting because, unable to afford the dowry being demanded, they had found it impossible to marry their only daughter. Conversion would mean not having to pay the dowry. Vimla said she convinced the family not to convert by promising that the movement would pay the dowry. In a similar vein, after vehemently condemning missionaries by saying, "I like everything about Christianity except for this hidden aim underlying all their activities to convert under the guise of helping,"[7] Ela told me that Sewa Bharati does provide material assistance to families to prevent conversions. If someone needs help with a daughter's wedding then Sewa Bharati can give a few pots and pans and a couple of saris. But, she claimed, Sewa Bharati's resources are limited, so they can do little to prevent a conversion if a missionary offers more. In each of these cases, although critical of missionaries who offer material rewards to converts, Hindu nationalist women do not problematize their own attempts to prevent conversions from taking place and to purchase allegiance to the Hindu nation by offering financial assistance to those in need.

Many Hindu nationalists assume that conversion takes people out of the Hindu fold. They assert that, unlike "foreign" religions, people cannot convert into Hinduism, so the religion can never replace those who convert. Apart from the existence of numerous Hindu sects that actively proselytize (ISKCON, Virashaiva), the Arya Samaj movement, mentioned earlier in this chapter, was responsible for mass "reconversions" (*shuddhi*) to Hinduism in the twentieth century. While the VHP recognized *shuddhi* as early as 1968 as a strategy to keep Hindus in the fold (S. Sarkar 2002: 239), Hindu nationalists insist that these practices are not a form of conversion. This allows them to engage in mass reconversions to Hinduism, as they have done recently among Christian *adivasis* in Gujarat and other places, while still criticizing missionaries for engaging in conversion. In the mass reconversions organized by Hindu nationalist groups in 1998 and 1999, the actual ritual varied. In an interesting parallel to Christian conversions, those who agreed to reconvert in Ahwa, Gujarat, were made to take a dip in the hot springs of a nearby village. Then the officiating priest tied a black string with a locket with the picture of the monkey-god Hanuman around the neck of the newly reconverted (*Hindustan Times*, January 16, 1999, 1). In Dandoli village, Madhya Pradesh, 176 Christians were reconverted after being made to take a dip in the Narmada River, followed by a sacred thread ceremony performed by priests from the Arya Samaj (*Indian Express*, February 15, 1999, 1). As it turned out, this ceremony was staged for the media invited to witness the event. Journalists found that most of the "reconverted" considered themselves Hindus to begin with.

In some cases, according to a Human Rights Watch Report, Christians in Dangs district in Gujarat were forced to participate in these reconversion ceremonies (Narula 1999). Manglu Bhai, an evangelical Christian who was severely beaten along with others in his family by members of the Bajrang Dal, says in this report: "Bajrang Dal and VHP people told us on December 25 to become Hindu. Since then they have been harassing us. They said, 'we will keep beating you until you become Hindu.' We said we wouldn't come for conversion. Then they said it is their government so they won't get arrested, and nothing will happen to them" (cited in Narula 1999: 29). In these cases, local cadres of Hindu nationalists clearly coerced Christians to participate in reconversion ceremonies with the threat of physical violence. This story is also interesting in that it reveals how local cadres draw on the power and authority of the state, led by a BJP government, to compel Christians to become Hindu.

Few have challenged the use of the term "reconversion" by the movement and the underlying assumption that *adivasis* were Hindu before they became Christian. Sumit Sarkar (1999) argues that the term is a form of "semantic aggression" for it suggests a natural reorientation of people back to their "original" state. Additionally, those who were Hindu tribals are also being converted to another form of Hinduism through the movement's "civilizing mission" run through educational institutions that cater to tribal populations (Hansen 1999: 106, 104–7). Using a term coined by M. N. Srinivas (1952: 65) to describe the process by which lower-caste groups adopted Sanskritic values to move up the caste hierarchy, Thomas Hansen describes it as "nationalist sanskritization" which appropriates the "little traditions" of Hinduism into the "Brahmanical great tradition" of nationalist Hinduism (Hansen 1999:107).

Of Culture and Morality: The Politics of Cultural Actualization

"Every Christian or Muslim today was originally a Hindu," said Sadhvi Kirin Bharati, a member of the VHP's organization for female ascetics, the Sadvhi Shakti Parishad. Striking a similar note, Taiji asked me, "Before they became Muslims and Christians they were Hindus, weren't they?" Implicit in these statements is the normative assumption that the convert was originally a Hindu who was tricked out of the fold. This made the construction of the moral though ignorant convert especially important in many of the stories women told me about conversion. During our conversation at Neera's house, Taiji told me a vignette, about a person in Varanasi who had become a Christian, that reflected this basic construction. Every morning, as he had done ever since he could remember, he would go to the River Ganga to take a dip and do his *surya namaskar* to salute the sun. Taiji told me that the local Christian priest asked him to stop doing this. The man refused, saying that while he was a Christian he could not give up what was part of his culture (*sanskriti*). In Taiji's story, such practices are manifestations of a cultural essence ingrained in all Indians. Christianity might take converts, but Hinduism is part of the primordial essence of the nation and its culture.

Other Hindu nationalist women also echoed the view that this primordial essence defines a Hindu, regardless of current religious affiliation. On one occasion I heard Payal try to convey this idea to young girls at a Samiti *shakha* in Budh Vihar. She asked them who a Hindu was and, clearly disappointed with their responses, told them to talk to their friends and family and find out before the next *shakha*. Then, hinting at the response she wanted, she pointed to Saira, the only Muslim girl present, and said perhaps even Saira would consider herself Hindu if she knew what this meant. Keen to hear how Payal would have answered her own query, I asked her the same question as soon as we left. Payal responded, "A Hindu is anyone who loves India. Hindus were the original inhabitants of the land around the Indus River and we are all their descendants. If we love the land that is called "Bharat" (India) stretching from the Indian Ocean to the Indus River, then we are Hindus. It is not only a religion. We should stop thinking in terms of sects."

Both Taiji's and Payal's narratives articulate with RSS constructions of Hindu identity as more than just a religious affiliation. Dr. Rajendra Singh, Rajju *bhaiya* to members of the movement, the former supreme leader (*sarsanghchalak*) of the RSS, was asked in an interview to define Hinduism. He responded, "Hinduism, for the RSS, is not any form of worship. Actually it is another name for nationalism" (1993: 7). As early as 1923, V. D. Savarkar asserted that a "Hindu" was a person who resided in the territory south of the Indus and the Himalayas and who shared "racial and cultural characteristics" that were primordially linked to the ancient Aryans (Jaffrelot 1999: 27). In these formulations, Hinduism is ineluctably linked to the blood, culture, race, and territory of the nation. Religions like Christianity and Islam, linked to other territories, are deemed alien to this Hindu nation. Critically, conversion is not only a religious transformation of an individual, but also an act that threatens the unity of this Hindu/Indian nation by separating people from their culture.

In the eyes of many Hindu nationalists, conversion thus becomes an immoral act that violates the integrity of the nation by stripping away the primordial essence of Hindus. During one of many protest rallies against the pope's visit to India on November 4, 1999, B. L. Sharma

Prem, mentioned earlier, used rape (*balatkar*) as a metaphor for conversion. Angrily addressing a large group of supporters at Badarpur near the Delhi-Haryana border, he asserted that missionaries used inducements and tricked people in tribal villages to convert to Christianity, thereby "raping" them of their culture. In his speech, Christianity becomes a threat to the cultural purity of the nation, an immoral violation of its "natural" state. This is powerful imagery, particularly since the nation itself is imagined as the body of Bharat Mata. In this gendered vision, conversion-as-rape not only violates the nation, it violates the pure and sacred body of the goddess. Interestingly, here, as in the anti-Muslim histories discussed earlier, sexual violation becomes the metaphor through which Hindu nationalists articulate the need for Hindu unity to combat the alleged persecution of the nation by religious "others." The moral outrage expressed by Sharma at these violent intrusions on sacred space is compounded by his claim that Muslims and Christians have denigrated Hinduism. He accused them of proclaiming that there is only one god, making fun of Hindu deities, and arguing that there is only one path to salvation. He asserted that Hinduism, in contrast to Islam and Christianity, was tolerant and recognized multiple paths to salvation and therefore did not engage in conversion. His speech drew cheers of support from the crowd that had gathered at Badarpur, many of whom were affiliated with various Hindu nationalist organizations or programs.

The image of India as the goddess Bharat Mata and the ineluctable link between territory, blood, and culture in the discourse of many women and men I worked with effectively cast Christianity as a "foreign" religion linked with both western values and western imperialism. This portrait of Christianity as a tool of empire was powerfully evoked at the rally in Badarpur. Organized to protest the pope's visit to India the next day (November 5, 1999), the rally marked the culmination of a *rath yatra* (chariot procession) from Goa to Delhi, ostensibly to raise awareness about the acts of missionaries during the "Goan inquisition"[8] five hundred years ago and to decry "forced conversions" (*Indian Express, Newsline*, November 5, 1999, 1, 3). The "chariot," parked near the stage that had been constructed for the event, was a Tata Sumo (Indian sports utility vehicle) made to resemble a chariot. It was elaborately painted with pictures of white missionaries blessing and healing dark-skinned "tribals." The paintings forcefully conveyed the assumption of many of those I worked with, that missionaries are white/foreign and not Indian. In the images of white missionaries converting brown people, religious/cultural difference is not only mapped onto territory, but also racialized and embodied. While India emerges as Hindu and non-white space, Christianity is constructed as "foreign" to India not only through its association with the discontinuous territorial space of "the west" but also through its projection as a "white" religion.

Interestingly, the "chariot" was supposed to bring the descendants of "victims" of forced conversion resulting from the Goan inquisition to Delhi, where they were to testify to their plight. However, neither Urvashi—who had brought me to the event—nor I could locate any of these "tribal" "victims" at the event. According to an article the next day in the major Indian daily, the *Indian Express,* "the promised tribal leaders, who had come to talk about 'forced conversions' of the Church, were not there. Neither were the Christians whose forefathers were tortured during the Goan inquisition, 500 years ago. The only ones who made it to the concluding ceremonies of the Goa-Delhi Rath Yatra were religious leaders from the Sangh Parivar outfits" (*Indian Express, Newsline,* November 5, 1999, 1, 3). Despite this absence, the racial and gendered imagery used by Hindu nationalists powerfully evoked a sense of moral outrage among those at the rally.

While the Goan inquisition provided an arena for Hindu nationalists to argue that indigenous populations had been forcibly converted to Christianity under the threat of violence, it also established a history of Christian atrocities against Hindus that predated British colonial rule. According to those I spoke to, this persecution was not limited to forcible conversions but included violence against Hindus and the desecration of sacred sites. For example, when I asked Aditya Trivedi why Hindu nationalists were protesting the pope's visit, he told me (in English):

When St. Xavier came to Goa and established his *raj* nearly three *lakh* (hundred thousand) Hindus were massacred. Just like Islam, theirs was also that either accept cross, Jesus, or get murdered. Three *lakh* Hindus were murdered. And hundreds of temples were razed. In the church where St Xavier's body is kept, that was basically a Shiv *mandir* [Shiva temple]. That is the only church in the whole world on top of which there is no cross. Many crosses have been put on it, even a cemented cross was put on it. But none of these stayed on for more than two nights. Then they had full security to make sure that Hindus weren't making the crosses fall. They automatically fell. Ultimately they have given up. But the people of that place say that there used to be a very nice temple there on top of which the church has been built.

Aditya claims not only that Christians destroyed Hindu temples, but also that such acts were intolerable not just to Hindus but to a higher power that miraculously prevented the mounting of a cross on the church. Stories such as these become crucial tools through which to create a sense of public outrage and mobilize people against Christians in India. For those who may remain unmoved by suggestions that Christianity, because it is inherently western, poses a threat to the Indian/ Hindu way of life, Aditya's narrative presents more tangible threats, such as those presented by forced conversions, massacres, or razing temples. The last, of course, had already proven to be highly successful in mobilizing support for destroying the Babri mosque in Ayodhya. Threats such as these were compelling not only to the women I worked with, most of whom were deeply religious, but also to many other Hindus listening to these narratives. While many of those at the rallies to protest the pope's visit may not have endorsed the violence between Hindus and Christians, the masses that Hindu nationalist activists had managed to assemble testify to the power these images have for ordinary people both within and beyond the movement. At the various rallies, most of those gathered joined members of the movement as they responded to the speeches with slogans that denigrated Christianity in various ways. Indeed, as I mentioned earlier, my own refusal to participate in these activities at the rally was noted, and criticized, by Urvashi.

While I was unable to further interview those in the crowd, it is clear from conversations with the women and men I worked with that the sense of outrage against the alleged activities of missionaries in India throughout history is deeply felt. Importantly, narratives such as Aditya's must also be understood as part of a concerted effort by members of the Hindu nationalist movement to shape public memory about Christians in India and mobilize communities for collective action.[9] These attempts to shape public memory about religious "others" in India are key to understanding what makes the Hindu nationalist political agenda compelling to ordinary people who have experienced multiple versions of the "history" being recounted.

Allusions to conversion-as-rape, duplicity of missionaries, forcible conversion of *adivasis*, destruction of Hindu temples, and conversion as colonialism all imply the moral depravity of Christian missionaries in India. Yet nothing more powerfully conveys the threat of Christianity than the skillful marking of women's bodies as sites of cultural purity/impurity, a common trend in nationalist discourses in India and elsewhere.[10] Hindu nationalist women often conjured up images of immoral, westernized, Christian women to construct the threat that Christianity posed to the morality and values of an ostensibly "pure" Hindu nation. On one occasion, after a visit to a Sewa Bharati school in a south Delhi slum, I asked Kalpana whether there was much missionary activity in the area. After saying that there were no missionaries active in this slum, Kalpana added that conversions by missionaries were a real problem in other slums. She asserted, "Missionaries bring girls to the slums with the expressed purpose of picking up Hindu boys, trapping them into marriage and then converting them. You don't see as many girls who have been converted . . . because the whole thing is that Christian girls with their loose morals come and trap these boys into converting."

While the image of Christian girls as bait to trap Hindu boys into converting to Christianity might seem absurd, it is important to recognize that the inherent immorality of Christian women is an image mobilized quite consistently in popular culture in India. Scriptwriters in countless Bollywood films have deployed the figure of the Christian woman who tempts good Hindu boys to stray—temporarily—from their moral bearings. Kalpana also suggests that Hindu boys—particularly those residing in slums—are innocent and gullible to Christian duplicity. Her narrative suggests that slum dwellers are particularly vulnerable (or ignorant) and in need of protection, an attitude that is relatively common in the movement and reveals its middle-class biases. Kalpana carefully builds on stereotypes of the poor and of Christian women to suggest that Christianity itself is morally depraved.

Like Kalpana, other women suggested that Christianity itself, not just the duplicitous activities of a few missionaries, was the problem. When I asked Vimla why the VHP had a problem with conversion, she explicitly condemned Christian morality by saying:

A *kunwari* [virgin, unmarried] girl gave birth to Jesus. So Christians do not believe that it is a matter of shame if someone gives birth to a child while they are still unmarried. They say, never mind, the lord Jesus is being born, this is how the lord Jesus was born. So since the day that the Christian faith first set foot in this country, since that day there has been rape and oppression of women in India. They come here and wear their short dresses, the Christians wear them. Even nine-year-old kids celebrate a festival where lovers exchange gifts, they call it Valentine's Day. We don't have such a tradition in Hindustan. And since the day the Christians arrived here, from that day, this tradition started here. Today's girls think that we should also make male friends and they wait for the time when their boyfriends give them presents. In our culture girls cannot even see their husbands before marriage. Without *parda* (veiling) they cannot go outside their homes. And after they are adults girls cannot even sit next to their fathers or their brothers. But today they wander around with strangers. All this should not happen. Whatever filth has spread in our nation has been spread by Christians.

In her narrative, Vimla refers to Mary as a *kunwari ladki* (girl). While *kunwari* literally means virgin, it is also used generically to refer to girls and unmarried young women. While this may simply be a reference to the Christian belief in the Virgin Mary and the virginal birth of Jesus, Vimla's next sentence suggests that Christianity condones the birth of children prior to marriage because of Mary's example. Through this juxtaposition of ideas, Vimla questions not only Mary's morality but also that of Christianity itself. The allegation is not new. In the late nineteenth century, Swami Dayananda Saraswati expressed his fear that the idea of virginal conception was dangerous because it enabled women to sanctify illegitimate births with the claim that they had "conceived through god" (S. Sarkar 2002: 230). Dayananda feared the "loss of control over women" (230), a theme also central to Vimla's words. Vimla's narrative is suffused with images of this loss of control over female sexuality, resulting in the moral degeneration of Hindu society. As she conjures up images of Hindu women who desire boyfriends, observe Valentine's Day, and wear short skirts, Vimla suggests that these desires threaten the very purity of the Hindu nation and reflect the infusion of western/Christian values into society.

Mary Douglas has argued that the "body is a model which can stand for any bounded system. Its boundaries can represent any boundaries which are threatened or precarious" (1966: 115). Women's bodies in particular are often used to symbolize the boundaries of the nation in nationalist discourses. For Kalpana and Vimla, the very purity of the Hindu nation is jeopardized when Hindu women are influenced by Christian/western values. Moral degeneration is linked not only to the infusion of these values, but also to the loss of control over female sexuality, considered dangerous in many Hindu traditions. Indeed, the control of female sexuality is the pivotal axis around which the essential morality of Hinduism is contrasted with the inherent immorality of Christianity in Vimla's narrative. The contrasting subjectivities of Christian and Hindu women are central to the way in which these Hindu nationalist women condemned Christianity, established the danger it presented to Hindu India, and crafted the necessity of engaging in Hindu nationalist politics to protect Hindu society from such immorality.

It is critical to note here, that although I was asking similar questions about conversion of both men and women, none of the men I spoke to discussed the sexuality of Christian women. Instead, their comments focused on critiquing missionaries for bribing or tricking Hindus out of the fold or, as I will discuss below, for their alleged involvement in antinational activities. While women also discussed these issues, they often articulated critiques about westernization and Christianity through discussions of western/Christian women's sexuality. In part this was because, in keeping with the gendered norms of the movement, women were more comfortable talking about sexuality with me than men were. However, I also believe this reflects how the particular concerns and points of intervention of men and women in the debate on Christian conversion are gendered. Women, as I have already noted, are responsible for ensuring that Hindu culture and values are channeled into their families and are transmitted to the next generation. As mothers of the nation, it is also their responsibility to promulgate Hindu cultural values in their social worlds. Consequently, it is not surprising that concerns about activities that threaten this culture, at home or in the world, were foremost in women's rather than men's narratives about conversion.

While Vimla's condemnation of Christianity centers around the control of female sexuality, I know from other conversations that she is aware of women in the movement who are having affairs. Interestingly, in these conversations she did not necessarily denounce their actions. Since Vimla and I got on very well, our conversations often shifted from my research questions to more personal issues, and she was willing to laugh and gossip with me about these relationships in casual conversations. But her tone and attitude were markedly different in the context of this formal taped interview. Unlike casual conversations that can be repudiated, a tape recorder captures voices, crystallizes words, and leaves a trace that individuals might be held accountable for. Consequently, as for other women I worked with, it prompted Vimla to abandon her usual flippancy regarding these transgressions for the stance of moral outrage expressed by leaders and official propaganda. On tape she reiterates normative constructions about the purity of Hindu women and the essential immorality of Christian women. In so doing, Vimla performs the norms that sustain the Hindu nationalist subject whose ontological existence requires, according to Judith Butler, the repetitive performance of norms (1997: 14). The subject, in this case Hindu women, is not fixed, and because it is dependent on performative acts like reiterating purity, is always open to contestation. Since there are multiple ideological systems in operation in contemporary India, the nature of the subject depends on the extent to which discourses—in this case Hindu nationalism—can fix the meanings attached to them (see Laclau and Mouffe 1985: 116, 111–12).

Vimla chooses to ignore affairs on tape, since any acknowledgment of the romantic transgressions of women in the movement would reveal the refusal of Hindu nationalist women to perform Hindu nationalist norms and expose the failure of the movement to fix its constructions of subjectivity and make its ideology hegemonic in the social world (see Comaroff and Comaroff 1991: 22–24). Here it is not only the women having affairs who transgressed the gender norms of the movement; Vimla also transgressed them when she gossiped about these women. Both failed to perform the movement's norms, revealing the chimerical nature of the Hindu nationalist subject and the limits of Hindu nationalist hegemony. In both cases, women are dissonant subjects—they fail to reproduce Hindu nationalist ideology and transgress it by citing norms of alternative systems. Thinking of these women as dissonant subjects rather than just hypocrites enables us to understand how women's subjectivity in the modern world is shaped by multiple ideologies even when they may belong to one ideological group. Their dissonant acts are of course subject to the regulatory regimes of the movement, which compel individuals to act in prescribed ways (Butler 1993: 95). To avoid potential disciplining, Vimla chooses to perform Hindu nationalist norms in the taped interview. Indeed, her reiteration of normative expectations and non-acknowledgment of dissonant acts of fellow activists, testifies to the way the acts of individuals can reflect a "tacit collective agreement to perform, produce, and sustain" Hindu nationalist ideology (Butler 1999: 178).

Insurgent Christians: The Politics of National Security

The politics of national allegiance is another central trope that is mobilized to generate fear about Christian conversion in India. According to many in the movement, the nationalist allegiance of Christians is questionable because their religious loyalties lie in the west. While the concern is grounded in the conflation of religious culture and territory in Hindu nationalism, it is an effective tool because of the extent to which religious identity is already implicated in the construction of nationalist subjectivity in India (Viswanathan 1996). Indeed, middle-class and upper-caste Hindu identity was central to the imaging of the nation in the colonial period and continues to underlie constructions of the "normative human-Indian subject" today (Tharu and Niranjana 1999: 498).

This implicit structuring of the nationalist subject as Hindu, along with the imagining of India as the sacred land of the Hindus formed by the body of the goddess, enables Hindu nationalists to assume Hindus' allegiance to the Indian nation. This argument not only presumes that national territories are inscribed with religious and cultural qualities, as I have already suggested, but also implies the primacy of religious identity in determining political allegiance. Many women argued that, since Muslims and Christians do not consider India their holy land, their loyalty to the political territory of India is questionable. For instance, Taiji told me that it is fine to be Muslim as long as you do not pray to Mecca and Medina. For her the ritual act of praying in the direction of Mecca engendered divided loyalties. More pertinent is the perceived threat to national integrity posed by conversions to Christianity, even though only 2.3 percent of Indians are Christian.[11]

Hindu nationalists argue that Christian missionaries threaten national integrity by using conversion as a ruse to harness political loyalty and fuel insurgencies against the Indian state. Given that powerful memories of religious mobilization in political movements like the Pakistan movement—resulting of course in the Partition of the subcontinent—already exist in people's minds, these claims are an effective means of conveying the need to mobilize against Christian missionary activity in India. The connection between conversion and national security was explicitly made by Nandini Bharati, a leader of the women's wing of the Delhi branch of Sewa Bharati. While explaining some of the "history" that made Sewa Bharati's work at the grassroots level necessary, Nandini told me that conversions from Hinduism are part of a larger world conspiracy to divide India along religious lines. She told me that this was how Pakistan was "taken away" and how "they" tried to take away Punjab by calling for the separate Sikh state of Khalistan. She informed me that when RSS *pracharaks* were sent to the northeastern state of Tripura to put an end to mass conversions to Christianity, Christian "terrorists" kidnapped four of them to prevent them from doing their work. She insisted that if Christian numbers increased, then they too would demand a separate state and weaken India. In a modern electoral democracy, where numbers matter and upper-caste Hindus are already feeling threatened by the rise of lower-caste groups and minorities, Nandini's argument, particularly the specter of "mass conversions," is an effective way to generate fear about Christian missionary activity.

Several Hindu nationalist men I spoke to linked the violent rebellions in many of the northeast states of India to Christian conversion. Aditya Trivedi said (in English):

The terrorist organizations in the northeast are getting support from international Christian missionaries. . . . When Staines was killed the whole world's newspapers wrote of this. Only three persons were killed. But here [in the northeast] five and a half thousand persons are killed, battered to death.[12] But not even a single Christian missionary or Christian organization uttered a word of condemnation against those killings.

Echoing the sentiments of Nandini, Aditya continued:

Their strategy is such that we will concentrate on certain pockets and those certain pockets will be made anti-Hindu. And anything which becomes anti-Hindu becomes anti-India. We believe that once somebody changes his religion he changes his nationality also. Solid proofs are Kashmir where Islam is the dominant factor. They say we don't want to live with India. Here the dominant factor is Christians. They say we are a different country.

Aditya uses insurgencies in the northeast as evidence of the antinationalism of Christian missionaries and their converts, and to argue that Hindus must join the movement's efforts to challenge missionary activity. His arguments gloss over the complex differences among the myriad political movements in the northeast, and assume the primacy of language and religion to these struggles, when, perhaps, "the main argument for separation and secession was that tribal peoples were simply not Indians at all" (Brass 1994: 202). A. J. Philip asserts that it is important to keep in mind that in the northeast "the church has in many ways stood for national integration. The Meiteis, Tripuris, Bodos, and Assamese ULFA cadres are not Christian. In Nagaland and Mizoram, the church has helped in restoring peace within the Indian framework" (Philip 1999: 8). In fact, high-caste Hindus participate in some of the most prominent and violent movements like ULFA (S. Sarkar 1999). ULFA, a secessionist movement in Assam, grew out of existing movements of Hindu Assamese who resented losing jobs and land to non-Assamese—particularly Bengalis—who had been migrating to the northeast and had dominated the government since the colonial period (Brass 1994: 213, 205).

What these arguments reveal is that, while missionaries have had a strong presence in the region, and may indeed have both targeted *adivasi* populations and other underprivileged groups throughout India (S. Sarkar 1999) and capitalized on their economic and social marginality by providing social services like schools and hospitals, it is simplistic to suggest that secessionist violence in the northeast has been caused by missionary activity. As some have argued, the problems of the northeast are multiple and complex, and derive in large part from the relationship the central government has had with these regions in the postcolonial period. Paul Brass suggests that these insurgencies highlight a "structural problem in the Indian political system" wherein conflicts are generated because of "the strongly centralizing drives of the Indian state in a society where the predominant long-term social, economic, and political tendencies are toward pluralism, regionalism, and decentralization" (1994: 227). Yet, despite the political and historical complexities of violence in the northeast, Nandini and Aditya clearly believe it is rooted in the work of Christian missionaries. Like many of their colleagues in the movement, they perceived it as part of a larger conspiracy against the Indian polity.

Some of those I spoke to asserted that the Church was also responsible for smuggling arms, ammunition, and foreign funds into India for these movements. While explaining to me why Hindu nationalists had been protesting the pope's visit, Jayant contended:

It has been said in the Lok Sabha, to the members of the Lok Sabha. . . . At this point I cannot remember the exact number of how much money . . . every year how many dollars come into India [*Bharat*]. How does it get spent? It comes in with the missionaries. Five thousand *crore* [ten million] rupees comes every year to India from foreign missionaries. Now where does it get spent? On whom?

Aditya claimed that a former deputy home minister of India was asked a question in Parliament in 1992 about the violence in the northeast. Aditya said (in English):

He replied that in the northeast the terrorist organizations are getting support from international Christian missionaries. Their money is coming from them. . . . Because others do not want to see India strong. And in fact in Burma, their authorities, they don't have any control in these areas, which are adjacent to our borders. So these people are freely conducting their training camps out of these areas. Then the ammunition they are getting is better than what our forces have got. So naturally some big force is supporting them and this is none else than these Christian missionaries.

At this point, in order to clarify whether he thought the trouble makers were all from the west, I asked Aditya whether the arms could possibly be coming from China. He quickly dismissed this possibility:

In Hindi we have a proverb: *dushman ka dushman dost* [the enemy's enemy is a friend]. . . . China also does not want India to be a strong nation. It is possible that they are providing some help. But the ammunition and all other equipment they are getting—these are all western. Most modern. Our boys say they have better equipment than ours. So that money which Christian missionaries are collecting in western countries is being spent in those operations.

Although there is little evidence to support these statements, they remain powerful ways to recruit people into the movement, because they capitalize on existing fears regarding threats to national security. Linking Christianity to violence in the northeast taps into an already existing sense of discomfort about the randomness of violence in the northeast to create outrage. It also suggests that such violence is a threat to the sanctity of India's borders, just like the Kashmir issue or the Khalistan issue, again tapping into fears and threats that are already part of public memory. By portraying their anti-Christian mobilization as a struggle against insurgency, Hindu nationalists are also able to depict themselves as true patriots called to action by threats to national security rather than divisive religious politics. Through connecting Christian conversion to the problem of insurgencies and foreign allegiances, the movement is able to present itself as the protector of Hindus in India against the insidious workings of the "foreign hand."

Conclusion

If Hinduism provides the matrix for national culture, then any threat to Hinduism is an attack on the nation. By suggesting that the Hindu nation is a primordial entity that is cartographically inscribed with the sacred body of the goddess Bharat Mata, Hindu nationalists establish their essential claim to the nation while rendering Islam and Christianity foreign religions. Through stories about missionaries' duplicity, collusion with foreign powers, forcible conversion of innocent Hindus, and denigration and destruction of Hindu culture, Hindu nationalists argue that Christianity is not only a foreign religion but one that threatens national culture. By linking conversion to Christianity with insurgencies in the northeast, they articulate the threat posed by missionary activity to the political integrity of India. These arguments present a portrait of an insecure nation under attack by antinational missionaries and suggest that patriotic Hindus should join in the struggle to protect the nation.

What is the purpose of this anti-Christian mobilization? How do we explain violence by the Hindu majority against the tiny Christian population of India? Mark Juergensmeyer has argued that religious violence tends to be spectacular and is often "almost exclusively symbolic" (Juergensmeyer 2000: 217). In other words, the point of religious violence is often to make a statement of symbolic importance. When one considers the violence against Christians in Gujarat, it is clear that such violence targeted at Christian communities is not an effective way to tempt Christians back into the Hindu fold. However, as a symbolic statement it draws attention to the fact of Christian conversion in India and provides a narrative through which to reiterate the normative construction of India as a nation of Hindus struggling for centuries against the "foreign" influences of Christians and Muslims. It also provides an arena to shape public memory about the relatively unknown history of Christianity in India and the relationship between Hindus and Christians throughout history. This revisionist history of aggression against Hindus, whether by the Portuguese Inquisition or by colonial missionaries, constructs an image of a nation under siege which Hindu nationalists must struggle to reclaim in the present.

Anti-Christian violence does more than send a message. Indeed, Arjun Appadurai has argued that extreme violence is an effective way to fix identities, particularly in a world marked by uncertainty (2006: 7). Violence against Christians not only establishes them as threats to the nation but also promotes Hindu nationalists as the true defenders of the Indian nation and creates a community of support for them. Fear of external threats becomes a way to unite people against a common enemy, a strategy that has been used extremely successfully by Hindu nationalists in various contexts. Indeed, "discourses of crisis and practices of violence" are necessary for the reiteration of the Hindu nation as an actual entity rather than an ideological fiction (74). The crisis of Christian conversion becomes a rallying cry for Hindu nationalists and provides an arena to reiterate Hindu nationalist claims to indigeneity and nation. Next, I examine a similar crisis presented by the Kargil War with Pakistan, which enables Hindu nationalists to argue that it is not just the patriotic duty but the sacred duty of Hindus to join the struggle to defend the Hindu nation.

Chapter 3
Violent Dharma

To live in the face of death? To live in the world and yet be free from the world? Have we ever fulfilled our duty by sitting in the forest? This is why even renouncers have to help society while staying free of human affairs (insani batein). *We have to fulfil our duty/responsibility* (daitva) *not run away from it. We should not run away from problems. Today it is very important for India* (Bharat) *to understand the message of the Gita.*

—Sadhvi Rithambara, August 22, 1999

Sadhvi Rithambara is a powerful female renouncer belonging to the Sadhvi Shakti Parishad, a branch of the Hindu nationalist movement in India whose membership is limited to Hindu female renouncers (*sadhvis*).[1] She was speaking to a rapt audience of men and women in Ramakrishna Puram in Delhi in 1999 during the Sri Mad Bhagavad Gita Gyan Yagya. This three-day event held in the large hall of the Sankat Mochan Ashram, had been organized by the Vishwa Hindu Parishad to spread the message of the Bhagavad Gita, an important Hindu scripture. Large speakers had been placed outside the hall so that anyone living in the vicinity or passing by could clearly hear the proceedings inside. Everyone had been asked to sit in neat rows by VHP men and women officiously milling around wearing saffron armbands with the Hindi word *raksha* (safety) printed on them. I was given one of these and, for a while, I helped seat men on the left side of the room and women and children on the right, facing the stage at the front where Sadhvi Rithambara was now sitting with two Jain *sadhvis* and another Hindu *sadhvi*. To Rithambara's left was a heavily garlanded gold statue of Krishna, a large poster of Bharat Mata, a lamp, a donation box, and other *puja* items. On her right were three musicians who had been leading the audience in *bhajans* (devotional songs) before she arrived. In the speech she delivered at this event, Rithambara used the Gita to argue that the principles of worldly involvement and renunciation are not opposed to each other. According to her, renouncers must fulfill their duty to society while also maintaining their detachment from the everyday involvements of human beings. Following many modern renouncers, Rithambara distances herself from the prevailing construction of renunciation in classical Hinduism, which suggests that a true renouncer is one who lives in the forest, distant from worldly passions and involvements.

Classical theories of renunciation suggest that the renouncer must remove him/herself from the world of attachments, desires, luxuries, and possessions in order to attain liberation from *samsara* (cycle of birth, death, and rebirth). Far from imbricating oneself in the attachments and passions that mark the social and political world that ordinary humans inhabit, the Mundaka Upanishad asserts that *moksha* (liberation from *samsara*) will be attained only by those who abnegate involvement in the world and live a life of "penance and faith" focused on penetrating the illusions of the world (Mundaka Upanishad 1.2.11, trans. Olivelle 1998). Yet, how should we understand the deep involvement of female renouncers in the political battles of Hindu nationalism? Rather than turning to the Upanishads to define their place and role in the world, Hindu nationalist *sadhvis* use the Bhagavad Gita to suggest that it is not only possible but in fact imperative for them to engage in righteous action that upholds *dharma*, the moral order of the world.[2] These female renouncers also argue that it is the sacred duty of Hindus to participate in this struggle for *dharma*, identified as the struggle to establish India as a Hindu nation.

I examine how Hindu nationalist female renouncers use religious texts and ideology to disseminate the politics of the movement as well as to justify their own worldly involvements. Through an examination of speeches and conversations with Hindu nationalist renouncers in Delhi, I analyze the way female renouncers interweave religious ideas with Hindu nationalist ideology. Their efforts not only imbue political action with a sacred injunction but also suggest that their calling is not to remove themselves from the world but rather to shape that world and infuse it with the values, ideology, and politics of Hindu nationalism. I argue that it is their ability to weave the political imperatives of Hindu nationalism with the realm of the sacred that makes renouncers such effective spokespersons for the movement. Indeed, by drawing an ineluctable link between religion and politics, *sadhvis* not only frame Hindu nationalism as a religious movement, but also suggest to deeply religious Hindus that it is their sacred duty to participate in its politics.

While most Hindu nationalist *sadhvis* do not make the headlines in India, some like Sadhvi Rithambara are among the most prominent figures in the movement. Her strident voice is instantly familiar to those within and beyond the movement, eclipsing the Hindu nationalist male renouncers. I suggest that it is their dual status as renouncers and as women that makes these *sadhvis* such effective voices for the values, morals, and politics of the movement. Indeed, women renouncers like Rithambara are vital to the expansionary power of Hindu nationalism because of their ability to appeal to Hindus within and beyond the movement, and to produce a nationalist Hinduism in which the movement's politics are inextricably intertwined with religious ideas and imagery.

While conducting fieldwork I had the opportunity to attend and record several *pravachans* (religious lectures) given by different female renouncers who belonged to the Hindu nationalist movement, as well as to analyze the ethnographic context in which they were uttered and made meaningful. Each of these *pravachans* addressed the politics of the movement in different ways, and the lectures varied in their emphasis on ongoing political debates over religious themes. Some only tangentially referred to religious themes, while others focused explicitly on religious ideas and used them to interpret the political world and frame activism within it. Here I am not suggesting that the *pravachans* of Hindu nationalist *sadhvis* are distinct from other religious lectures because they are imbued with political ideas. Rather, following Talal Asad (1983), it is my contention that religion should not be viewed as a sphere distinct from the social or the political and, consequently, all *pravachans* are shaped by the particular contingencies of their worlds. Produced by *sadhvis* involved in the Hindu nationalist movement, the *pravachans* examined here are inflected with the values and politics of Hindu nationalism. Indeed, they embody a peculiarly Hindu nationalist version of Hinduism in which ancient Hindu texts are infused with new meanings that reflect the contemporary struggles and aspirations of the movement.

At these events, it is the audience's acceptance of these women as religious renouncers who have the wisdom to penetrate the everyday illusions of the world that gives their words added power and efficacy. Delivered by renouncers believed to have transcended the pettiness of everyday life, for those who listened to them these *pravachans* carried the weight of a higher spiritual authority. To the Hindus present at these events, whether or not they were part of the movement, these *sadhvis* were accepted as religious authorities and accorded the respect commanded by such figures. For deeply religious Hindus already familiar with a long tradition of modern renunciation that includes serving the world, the *sadhvis'* discussions of social and political events would not have been unusual. In fact, this acceptance is precisely what makes the political interventions and interpretations of *sadhvis* so pivotal to the Hindu nationalist movement. It is therefore critical to examine the gendered religious politics of Hindu nationalist *sadhvis* in contemporary

India to see how they frame Hindu nationalism as a religious movement and mobilize support for its politics among diverse groups of Hindus. After a brief discussion of renunciation and violence in contemporary India, I analyze how the Bhagavad Gita offers an ideology of action. Then I show how invoking religious texts is a way to encourage participation—even violence—in the struggle for a Hindu nation. Finally, I look at the degree to which the movement relies on *sadhvis* to mobilize Hindus to engage in the violent politics of Hindu nationalism.

Renunciation and Violence in Contemporary India

Hindu renouncers became prominent in the cultural politics of the movement during the Ramjanmabhumi movement to build a Ram temple at the site of the Babri Masjid destroyed by Hindu nationalists in 1992. In rallies and events leading up to the destruction of the mosque, Hindu nationalist renouncers used religious ideas and their renunciant authority to rouse Hindus to destroy the mosque and build a temple in its place. While both male and female renouncers joined the movement, it is important to note that female renouncers, often less visible in traditions of renunciation (Khandelwal 2004), became quite prominent during the Ramjanmabhumi agitation. The VHP established the Sadhvi Shakti Parishad (Organization of Sadhvi Strength) to create a platform through which Hindu female renouncers could participate in the Ramjanmabhumi movement. In particular, two female renouncers, Sadhvi Rithambara and Uma Bharati, escalated to fame as they stood in front of crowds of Hindus exhorting them to defend Hinduism, destroy the mosque, and kill Muslims, who were constructed as the paramount threat to Hindu India (see T. Sarkar 2001: 269). Scholars have noted the highly sexual and gendered imagery employed by these *sadhvis* (A. Basu 1995; B. Ghosh 2002) in their condemnations of Muslim men. In their speeches they suggest that Muslim men committed atrocities against Hindu women and figuratively violated the honor of India, conceived as the goddess Bharat Mata. The power of women (albeit renouncers) calling on men to avenge the honor of Hindu womanhood is central to the successful mobilization of men to engage in acts of violence against Muslims.[3] While most Hindu nationalist ideologues are men, it is important to understand how the agency of *sadhvis* is critical to constructing the affective power of Hindu nationalism in the minds of ordinary people.[4] Their performative acts interlace religion and politics, imbuing Hindu nationalism with a sacred injunction and recruiting their audience as subjects of a Hindu nation under siege.

The acts and events discussed in this chapter occurred in the context of the Kargil War between India and Pakistan in 1999, an occasion that charged these injunctions with a particular urgency. Female ascetics alluded to an emerging national narrative on the war to infuse religious symbolism with significance, making religious imagery a compelling lexicon through which to interpret the violent conflagration between India and Pakistan. In their speeches the Kargil War was ineluctably linked with the sacred battles between morality and immorality described in ancient sacred Hindu texts. Indeed, the imagery of cosmic war that Mark Juergensmeyer (2000) has argued is central to understanding the appeal of religious imagery in contemporary conflicts in the world was indispensable to Hindu nationalists as they recruited support for their agenda during this period. Below I provide a brief and necessarily sketchy description of the events leading to the Kargil War, since many of these details are woven into the religious sermons that I discuss later.

In February 1999 Atal Behari Vajpayee, prime minister of India, traveled to Pakistan to meet his Pakistani counterpart, Nawaz Sharif, on the newly established bus service between the two countries. The event was a media spectacle in which many saw a dissipation of the tensions that had arisen the previous year after both countries had conducted nuclear tests (in May 1998). In February the prime ministers of India and Pakistan signed the Lahore Declaration, in which both pledged their commitment to previous agreements to resolve the Kashmir issue peacefully rather than militarily, and, in recognition of their nuclear capabilities, sought to work toward reducing the risks of a nuclear conflagration in South Asia (Ganguly 2001: 115). In May 1999, the Indian army discovered that Pakistanis had breached the line of control and occupied several Indian army positions in Kargil district in the state of Jammu and Kashmir (116). This discovery resulted in the Kargil War, during which the Indian Army sought to wrest the strategic positions from Pakistani control.

As the Kargil War raged from May to July 1999, the media began to point to the inexplicable failure of the Indian government to further investigate or act upon intelligence—available in September 1998—regarding the possibility of Pakistani incursions across the line of control (Ganguly 2001: 124–25). The government led by the Hindu nationalist political party, the BJP, concerned about the upcoming national elections, sought to deflect such criticism by focusing instead on the creation of national affect through screening clips on national television about the soldiers who were dying in Kargil. At the grassroots level, organizations associated with the Hindu nationalist movement such as the VHP framed the breach of the line of control as a violation of the sacred body of goddess Bharat Mata. They organized several events to honor the soldiers who had died in Kargil, whom they referred to as "martyrs."

Much of the material I examine here is derived from speeches given by religious renouncers at these events. The *pravachans* discussed here are absolutely central to the production of self and "other" in the Hindu nationalist movement. *Sadhvis* play a critical role both in establishing a Hindu identity for the nation and in constructing Muslims as the enemy of a Hindu India. Using religious texts to interpret contemporary politics, they engage religious motivations to mobilize Hindus to participate in the politics of Hindu nationalism. In what follows I examine the religious sources used by Hindu nationalist renouncers to justify their worldly involvements in the politics of Hindu nationalism.

Renunciation and Action

> But those in the wilderness, calm and wise,
> Who live a life of penance and faith,
> As they beg their food;
> Through the sun's door they go spotless,
> To where that immortal Person is,
> That immutable self. (Mundaka Upanishad 1.2.11; trans. Olivelle 1998)

Living in the wilderness, practicing various austerities, holding no possessions, and devoting oneself entirely to the experience of oneness with ultimate reality—such is the life of a renouncer according to classical Hinduism. Fulfilling one's duty belongs to those caught in the web of *samsara*, that endless cycle of birth and rebirth that the renouncer seeks to escape. As the above excerpt from the Mundaka Upanishad suggests, the goal of renunciation is to attain *moksha* through the merging of the individual *atma* (self) with Brahman (ultimate reality), "that immortal person" (Mundaka 1.2.11). Part of the corpus of ancient Vedic texts that most Hindus consider to be divinely revealed, the Mundaka is one of the later Upanishads and was probably composed in the last centuries B.C.E. (Olivelle 1998: xxxvii). In the Mundaka Upanishad, Sage Agniras, speaking to the householder Saunaka, attacks those who believe that they will attain *moksha* through performing the fire sacrifices that were central to the early Vedic period. Agniras says:

> The fools who hail that as the best,
> Return once more to old age and death. (Mundaka Upanishad 1.2.7)

In other words, those who believe that liberation will be achieved through performing Vedic rituals and elaborate fire sacrifices will only be reborn again, bound as they are to that endless cycle of *samsara*. These words suggest that actions bind one to *samsara*, an idea that is important to the Upanishads. To attain liberation one must enter a state of non-action. A renouncer is required to stop performing rituals and tending the sacred fire. S/he is also required to enter a state of complete detachment from relationships, events, and the world in general to focus on understanding the nature of ultimate reality.

Clearly, Sadhvi Rithambara's claim that renouncers must learn to maintain their detachment from the world of humans and yet continue to serve society contrasts with the prescriptions for renunciation that one finds in the Upanishads. However, while many renunciant traditions in contemporary India continue to emphasize detachment from the social world, the worldly involvements and concerns of Hindu nationalist *sadhvis* are not unusual. In the nineteenth century, Swami Vivekananda established the Ramakrishna Order that required its members to perform *seva* (service) (Elder 1990: 32). He argued that renouncers should participate in the religious and cultural revival of the nation and engage in efforts to ameliorate the socioeconomic conditions of the country (Sinclair-Brull 1997: 32, cited in Khandelwal 2004: 115). Swami Chinmayananda, an important and respected figure in modern Hinduism, was also deeply involved with the Vishwa Hindu Parishad's early activities to revive Hindu culture in independent India (Jaffrelot 1999: 194–96). More recently, Swami Ranganathananda, the late president of the Ramakrishna Math and Mission, asserted that the idea that liberation is gained through inaction has deluded both renouncers and householders and "ruined the nation" (Ranganathananda 2000: 258). He argued that it is only in the modern era, through the ideas of people like Swami Vivekananda, that people are beginning to understand the importance of action. As Meena Khandelwal contends in her ethnography of female renouncers in North India, in the modern period renouncers have often included social engagement as part of their spiritual practice (2004: 115–16). Indeed, for Baiji, one of the female renouncers Khandelwal discusses, *seva* is central to spiritual practice. As Khandelwal argues, in contemporary renunciation, what is crucial is to maintain detachment from the actions one performs.[5]

Hindu nationalist *sadhvis* view their political activity as *seva* and, like other renouncers, use later texts like the Bhagavad Gita to suggest that there is religious justification for worldly involvement.[6] Revered by many Hindus today, the Bhagavad Gita is a text found in the ancient Hindu epic, Mahabharata and was written between 400 B.C.E. and 400 C.E. The Mahabharata tells the story of the battle between the Pandavas, the sons of Pandu, and their cousins the Kauravas, the sons of Dhritarashtra, Pandu's brother. In a story most Hindus are intimately familiar with, the Pandavas engage in war to reclaim the kingdom that their cousin Duryodana has usurped from them. As the armies line up on both sides of the battlefield, Arjuna, a great warrior and one of the five Pandava brothers, gets cold feet when he sees the family, teachers, and friends he will have to destroy to win the war. His charioteer Krishna, as Arjuna is yet to discover, is an incarnation of Lord Vishnu. In the seven hundred verses of the Bhagavad Gita, Krishna tells Arjuna that he must engage in this epic battle for *dharma*, the moral order of the world.

The Gita became popular during the Hindu reform movements of the colonial period[7] and is now widely read and sold as an independent text. It has remained an important vehicle for religious politics and religious actions since Gandhi's use of the text to construct his own philosophy of nonviolent action. In contrast to Gandhi's interpretation, Sadhvi Rithambara argues that according to the Gita worldly involvement—even violent action—in defense of the moral order is justified and can lead to liberation. While in the Upanishads the path to liberation is through a transforming wisdom, the Gita suggests that in fact action is more powerful than knowledge in the pursuit of liberation. Krishna tells Arjuna the following:

A man cannot escape the force
of action by abstaining from actions;
he does not attain success
just by renunciation.

No one exists for even an instant
without performing action;
however unwilling, every being is forced
to act by the qualities of nature. (Bhagavad Gita 3. 4–5, trans. Miller 1986)

Here Krishna argues that a person cannot escape action. Even a renouncer, who has supposedly entered a state of inaction, continues to perform actions because s/he is human. According to Krishna, renunciation of action does not necessarily lead an individual toward *moksha*. Krishna argues that *moksha* is achieved not through renunciation of action but rather through performing "necessary action" with complete detachment (Bhagavad Gita 3. 8–9), an idea which Hindu nationalist *sadhvis* rely on—explicitly or implicitly—to promote their vision of a unified India.

However, if actions bind one to *samsara*, then how is Krishna able to argue in the Gita that actions can also liberate one from the cycle of *samsara*? While Krishna accepts that most actions bind you to *samsara*, he posits that sacrificial actions performed simply for preserving the universe, rather than for personal gain, can be liberating. Thus he tells Arjuna to "perform action as sacrifice" (Bhagavad Gita 3.9). Krishna argues that sacrificial actions performed with complete detachment from the fruits of action cannot bind one to the cycle of birth and rebirth. He reminds Arjuna that it is because action is necessary for the universe that Krishna himself must return in successive incarnations to perform actions (3.24). Therefore, according to Krishna, "wise men should act with detachment to preserve the world" (3.25).

This last statement is central to understanding the worldly involvements of Hindu nationalist *sadhvis* today. Krishna's counsel in the Gita enables these *sadhvis* to argue that it is their duty to perform actions that lead to the preservation of the world. They must do so with complete detachment, however, or they risk performing action that will carry *karmic* repercussions. This is why Sadhvi Rithambara argues that it is the duty of renouncers to "help society while staying free of human affairs." In the language of Hindu nationalism, it is not appropriate for a renouncer to search for liberation alone in the forest; rather, it is necessary for the renouncer to live in the world while being detached from it. Yet, how does a renouncer "help society"? Below I analyze how Hindu nationalist female renouncers interpret necessary action for those who listen to their religious discourses.

Awakening Sadhvi Shakti

Sadhvi Kamlesh Bharati, head of the Sadhvi Shakti Parishad, argued in a speech at the Sri Mad Bhagavad Gita Gyan Yagya that, in addition to attacks on "mothers and sisters" and attacks on Hindu values, in recent years "two *lakh* Hindu girls are converted by Christians and Muslims every year. Our temples are being converted into mosques. If our *sadhvi shakti* (strength) is awakened then these attacks on our *dharma* (religion) will stop." Building on the common Hindu nationalist construction of a Hindu nation under siege, her brief speech explained to those assembled why *sadhvis* and people of faith needed to organize and engage in the struggle to protect India. The role of the Sadhvi Shakti Parishad was to organize programs such as the Sri Mad Bhagavad Gita Gyan Yagya in order to promote Hindu values, culture, and rituals, as well as to teach people to "consider Bharat Mata as a mother and seat her on the throne of the universe."

As I have already suggested, the vision of India as Bharat Mata has profound implications for the politics of Hindu nationalism. A relatively new form of the goddess, Bharat Mata was first conceived in Bankimchandra Chattopadhyaya's novel *Anandamath* in 1882 (McKean 1996: 44). In Vande Mataram, a hymn Bankimchandra composes to the goddess in *Anandamath*, Bharat Mata is variously portrayed as Annapurna who symbolizes the rich past of the nation, as Kali who symbolizes the angered and violated nation under colonial rule, and as Durga who symbolizes the victorious and powerful future of the nation freed from colonial rule (T. Sarkar 2001: 274). Here the goddess is depicted as both vulnerable and powerful, violated by the enemy and then empowered by the faith of her devotees. For the protagonists of *Anandamath*, as for Hindu nationalists today for whom Vande Mataram remains a daily prayer, both spiritual and political liberation come from devotion to the goddess (McKean 1996: 145). Importantly, here Bankimchandra clearly links Bharat Mata to ancient forms of the goddess—Kali and Durga. For most Hindus, Kali and Durga, like other goddesses, are understood to be different manifestations of the great goddess Devi. The relatively recent provenance of Bharat Mata is thus not an issue; they can easily incorporate her into a constellation of goddesses who are part of their daily rituals of worship.

In her speech, Sadhvi Kamlesh Bharati argues that the dishonor of Hindu women and girls must be fought against alongside the greater dishonor of Bharat Mata and the Hindu values that both represent. Central here is the image of women's honor that must be protected from violation, an image that is central to Hindu nationalism and to nationalist movements all over the world.[8] Yet, instead of simply portraying women/goddesses as victims of violence, Sadhvi Kamlesh Bharati asserts that *sadhvi shakti* can stop attacks on *dharma*. *Shakti* can be translated as strength, but it also specifically refers to the female creative principle that women are thought to embody. Although *sadhvis* are supposed to be neither male nor female, they continue to be viewed as women and often continue to play roles that are consistent with those of female householders (Khandelwal 2004). Given that women bear the unequal burden in Hindu nationalism of both embodying and transmitting cultural traditions, values, and morals, it is perhaps the femaleness of *sadhvis* that uniquely positions them to prevent attacks on *dharma* and also to organize events to promote Hindu ideas. Tanika Sarkar argues that Hindu nationalists believe that women are the "custodians" of Hinduism and "that therefore they can respond to a call that comes from the heart of age-old Hindu beliefs" (T. Sarkar 1995: 209). Thus, it is not surprising that *sadhvis*, rather than male renouncers, play such a prominent role in the cultural politics of Hindu nationalism. Indeed, *sadhvis* may be visible precisely because they are female and are able to deploy their gendered identities as "custodians" of culture to produce, disseminate, and recruit Hindus into a uniquely Hindu nationalist construction of religion.

The image of India as Bharat Mata also suggests that it is not simply the patriotic but also the religious duty of all Hindus to participate in the struggle to defend this goddess/nation. As Sarkar (2001: 278) has argued, Hindu nationalists envision the struggle to defend the integrity of India's borders as a religious necessity because an attack on territory is a violation of the sacred body of the goddess. This image was powerfully invoked by *sadhvis* when speaking about the Kargil War between India and Pakistan in 1999. At a speech to members of the Hindu nationalist movement gathered to honor soldiers who had died in the war, Sadhvi Rithambara evoked the image of soldiers sacrificing their lives for this goddess/nation:

> Our greatest respects at the feet of those who gave their lives at the feet of Bharat Mata. We salute that mother's womb, that mother's lap, that mother's love, her affection, in whose shadow our country's brave soldiers learned to sacrifice for their motherland. We salute those widows who laid their *sindhuri* (married) nights, their happy days, at the feet of Bharat Mata.[9]

In this passage, both men and women must sacrifice for Bharat Mata, yet these sacrifices are clearly defined according to Hindu nationalist constructions of gender. Here violence is glorified and men are asked to embrace death in defense of Bharat Mata. Women are applauded for their ability to sacrifice the pleasures of motherhood and sex (codified in the reference to *sindhuri* nights) and for teaching their sons to be brave and patriotic. Indeed, as I demonstrate below, references to the sacrifices of both soldiers and their widows greatly affected the audience. The images of a mother sacrificing her son or of a wife sacrificing her husband resonate with a broader cultural glorification of female sacrifice and are powerful ways to recruit women into the movement.[10] In this discussion of female sacrifice, Rithambara makes a reference to women's sexuality. While this is a relatively tame allusion to sexuality, Rithambara is known for fiery speeches in which she explicitly discusses the sexuality of Muslim men (see A. Basu 1995). Such discussions of sexuality at public venues violate the gendered norms of the movement, making Rithambara's speeches "highly sexual and transgendered" moments in which she "adopts the privileges of male speech (sexual aggression, intimate vulgarities, suggestive insinuation)" (B. Ghosh 2002: 270–71). Yet, while her status as a renouncer allows her to distance herself from the restrictions on women's performance, it is her femaleness, as I argue below, that empowers her words.

Sadhvi Rithambara is one of the most skillful orators in the movement. Tapes of her passionate speeches circulate among members of the movement and are sold at events such as the Bhagavad Gita Gyan Yagya. After the Gita event, a man approached Urvashi and me as we were waiting at the bus stop, to find out where he could purchase tapes of Sadhvi Rithambara's speeches. After responding to his question, Urvashi asked where he was from. We discovered that he had come from Kota, Rajasthan, about 500 kilometers away, to hear Rithambara speak. This encounter illustrates the powerful appeal of Rithambara's words. In these speeches, Tanika Sarkar has argued, her "voice seems always almost about to crack under the sheer weight of passion. The over-whelming and constant impression is one of immediacy, urgency, passion and spontaneity" (1993: 30). Bishnupriya Ghosh argues that Sadhvi Rithambara is one of the key women in the movement who engage in public performances as "instigators of affect and emotion, and as progenitors of non-rational collective identifications" (2002: 259).

That Rithambara is a woman is not incidental to her popularity. Amrita Basu has argued that in Hindu nationalist imagery women are closely associated with "emotion rather than reason" (1995: 164). I believe this is central to understanding why *sadhvis* play such a prominent role in the movement. Although female renouncers are supposed to have transcended gender (Khandelwal 2004), it is because they are identified as women that they are able to forge the patriotic ardor that drives Hindu nationalism.[11] As a renouncer, Sadhvi Rithambara is supposed to be detached from passions. However, as a woman she is expected to be emotional. Arguably, Sadhvi Rithambara's prominence in the movement is related to the ambiguity of her own subject position as a passionate renouncer.

This production of affect and emotion was central to Rithambara's performance at the Kargil event. The large auditorium of the Constitutional Club on Rafi Marg in New Delhi was filled to capacity, and yet the room was quiet as Sadhvi Rithambara's voice trembled with emotion, and tears streamed down her face. Several in the room wept along with her, caught in the spell of her powerful oratory. As she continued her speech her voice became more angry and passionate until she was almost screaming the words to a silent auditorium: "on Islamabad's chest will rest India's flag, up till Rawalpindi and Karachi . . . up to the Indus River it will all become India.[12] Then for eons and eons there will not be a devil like Jinnah.[13] There will be a Kashmir but there will not be a Pakistan."[14]

As the audience cheered in response to these statements, it became clear that Sadhvi Rithambara's passionate anger inflected the imaginations of those present and perhaps recruited them into the discursive constructions of Hindu nationalism. When studying such movements it is important to recognize the processes through which individuals come to view themselves as subjects within specific ideological formations (Mankekar 1999: 17). At this event, the affective power of Rithambara's speech clearly resonated with those present, creating an arena in which individuals could embrace the politics of the movement and envision themselves as subjects in its particular ideological formations. As a woman, Rithambara can be a passionate renouncer who generates the affect necessary to recruit individuals into the movement.

The image of Bharat Mata torn asunder by Partition, whose sacred body will be reintegrated in an undivided Hindu India is important in Rithambara's speech. The idea of *akhand Bharat* (undivided India) is central to Hindu nationalists and is called upon repeatedly in speeches by *sadhvis*, including Rithambara. She refers to it at the Sri Mad Bhagavad Gita Gyan Yagya as well, suggesting that it is the sacred duty of Hindus to fight for an *akhand Bharat*. At this event she skillfully integrates Hindu nationalist politics into her exegesis of religious texts to suggest that the struggle for *akhand Bharat* is a struggle for the very moral order of the world—for *dharma*. She begins by saying, "the martyrs of Kargil, according to the guidance of the Gita, sacrificed themselves for their country. They gave their bodies for their country. What will we give? We will listen to the *pravachan* and then go home and live surrounded by comforts." In Sadhvi Rithambara's speech, the battle against Pakistan to defend the territories of India was a sacred war, similar to the War of Kurukshetra that forms the backdrop to Krishna's conversation with Arjuna in the Gita. Krishna suggests that it is Arjuna's sacred duty to fight, and revealing his cosmic form, Vishvarupa, he shows Arjuna that the relatives and teachers he is so reluctant to fight are already dead. He tells Arjuna that they will die regardless of Arjuna's actions because their death is necessary to uphold *dharma*.   Arjuna is to act as Krishna's "instrument" so that he may "win glory" (Bhagavad Gita 11. 32–33). Referencing this, Sadhvi Rithambara says:

Bhagvan Krishna says, Arjun, the Kauravas standing in front of you are evil. They endanger *dharma*. If you do not kill them Arjun then I will. If the enemy does not understand friendship then it is necessary to give them a strong reply. This is the goal of the Sadhvi Shakti Parishad. I want to make a request to Atalji that you had gone there taking a bus with the message of friendship. But that rogue called Sharif[15] did not understand your friendship. Now it is necessary, instead of taking a bus to take a tank and go. In Pakistan go up to Rawalpindi, Lahore, and Karachi. . . . Because we know that those who don't make mistakes we call god. Those who make mistakes and repent we call humans. And those who make mistakes and don't repent we call the devil. But those who make mistakes again and again without repenting we call Pakistan.

The audience began to cheer and clap loudly, clearly delighted by Sadhvi Rithambara's indictment of Pakistan. By juxtaposing the Gita and the Kargil War, Rithambara suggests that both are *dharmic* wars. In the Mahabharata the Pandavas attempted to prevent war with the Kauravas by trying to convince Duryodhana to concede their share in the kingdom. Alluding to Vajpayee's visit to Pakistan on the newly established bus service between New Delhi and Lahore, Rithambara argues that Pakistan responded to this overture of friendship with an act of aggression—crossing the line of control in Kashmir—resulting in the Kargil War. Rithambara sees this as reason not only to defend territory but also to fight to regain the *dharmic* order that, from her perspective, requires *akhand Bharat.*

I once asked a male member of the movement what *akhand Bharat* included. He informed me that India, Pakistan, Bangladesh, and Afghanistan were all part of *akhand Bharat.* When I expressed surprise at the inclusion of Afghanistan, he responded by saying: Yes, Afghanistan—for after all Gandhari from the Mahabharata is from Gandhar or Kandahar, which is in Afghanistan.[16] Many in the movement believe that all these countries are part of the sacred soil of the Hindu nation, resonating with a common claim of nationalisms that culture, blood, and nation are not imagined but instead firmly rooted in territory (Ferguson and Gupta 1992). This territory is included in the landscape of the nation through imagined networks forged through folklore—in this case the ancient Hindu epic, the Mahabharata. Also linked to this notion of *akhand Bharat* is the related sense of injustice that this land, firmly linked to the imagination of nation, has been taken away from its rightful claimants. Sadhvi Rithambara asserts that it is only with the creation of *akhand Bharat* that the "river of peace will flow" and the "sacrifice" of the soldiers will be honored. Until then the intrusions will continue, the violence will continue, and such violence, on the part of Hindus fighting for a moral order, will continue to be justified.

During these events, the affective oratory of *sadhvis* like Rithambara becomes central to the movement's ability to frame Hindu nationalist politics within a religious lexicon. This lexicon invokes images of cosmic war, suggesting that violence is necessary to rid the world of immorality (Juergensmeyer 2000). While some might argue that these renouncers are simply using religion to further their political agenda, I would like to suggest that, like the religious militants that Mark Juergensmeyer (2000), Jessica Stern (2003), and Cynthia Mahmood (1996) have written about, for Hindu nationalist renouncers too, their construction of religion is inextricably linked with their politics. Indeed, following Talal Asad (1983), religious belief and practice are inseparable from the world of power and politics, and it is analytically problematic to imagine a pure religious space untainted by politics. As Asad so eloquently argues, the distinction between religion and politics is rooted in the history of the western world, and we need to be cautious of how we use these analytical categories in other contexts where such distinctions may not be as relevant. Religion was inseparable from politics in the words and deeds of the Hindu nationalist women I worked with. For their mobilizing strategies to be effective, it was necessary to ensure that this religious lexicon could be interpreted in ways conducive to their politics. Below I examine how *sadhvis* interpret the message of the Gita for their audiences so that it can become a tool for mobilizing people toward Hindu nationalist politics.

"The Time for the *Sudarshan Chakra*": Hindu Nationalism and Sacred Duty

In this world if you have to leave acquaintance for the sake of god then leave them. However, don't ever leave god for the sake of acquaintances. If in this world you have to forget acquaintances for god's sake then do so. However, don't ever forget god for the sake of acquaintances. And when a person's mind becomes joined with god then there is no duty that is too much for a person to perform. (Sadhvi Shiva Saraswati, August 21, 1999)

Sadhvi Shiva Saraswati uttered these words in a speech delivered at the Sri Mad Bhagavad Gita Gyan Yagya. This speech, heavily laden with Sanskrit verses recited from the Bhagavad Gita and delivered in a flat voice, did not raise as much audience participation as Sadhvi Rithambara's. Perhaps the monotonous tone had something to do with her own irritation at the fact that her entrance had been mistaken for Sadhvi Rithambara's. A man who had been leading the audience in devotional songs before any of the *sadhvis* arrived spotted the entrance of a *sadhvi* and declared energetically into the microphone, "Sadhvi Rithambara *ki jai*" (glory to Sadhvi Rithambara). The audience immediately stood up and began showering her with flowers and saying, "Sadhvi Rithambara *ki jai.*" It was a while before the man on stage and the audience were able to discern Sadhvi Shiva Saraswati's short form through the crowd to realize their error. Ignoring the embarrassed and profuse apologies (also made into the microphone), Shiva Saraswati sat down on the mattress prepared for her at the center of the stage in what seemed like a huff. She did not acknowledge the apologetic gentleman or smile in his direction, but sat sullenly staring at the audience in front of her. Another young *sadhvi* who had come in with her began to sing a devotional song to the sound of an electronic keyboard she was playing. During this song, I began to talk with one of Sadhvi Kamlesh Bharati's two young nieces who had escorted Sadhvi Shiva Saraswati in and were now sitting with me in the audience. I found out from one of them that Sadhvi Shiva Saraswati was about thirty years old. Whether it was due to her youthful lack of control over emotion or not, the speech itself, which ran for well over an hour, was monotonous. Yet, although they were not clapping and participating in her speech, the members of the audience sat with their hands folded in their laps and seemed to be listening reverently to what Shiva Saraswati had to say.

All the speeches delivered at the event expressed Hindu nationalist politics in a religious framework. Sadhvi Shiva Sarawati's speech focused specifically on sacred duty and attempted to define how Hindus should act according to their duty. She used Krishna's discourse in the Gita to argue that all actions in which a person engages must be undertaken as acts of devotion.[17] She said, "Whatever you do, do it as if it were an act of devotion to god. Now even if you are sweeping the floor or cooking a meal, as long as you are doing this without selfishness and you are doing it as an act of devotion to god, you will show your devotion. If you think of the whole world as god's feet, then any act you do in this world is an act of worship at god's feet." Her use of domestic roles usually performed by women in a discussion of duty and devotion is important since it reinforces the Hindu nationalist presumption that women's activism in the movement should not challenge their roles in the patriarchal family (see A. Basu 1995).

Having spelled out the need to show devotion to god through performing one's duty, Sadhvi Shiva Saraswati asserted that everyone must give a percentage of their earnings to god by "giving to national organizations." She did not name any of the organizations in the Hindu nationalist movement, yet, given that the event had been organized by the Vishwa Hindu Parishad, her statement could be interpreted to mean contributing money to organizations like the VHP. In an interesting interpretation of the Hindu *ashramas* (stages of life)[18] Sadhvi Shiva Saraswati said:

Give a few years of your life to society. When the children get older and start taking care of the business, when you get old, then the mother thinks, the time for *vanaprastha* has come; the father thinks, the time for *vanaprastha* has come. Don't leave everything behind and go off to the jungle.[19] Stay at home. Put all your worry and all your efforts into serving the society that has given you strength.

She repeats these lines later in her speech after saying that Ram *rajya* (kingdom), the lengendary kingdom that Hindu nationalists identify with a Hindu India, comes not from speeches but through actions. Shiva Saraswati is not simply telling people to work toward the betterment of society, she is identifying the goal of social work as the establishment of Ram *rajya*, a Hindu nation in India. She asserts that the best way to attain Ram *rajya* is not to "stay at home and admit defeat," but rather to join a "social organization or a national organization." But, she warns, one must perform social work without any ego because that is the message of the Gita. She says, "The life that has ego, it attaches a human. The life that has desire, it attaches a human. The life that brings another misery, that attaches a person. The person who has pride, it attaches a human. But the person who wants to be like Lord Krishna, s/he (*voh*) will be freed from attachments." In other words, engaging in necessary action to uphold *dharma*—like Krishna in the Gita—will not attach an individual to the cycle of *samsara*, but will lead to *moksha*.

Krishna says in the Gita that he engages in action in the world to prevent disorder and the destruction of living beings (Bhagavad Gita 3.24). He also tells Arjuna that those who perform actions in devotion to him will attain liberation and become a part of him (Bhagavad Gita 9.27–29). Shiva Saraswati builds on these ideas, claiming that if one performs actions like Krishna, for the preservation of *dharma* rather than for personal gain, one will be freed from all attachments. She emphasizes that all actions must be performed as acts of devotion to god, and since the entire world is god, anything one does, including participating in the Hindu nationalist struggle for Ram *rajya*, is an act of devotion. She suggests that god is more important than any human relationship, and ultimately human relationships should not guide our actions. Viewing those involved in India's independence movement through a distinctly Hindu nationalist lens she argues, "Those people who sacrificed their lives to make this country free. . . . On the outside they were fighting a war. They were struggling. But on the inside their minds were focused on Bharat Mata." According to Shiva Saraswati, wherever duty takes a person, even if it means fighting a war, one must perform it thinking not of oneself or those one is about to destroy, but only of how one can serve Bharat Mata.

While Sadhvi Shiva Saraswati expresses the political aspirations of Hindu nationalism, she does not explicitly discuss the Kargil War or prescribe a role for Hindus in the battle. Sadhvi Rithambara, on the other hand explicitly prescribes a role for Hindus in the conflict with Pakistan. She ends her speech at the Sri Mad Bhagavad Gita Gyan Yagya saying: "My request to you is when the time is right to play the *bansuri* (flute), then do so. Now it is the time of conflict. It is the time for the *sudarshan chakra* (Krishna's sacred weapon).[20] Join the war. Learn about the circumstances all around you and fulfill your duty." Krishna of Jayadeva's erotic twelfth-century poem Gitagovinda, which has inspired Vaishnava[21] devotional movements for centuries (Miller 1977: ix), is the cowherd who sits in the secret grove playing his *bansuri* and awaiting his lover Radha. This powerful metaphor for devotion to god, where the worshipper is cast as the lover longing for union with his/her beloved (god), is all right, says Sadhvi Rithambara, at certain moments. However, she argues, a time when India and Pakistan are at war is not the moment to sing devotional songs. This is the time to pick up weapons[22] and participate in the battle. She continues a few sentences later, "Lord Krishna says: Arjun, those who have to die, they will surely die. . . . Death is simply a change of clothes, a few moments of rest. To live is the greatest art. But this is also the truth. Those who are scared of death have no right to live."

As Rithambara ended her speech the audience burst into enthusiastic applause. She suggests that it is the duty of all Hindus to pick up their weapons and fight in the battle without fearing death. These words, which combine vigilante heroism with religious imagery, clearly animated the audience in ways that Shiva Saraswati's speech, drawing as it did more directly from the actual Sanskrit text of the Gita, did not. Yet in both the message is clear: the sacred duty of Hindus is not to live in the jungle and contemplate detachment, it is not to sing devotional songs at gatherings such as these, and it is not, in Sadhvi Rithambara's words, simply "to listen to the *pravachan* and then go home and live surrounded by comforts." Rather, a new nationalist Hinduism is being crafted wherein it is the religious duty of all Hindus to act, and act violently in defense of the sacred land of Bharat Mata.

What's in a Speech? The Religious Lectures of Hindu Nationalist Women Renouncers

Using ancient Hindu texts like the Bhagavad Gita and the Mahabharata, and images of gods and goddesses, Hindu nationalist *sadhvis* construct a nationalist Hinduism in which the movement's politics are ineluctably linked to religious duty. As religious renouncers whose task it is to make esoteric religious ideas speak to the intricacies of life in the contemporary world, Hindu nationalist *sadhvis* are uniquely positioned to inscribe Hindu nationalist politics with a sacred injunction. In the landscapes of Hindu nationalism, it is renouncers who become charismatic leaders bridging the gap between the sacred and the mundane. Yet the question remains, how are these powerful acts of oratory viewed by the audience? Below I examine the ways members of the movement variously responded to the speeches by Hindu nationalist *sadhvis*, and the ways *sadhvis* themselves construe their involvement as exclusively *dharmic* rather than political.

The speech by Sadhvi Rithambara at the event organized to honor the "martyrs" of the Kargil War was an eloquent lesson to me about the impact of the words of religious renouncers. While most in the audience were either members of the movement or people involved in Hindu nationalist grassroots campaigns at their schools or vocational training classes, a few individuals I met were attending because of personal relationships with members of the movement. Hindu nationalist women play a central role in recruiting other women. One young woman, Priya Trivedi, who was sitting next to me, was not a member of any of the wings of the movement but had begun attending events at the invitation of Jamuna Sinha, a leader of the Delhi Vishwa Hindu Parishad's women's wing. She told me with awe in her voice that she had heard Atal Behari Vajpayee speak at such an event the previous week. Clearly, her association with Jamuna was giving her access to powerful people, which she may not have had before.

In this example, Jamuna's befriending of Priya and her gradual introduction to the movement illustrate a strategy commonly used by members of the movement and in many right-wing movements in other parts of the world. Amrita Basu discusses how Hindu nationalist women, because they straddle the public-private divide, are well suited to bring other women into the fold (A. Basu 1998: 179–80). Kathleen Blee also illustrates this process in her analysis of racist women in the United States, arguing that these women understand the importance of personal contacts when recruiting new members into the movement (Blee 2002: 133). Both cases highlight the important role played by women in right-wing movements as they mobilize support using gender-based strategies and networks.

Although Priya was relatively new to Hindu nationalist politics, she was deeply moved by Sadhvi Rithambara's speech. She had been extremely friendly and vivacious as we conversed before the event began. Her mood was transformed, however, during Sadhvi Rithambara's speech. As Rithambara spoke of the women who had lost their husbands and sons in Kargil, Priya sobbed in the seat next to me. As widows and mothers walked across the stage to receive awards recognizing their loss, Priya continued to cry, empathizing with the loss these women had experienced. Rithambara's words resonated deeply and evoked in her the emotional power of national belonging and national loss.

While the references to religion in Rithambara's Kargil speech were fewer than at the Bhagavad Gita Gyan Yagya, for those in the movement the speech was seen to convey a religious message because it was delivered by a renouncer. At both events, members of the audience crowded around the *sadhvis* after the speeches to touch their feet and be blessed by them. At the event organized to teach people about the Gita, we were all given *prasad* after the prayer led by the *sadhvis* was performed at the end of each day. *Prasad* is blessed food that is traditionally given to devotees at a temple, ritual, or other religious function. To give *prasad* to those in the audience clearly marks the event as a religious occasion. I had taped all the speeches, and after each of these events several women I worked with asked me for copies so that they could listen to, in their words, the *pravachan* again. The choice of language is significant here. A *pravachan* is a religious lecture usually delivered by a Hindu renouncer. By calling these speeches *pravachans*, women were clearly coding these events as a religious occasions. In fact, most of the women I worked with were deeply religious, and it was clear from their language and actions that they viewed these women as spiritual authorities.

Another example illustrates the attitude that those attending these events had toward Hindu nationalist female renouncers. At the Bhaga-vad Gita Gyan Yagya, the audience, including myself, were seated on the ground in front of the stage where the *sadhvis* were sitting. I have never been able to sit cross-legged for any length of time, so my knee soon began to cramp and I tried to stretch my leg to relieve the pain. I had barely stretched it out when an older woman seated near me smacked my leg and told me crossly that one does not point one's feet at *sadhvis*. Suitably reprimanded, I sat upright, swallowed my pain, and digested the reverence with which the woman viewed the *sadhvis*. This incident clearly revealed that while many secular Indians might view Hindu nationalist *sadhvis* as charlatans who fabricate religious meaning to fur-ther their political aspirations, for those attending the events they are religious figures whose words have sacred authority. Indeed, this is why women renouncers are so effective at constructing Hindu nationalism as a religious movement and weaving its political ideals into the religious imaginary of those present.

At these events, the acceptance of *sadhvis* as religious renouncers, who have distanced themselves from the cycle of *samsara* and have the wis-dom to penetrate the everyday illusions of the world, gives their words power and efficacy. Amrita Basu asserts that the celibacy of these *sadhvis* is associated with "spirituality, purity, and other worldliness" (1995: 161), which makes them powerful voices for the movement's visions. Arvind Rajagopal contends that renouncers like Sadhvi Rithambara are powerful precisely because as *sadhvis* their motives are above reproach (2001: 232). In other words, the authority that their religious status as renouncers confers on them allows them to translate their political zeal into a "pure religious passion" supposedly removed from what many in the movement view as the corruption and immorality of politics (T. Sarkar 2001: 286).

A conversation with a senior member of the Sadhvi Shakti Parishad about her life and her decision to join the Hindu nationalist movement reveals that Hindu nationalist *sadhvis* construct their own action as *dhar-mic* and as distinct from politics. Sadhvi Kiran Bharati became a renouncer at the age of thirty. However, she told me that since early childhood she had known she was somehow cut off from the world and interested in spiritual work. In fact, she claimed, nobody who knew her was surprised when she became a *sadhvi*. She joined the movement some years after her decision to become a *sadhvi*, at the time of the Ayodhya agitation over the 400-year-old Babri Masjid that Hindu nationalists claimed was at the site of a temple dedicated to the birthplace of the god-king Ram. At this time Sadhvi Kiran Bharati set off for Ayodhya to find out why Hindus were demanding a temple in the place of the mosque and why Muslims objected to this. She received the confirmation she needed in the form of the idols of Ram present in the temple, which she felt proved the existence of a temple at the site of the mosque.[23] She told me that this made her very angry and she joined the Ayodhya agitation.

The *sadhvi* told me that the VHP had not been responsible for destroying the mosque, since most of its workers were still in Delhi at the time.[24] She explained that the workers of the various wings of the movement present in Ayodhya had managed to attract a large crowd to the site of the mosque. They had all been sitting around when some monkeys began to play on the roof of the mosque. Given the significance of monkeys in the Ramayana, people viewed this as a sign that this was indeed Ram's birthplace, and several rose spontaneously and began to destroy the mosque.[25] She insisted that L. K. Advani and Ashok Singhal, who were prominent in the movement to destroy the mosque, tried very hard to stop the crowd from destroying it, but there was nothing to be done about it. However, she insisted, now that the mosque had been destroyed the temple was definitely going to be built.

Sadhvi Kiran Bharati sees her role, and the role of all the *sadhvis* in the movement, as defending Hinduism from perceived attacks from other minority religious communities. Clearly, in her narrative it is not the compulsions of electoral politics but rather the anger, or the "pure religious passion" (Sarkar 2001: 286), provoked by the sense of injustice to Hindus that motivated her to become a part of the movement. She informed me that the Sadhvi Shakti Parishad itself was founded because of this feeling of injustice a sentiment echoed by Sadhvi Kamlesh Bharati's claim that the organization was established to stop attacks against *dharma*. These narratives are not innocent of political agendas, however, even if *sadhvis* themselves and their supporters place their actions in *dharmic* rather than political categories. Laura Ahearn argues that language must be viewed as a "form of social action" that actually helps to create the very reality it is supposed to reflect (Ahearn 2001: 110, 111). Similarly, in her analysis of women's life narratives, Sarah Lamb contends that narrative, even if inaccurate, must be viewed as "a mode of social action, a creative act of self making and culture making, through the telling of words" (Lamb 2001: 20). While we cannot verify whether Kiran Bharati was in fact committed to Hindu nationalist politics prior to her visit to the Babri Masjid, her narrative on this point is instructive in its portrait of a renouncer moved by the passion of perceived religious persecution rather than by the seamier world of electoral politics.

By emphasizing her sense of religious wrongdoing, Sadhvi Kiran Bharati reveals her own agendas. First among these is the desire to present herself as a religious figure and to suggest that it is a threat to *dharma* that motivated her to get involved. Second, her narrative legitimizes the destruction of the 400-year-old mosque by claiming, as does the movement, that it was built on the site of a temple commemorating the birthplace of Ram after this temple was unjustly destroyed by the Muslim emperor Babur. Third, using a story also related to me by Sita Mishra, a senior member of the Delhi VHP, she suggests that the destruction of the mosque had divine sanction as evidenced by the presence of the monkeys, symbolizing the monkey-god Hanuman, one of Ram's greatest devotees. And fourth, her representation claims, contrary to evidence and in the light of ongoing legal processes, that the movement, particularly leading figures like Advani and Singhal, was not responsible for the destruction of the mosque. All these are political agendas that are linked to the larger goals of the Hindu nationalist movement and are iterated through the *sadhvi*'s performative act (Butler 1999). Sadhvi Kiran Bharati's articulation of Hindu nationalist politics as a defense of *dharma*, and her use of Hanuman to explain the destruction of the mosque, illustrate the ways in which religious symbols are given meaning through their complex interactions with the workings of power in the world (Asad 1983).

In each of these examples the ability to infuse politics with a sacred sanction, as well as the ability to portray their own political participation as primarily a religious act in defense of *dharma* rather than one undertaken for electoral politics, arises from the status of these women as religious renouncers speaking from a position of religious authority. To maintain this status it is critical to promote the idea that these renouncers exist outside the world of politics, although they participate in the process of cleansing the political world of corruption and immorality (Rajagopal 2001: 232). Speaking specifically about Sadhvi Rithambara, Rajagopal argues that she invests renouncers with the responsibility of "cleaning up politics" (232), thus transforming religion "from being the object of action to serving as the means by which the objective is accomplished, and the guarantee that it will be honestly done, given the purity of the leaders and the power of the Hindu tradition" (233). These ideas need to be situated in the larger context of Hindu nationalist discourse on corruption and politics. Many in the movement believe that the world of politics, narrowly defined as electoral politics and government, is corrupt. The RSS, using this narrow definition of politics, claims that it is not a political organization (Bacchetta 1996: 128). This is also a definition subscribed to by many members of the movement—including renouncers—in their attempts to distance themselves from the seamier world of politics (T. Sarkar 1995: 209). For many Hindu nationalists, this corruption in contemporary India will be ameliorated in a Hindu nation guided by the morality and values of Hinduism.

Hindu nationalist *sadhvis* draw on religious tradition to establish their authority as renouncers with the ability to penetrate worldly illusions. For those listening to their speeches, their words come with the sacred authority of a religious sermon delivered by individuals believed to have attained detachment from the world. Yet, clearly, Hindu nationalist religious exegesis cannot be separated from the political aspirations of Hindu nationalism. Talal Asad asserts that "religious symbols . . . cannot be understood independently of their relations with non-religious 'symbols' or of their articulation of social life in which work and power are always crucial" (Asad 1983: 251). In other words, the meaning of religious symbols cannot be separated from the contexts in which they are deployed. Asad also argues that the symbolism of a sacred text is contingent on the workings of power through which "their correct reading is secured" (251). The *pravachans* of Hindu nationalist *sadhvis* were delivered in the context of Hindu nationalist politics and the accompanying chauvinism and xenophobia that inflects their exegesis.

Given my interest in dissonant subjects, I do not want to suggest that all members of the movement seamlessly reproduce this image of Hindu nationalist *sadhvis*. Indeed, like any cultural system, Hindu nationalism is not a bounded totality but contains within it diverging tendencies, ambiguities, and inconsistencies. It is important, as several feminist scholars have noted, to analyze not only dominant ideologies, but also the perspectives of those on the margins, and the alternative visions, challenges, and ruptures that may be contained therein (see Raheja and Gold 1994; Mankekar 1999: 255). Over the months I engaged with them, Hindu nationalist women not only reproduced Hindu nationalist norms, but also transgressed them in everyday life. One such transgression, what I call a dissonant act, came from Vimla when she questioned renunciant authority by not only failing to reiterate the normative constructions of them as pure and otherworldly, but conjuring up a very different representation. Vimla and I spent an entire afternoon irreverently gossiping about the romantic involvements of renouncers in a conversation that implied that at least some of them were frauds. She told me with a laugh that there is nothing difficult in being a renouncer: "You just have to look spiritual and then people will give you Mercedes cars and you will live in luxury." Here Vimla is a dissonant subject, who transgresses the movement's norms and thereby challenges us to move beyond a vision of Hindu nationalism as a bounded and coherent discursive totality. Her act is indicative of how Hindu nationalists are affected by other ways of being and knowing and do not always inhabit the subject position created for them by the movement. As they negotiate their way through the multiple ideological systems that inform their plural worlds in everyday life, women can be drawn to other ideologies, may perform other norms, and consequently may become dissonant subjects. Yet, while Vimla was a dissonant subject, her critique was not the view that I commonly encountered in my conversations with Hindu nationalists. Instead, for the most part, as is clear from the discussion above, *sadhvis* were talked about and treated with deference.

Conclusion

Sadhvis play a critical role in disseminating Hindu nationalist ideology to those within and beyond the movement. Using the Bhagavad Gita to justify their worldly engagements, these passionate renouncers straddle the boundaries between the sacred and the mundane and become compelling spokespersons for the movement's vision of the world. They strategically employ their dual subjectivity as women and as renouncers to effectively mobilize Hindus to participate in Hindu nationalism. Using religious images from sacred Hindu texts and their renunciant authority, *sadhvis* imbue Hindu nationalism with a sacred mandate and suggest that it is the *dharmic* duty of Hindus to participate in its violent politics.

Through their acts, Hindu nationalist *sadhvis* skillfully intertwine the political and the sacred and reinforce the normative presumptions of Hindu nationalist politics. Mapping allegories of cosmic war onto the political geography of contemporary India, they ensure a reiteration of some of the key constructions of Hindu nationalism: that India is a Hindu nation, that Muslims pose a threat to both the political integrity and the spiritual purity of the nation, and that it is the duty of all Hindus to participate in the battle to liberate the sacred body of Bharat Mata. Although some like Vimla question the authenticity of these renouncers, the majority of those I encountered interpret their words as *pravachans* backed by spiritual authority. It is through these women renouncers that the movement is able to construct a new nationalist Hinduism that not only is ineluctably linked to Hindu nationalist politics, but also provides a vehicle to disseminate images of nation and subject that further its violent, xenophobic, and exclusionary agenda.

A question implicit in this chapter that remains to be discussed has to do with the relationship between the actions of devout Hindu nationalist *sadhvis* working at the grassroots level to recruit support for the Kargil War, and the actions of a supposedly secular state in its violent conflagration with Pakistan. While the Hindu nationalist BJP, as the leader of a secular coalition government, was limited from drawing on the power of religion to strengthen its floundering electoral position, Hindu nationalist *sadhvis* were able to cast the leaders of the state as struggling for *dharma*. Next, I explore these "blurred boundaries" (Gupta 1995) between state and society through an analysis of the practices of Hindu nationalists working at the grassroots level in Delhi, reaching out to widows of the Kargil War, establishing schools for the impoverished, and conducting social work at government hospitals.

Chapter 4
Benevolent Hindus

.

I spent several afternoons working with Urvashi and Shashi in the obstetrics and gynecology wing of a government hospital in central Delhi. Referred to by the hospital staff as the "VHP social workers," Urvashi and Shashi helped process female outpatients seeking prenatal care, every Monday, Wednesday, and Friday afternoon. In the overcrowded room, while nurses and doctors wove their way through meandering lines of pregnant women and their families, and hospital orderlies barked out peremptory instructions to women to line up and make way for the staff, the three of us performed tasks that were vital to the smooth functioning of the hospital. We filled out the name, age, and patient number of each woman present and recorded her weight before sending her to the nurses for blood pressure checks and other tests. Most of the patients were extremely poor, and many lived in the slums scattered throughout Delhi or worked as servants in middle-class homes. As I performed my assigned task of weighing the women, I became aware of how young and underweight many of them were and how daunting their experience at the hospital was.[1] They shied away from the authoritative orderlies even as they quickly followed their instructions, and timidly answered my questions as I filled out their forms for them. I realized, when a couple of young women pointed to the scale and asked me what it was or what they should do, that some had probably never been to a hospital before. It was clear to me that these women relied on the "VHP social workers" to mediate between them and the complex bureaucratic processes and domineering individuals at the hospital.

The social work performed by Urvashi and Shashi at the government hospital is only one of a range of activities undertaken by various wings of the movement to reach out to impoverished and needy communities in Delhi. As a neoliberal framework of governance replaces the shrinking welfare state in India, many of these communities are the first to experience the cuts to government programs in health care, education, and other social services. Capitalizing on the changes wrought by neoliberal policies, organizations in the Hindu nationalist movement position themselves as the caretakers and quintessential leaders of the poor and marginalized by providing invaluable assistance at government hospitals, running health clinics, schools, and vocational training workshops for those unable to access government facilities, and raising funds for widows whose husbands died in the Kargil War. As they conducted social work at these different venues, Hindu nationalist women responded to the everyday needs and demands of the urban poor and in the process skillfully articulated disparate interests toward their political agenda. Indeed, social work is a key expansionary strategy through which women disseminate Hindu nationalist ideology to new audiences, mobilize support for the movement, reach out to the diverse individuals they encounter, and, perhaps, recruit them into the movement.

Through their daily acts, women not only reached out to new audiences and reiterated normative Hindu nationalist constructions of the subject, but also performed the crucial tasks of disciplining these subjects and governing their conduct both in these venues and in their larger communities. Foucault defines "government" as the "conduct of conducts," a process through which the actions of subjects and groups are shaped by structuring the "possible field of action" (2003: 138). I find this conceptualization of the exercise of power through "governmentality" particularly useful for understanding the social work activities of Hindu nationalist women discussed here. These activities bring them into contact with populations who traditionally have not been drawn to Hindu nationalism, and allow them to shape the conduct of those they encounter in ways that are conducive to the movement's goals. As they deliver lectures, discipline their subordinates, or reprimand individuals who do not conform to their expectations, they infuse Hindu nationalist morals and norms in the social world.

Whereas in the early decades of postcolonial India the Nehruvian model promoted a developmentalist state that sought to provide health care and education to its citizens, James Ferguson and Akhil Gupta argue that we have entered an era of "transnational governmentality" characterized by the "outsourcing of the functions of the state to NGOs and other ostensibly nonstate agencies" (2002: 990). Hindu nationalism with its vast networks of financial and ideological support that transcend national boundaries, and its engagement in "state-like" practices that both enhance and contest the reach of the state (994), exemplifies this transnational governmentality as it reaches out to the marginalized urban poor in Delhi in its attempts to crystallize a base of support for the movement. Here I examine the processes through which Hindu nationalist women draw people into the movement, exercise power through disciplinary and regulatory mechanisms (Foucault 1980b: 139), and govern the subjectivities of those they encounter. I look at the work of VHP women in the government hospital above before turning to a discussion of schools run by Sewa Bharati in Delhi slums and resettlement colonies, and finally to work with widows of the Kargil War. I examine the way religious ideas are mobilized to shape and reiterate constructions of the subject and to craft a new nationalist Hinduism that can unify these disparate populations. Through their work in these venues, Hindu nationalist women are able to appeal to new audiences outside the movement's traditional middle-class/caste base, resonate with everyday needs, fears, and desires, and recruit support for Hindu nationalism in contemporary India.

"Social Work" at the Government Hospital

Every time I walked into the government hospital to join Urvashi and Shashi in their work with outpatients in the obstetrics and gynecology ward, I was struck by the pungent odor of Phenyl (a phenol-based disinfectant) that enveloped the small area crowded with pregnant women waiting for medical attention. It was as clean as it could be, given the dwindling resources and the heavy traffic of doctors, nurses, staff members, and patients. The VHP paid Urvashi and Shashi a small stipend to help the severely understaffed hospital process patients through the ward on three afternoons a week. Their superiors would occasionally stop by to check on them, a process that not only ensured their presence at the hospital but also reinforced their position in the VHP hierarchy. These checks can be conceptualized as practices of "vertical encompassment" discussed by Ferguson and Gupta in the context of the state (2002: 982), which reinforce both the hierarchy and the spatial reach of the Hindu nationalist movement. In addition to recording information on patient numbers, ages, and weights, the VHP women also played a critical role in mediating between patients and hospital staff. According to Urvashi, those who worked in the hospital were not particularly helpful or nice to the women, so it fell to the two of them to help women negotiate the complex "system" and get medical care. Indeed, their work was essential to the smooth running of the hospital ward. On the days Urvashi and Shashi were not present, when the ward tended to be less crowded because it focused on other gynecological issues, male orderlies took over these tasks. However, it was difficult for them to do so while also keeping an eye on who was present and where they were going.

Like many government establishments, the hospital had rigid rules and hierarchies. Since there was no system to communicate this to the uninitiated, it fell to the VHP workers to ensure that the rules were followed. For example, tests had to be done in a particular order. Urvashi would intermittently stop her work to stand up and shout above the voices of those gathered that if women had not had their blood tests and tetanus shots they had to stand in another line in another ward before coming to this one. On the days Urvashi and Shashi were present, the ward only saw pregnant women for prenatal care. A patient who was experiencing post-partum issues, or had complications or pain from an abortion or sterilization operation, could not be seen by the hospital staff on these days. I discovered how rigid the hospital staff were about these rules when I sent a woman who was experiencing extreme pain after a sterilization operation to one of the nurses, only to discover that the nurse had dismissed her complaint and instructed her to return the next day.

As I sat there recording data for women outpatients seeking prenatal care, I often encountered women who were there for other reasons. They usually came to Urvashi, Shashi, or myself rather than to the authoritarian male orderlies or nurses, to seek medical attention. In these situations, Urvashi, who is senior to Shashi in the VHP hierarchy, would act as a filter for the hospital, deciding which patients could be asked to return the next day and which were in such critical condition that they had to be attended to despite hospital rules. In critical cases she would try to pressure the doctors to see the patient, failing which she would accompany them to the emergency room and use her author- ity and familiarity with the people and the system to get medical atten- tion. In these cases, Urvashi arbitrated on the seriousness of the situation and decided whether the patient required immediate medical attention.

Usually Urvashi listened to the issue and firmly instructed women to return the next day, or sent them to the emergency room if they were persistent about needing medical attention. However, one day in late September a young woman came up to me and said that she was bleed- ing very badly because of her "menses."[2] She informed me that she had already spoken to the nurses, but they had asked her to come the next day. Since the woman was looking pale, I called Urvashi and told the woman to tell her what the problem was. At first Urvashi also told her to come the following day. Then an elderly woman who had escorted her (perhaps her mother-in-law or mother) intervened and explained that she had brought the young woman to the emergency room because she was dizzy from the blood loss, but the doctor had simply instructed them to return the next day. Urvashi began to recognize that the problem was serious and escorted both of them to the doctor. When she returned thirty minutes later, she informed me that the woman had been preg- nant but had begun to hemorrhage and had lost her baby. Everybody dismissed her because she had used the wrong terminology (menses) to describe the blood loss (hemorrhage). I could not help wondering whether the woman would have survived the hemorrhage if Urvashi had not been there to interpret the unclear allusions to blood loss and dizziness made by the young woman and her escort.

The rules for when doctors will see patients are there to maintain order. In an understaffed government hospital these rules become a way to regulate the flow of patients. It is also a way to discipline those present in ways that reinforce hierarchies and create pliant subjects, who follow the rules and reinstate order. For instance, while most patients are ordered to line up, those who accompany hospital staff do not have to stand in line, practices that testify to the authority of those working for the hospital over everyone else present. Foucault describes two poles of power: disciplinary power, "an anatomo-politics of the human body," and regulatory power, "a biopolitics of the population" (1980b: 139). The attempts to enforce rules, the practices through which patients are disciplined into seeking medical attention on certain days, and the disciplinary actions of the brusque orderlies who flit around ordering women to stand in lines are all part of this "anatomo-politics" through which power is exercised and the hierarchy of the state is made apparent to all those present. Indeed, as Ferguson and Gupta have argued, it is through practices such as these that we "experience" the state as an authoritative body that stands above us and also encompasses us (2002: 985).

At the same time, hospital staff and VHP women are fundamentally engaged in the management of life, what Foucault calls "biopolitics." As they record information about patients, conduct basic health tests such as weight and blood pressure checks, and dispense prenatal care at the government hospital, they are regulating the health of the population and accessing important information about health and well-being. These mechanisms very clearly institute a hierarchical division between the patients and those in charge of dispensing health care. This division lends itself to the separation between the state that benevolently provides services and the people who access its resources. It also reinforces class divisions between the patients, who are mostly urban poor, and the health care workers, who are lower-middle-class (orderlies, Urvashi, Shashi) and middle-class (nurses, doctors). This distinction was also clear in the class-based attitudes of health care workers toward patients. For example a hospital administrator told me to keep an eye on my purse because "these people" might steal my money.

Although Urvashi and Shashi are part of the mechanisms through which hospital hierarchies are crystallized, these examples show that they are also the ones who are in a position to challenge them. While they are not considered "staff," they know all the staff in this particular wing and have contacts with staff and administrators in other parts of the hospital. For those who are unfamiliar with her, Urvashi has no problem claiming the status of a staff member. On a couple of occasions when I was with her, she blithely announced that we were "staff" in order to take a short cut to the bus stop through a restricted wing of the hospital. Unlike most of the patients in the room, she refuses to be intimidated by government bureaucracies. As a VHP activist she has been trained to assert herself, and she uses this training to advantage in the government hospital. This attitude enables her to pressure doctors and nurses to see patients she deems to be in critical condition. However, there are boundaries to what she can do as a social worker rather than a staff member. She grumbled to me about how she was not able to jump the line like hospital staff members despite having worked in this ward for several years. However, for the patients, Urvashi and Shashi appear to occupy authoritative positions because they give orders and perform critical functions. They also derive authority from other forms of assistance they provide for women at the ward. For example, they buy medicines for patients who cannot afford to fill their prescriptions and keep a collection of old clothes to distribute to the needy. They also assist unwed mothers that they encounter through work. On my first visit to the hospital, Urvashi told me in a conspiratorial tone:

You know how it happens some times that girls get pregnant outside of marriage. Well these girls often give their babies to adoption agencies who send the children abroad. In order to prevent these children from being sent abroad, so that they can be brought up within our own *dharma*, we run our own orphanages and take these children of unwed mothers in them. Sadhvi Rithambara runs one such orphanage.

Through their presence at the ward and the help they provided as social workers in the hospital, Urvashi and Shashi managed to reach out to women to whom they might otherwise not have had access. Indeed, their work here is a key expansionary strategy of the movement as it seeks to reach out to, and recruit, new groups through engaging in social work. Their gendered position as women activists facilitated their access to the women at the hospital, not only because it made it easier for them to work in the obstetrics and gynecology ward, but also because other women considered them more approachable than the male orderlies. They, and by extension the VHP, could interact with diverse groups of women and perhaps draw them into the movement.

In their capacity as social workers, Urvashi and Shashi were also responsible for representing the benevolent side of the movement, concerned for all and providing service without regard to caste, religion, or class. While to my knowledge they did not use the hospital space to spread Hindu nationalist ideas and politics, they made it very clear to the women they encountered that they were not part of the hospital but VHP social workers. Through their work they contested the communal representation of the VHP in the media and distanced themselves from the social work of Christian missionaries who, they claimed, always had the ulterior motive of converting people. Importantly, in the eyes of all those at the hospital, these women were performing an integral task. They were filling a need made urgent by increasing numbers of urban poor and decreasing social sector expenditure.

At these sites the movement is no longer the vehicle of an overt cultural chauvinism, but rather paternalistically reaches out to all the poor, Hindu and non-Hindu, and projects itself as the *mai-bap*, the provider and nurturer (Menon and Bhasin 1998), of the poor. By taking over tasks that are essential to the functioning of the ward, these Hindu nationalist women are not only engaging in practices that were formerly within the purview of the welfare state, they are also establishing their own authority and claim over the patients. Challenging the state's claims to vertical encompassment, these VHP women are engaging in practices that position the organization as a "horizontal contemporary" of the state that engages in a "transnational governmentality" alongside it, a phenomenon increasingly common in the neoliberal era (Ferguson and Gupta 2002: 994). Their work in the hospital creates an arena in which to insert themselves in the state's framework and to "conduct the conduct" of those it encounters. This transnational governmentality is central to understanding the ability of Hindu nationalists to shape and govern those it encounters.

Educating Consent

Nowhere is this process more apparent than in schools run for the urban poor by Sewa Bharati in slums and resettlement colonies throughout Delhi. The provision of essential services like health care, schools, and vocational training to the urban poor in cities like Delhi is a key strategy through which the movement reaches out to those in need and expands its base. While many wings of the movement run programs for the urban poor, for Sewa Bharati such work is its raison d'être. Although they do run programs for *adivasis* and widows in rural India, I was told that the organization works primarily in urban areas, providing schools, mobile health clinics, and vocational training (electronics, sewing, typing) workshops in slums and other low-income neighborhoods that have been long neglected by the government and the private sector. Nita Mahajan, one of three women in charge of the Delhi women's wing of Sewa Bharati, informed me that the organization works in 350 slums in and around

Delhi. There are eleven subdivisions of Sewa Bharati in Delhi, each with
separate male and female wings, although a man is assigned to oversee
each of the women's wings. Most workers are volunteers, though some,
the teachers who are often local to the area, are given a token stipend.
Nita informed me that, although most members of Sewa Bharati are
from RSS families, recently the organization has drawn members from a
variety of backgrounds. This is not surprising, since Sewa Bharati has
extensive networks throughout Delhi and does not advertise its links to
Hindu nationalism. I was made aware of the extent of Sewa Bharati's
access to people in Delhi slums when, at the end of my meeting with
Nita, a woman from an independent NGO on women's reproductive
health came to discuss potential collaboration in some of these areas.

I learned about the philosophy guiding Sewa Bharati's work from
Nandini, a soft-spoken woman who was also a leader of the Delhi wing of
the organization, and who informed me that she had a Ph.D. in modern
political thought from Patna University. Illustrating the strong connections between the RSS and Sewa Bharati, Nandini told me (paraphrase):

The RSS was started in 1925 by Hegdewar who saw the need for social work.
After two hundred years of slavery (*gulami*) our society was destroyed. Hegdewar
believed that an individual cannot do anything without society and so he wanted
to build a society that was strong and good. He wanted to build a society according to the scientific values of Hinduism. Accordingly he started up the RSS and
this was initially an organization of men. The Rashtra Sevika Samiti was formed
some years later for women. The Sangh *parivar* (family) was greatly oppressed
by those who preferred western culture both before and after independence. . . .
Vedic culture is the best for our society. Now however, conversions from Hinduism are part of a larger world conspiracy to divide India along religious lines. . . .
Sewa Bharati was created to serve society regardless of religious background—
for Christians, Muslims and Hindus.

Although she does not explicitly say so here, Nandini is distinguishing
Sewa Bharati's work from that of Christian missionaries, who, according
to Hindu nationalists, as we have seen, use social programs to convert
people. Equating colonial rule with the enslavement of Hindu society,
Nandini demonstrates the links between Sewa Bharati's social programs
and the Hindu nationalist project of prioritizing religion as a basis for
national unity. It is not the myriad traditions of Hinduism that we see in
contemporary India that form the basis of Hindu nationalist culture, but
rather a Hindu nationalist reconstruction of "Vedic" religion. Indeed,
although the focus of Sewa Bharati's work is social uplift, I demonstrate
below how Hindu nationalist religious ideas and traditions are disseminated in these venues. In these contexts, religion is not only central to the
reconstruction of national subjectivity, citizenship, and social order, but
also an "invented tradition" to symbolize and indeed produce the

nation (Hobsbawm 1983; Handler 1988). Sewa Bharati's vision of society involves the moral improvement of all members of society, through economic and social reforms aimed at "appropriat[ing] the support of the popular masses but keeping them out of any form of direct participation in the processes of governance" (P. Chatterjee 1986: 45).

Although I spoke to members of Sewa Bharati in different parts of Delhi, my primary exposure to their activities was in the South Delhi women's wing (Dakshini Mandal), which covers the area from Badarpur to Sangam Vihar and from Madangir to Lajpat Nagar. In slums and resettlement colonies in South Delhi, I visited various different types of schools including day care centers (*balvadis*) for preschool children, and attended a few *bhajan mandalis* (devotional song sessions) organized as part of their adult outreach. Ela told me that most of Sewa Bharati's work in this sector involved children's education and cultural training. In addition to the CBSE curriculum used in schools run by the national government in India, the Sewa Bharati curriculum also included values training.[3] According to Ela, this training incorporates everything from how to behave in school and at home to celebrating religious festivals. By way of example, Ela said that children are trained to speak to their parents and teachers in a respectful manner. School children are taught the stories behind religious festivals and are encouraged to perform plays on them as part of the celebration. Ela made a point of telling me that it is not only Hindu festivals that are celebrated, since they want children to learn about all religions, but she only mentioned Independence Day, Republic Day, and the Sikh Guru Govind Singh's birthday to make her case.

My conversation with Ela was instructive in that it illuminates how schools become central sites for the construction of nationalist subjectivity and moral disciplining. Aihwa Ong has argued that educational institutions are key sites of governmentality, since they are focused on producing "morally normative and economically productive citizens for the nation-state" (2006: 139). Schools become powerful places for the construction of the subject not only because of the values education described by Ela but also because of the daily rituals through which emotional attachments to the nation are constructed and, indeed, embodied, as Véronique Bénéï (2000) demonstrates in her study of nationalism in schools in Maharashtra. As I illustrate below, much of the values training conducted by Sewa Bharati has a distinctly Hindu flavor and becomes a vehicle for reiterating Hindu nationalist constructions of nation and subject. Yet Sewa Bharati's willingness to celebrate Sikh festivals suggests that this construction of nation does not preclude all non-Hindus. Like others in the movement, Sewa Bharati women believe that the term "Hindu" encompasses all those whose religious traditions originated within the boundaries of India. At the same time, their unwilling-ness to celebrate Muslim and Christian festivals indicates that some religious minorities are clearly excluded from the Hindu nation. Thus while Sewa Bharati schools construct the nation as more than simply a vehicle for cultural chauvinism, they also set the boundaries of national culture. Through a discussion of three different kinds of Sewa Bharati schools in Delhi, I examine how these become sites for disseminating normative Hindu nationalist ideas, practices, morals, and sentiments.

Sewa Bharati runs several different types of schools depending on the income level of the community in which the center is situated. The first school I visited was in a resettlement colony[4] in Dakshinpuri. The small four-story building accommodated about a hundred students. There were two classrooms on each floor (a total of five since one of the rooms on the ground floor was the principal's office); the top floor was a large hall. The school uses the CBSE Hindi-medium curriculum and caters to local children enrolled in classes one through five who, according to Kalpana Saxena, a Sewa Bharati school supervisor, represent diverse reli-gious backgrounds. As in all Sewa Bharati schools, there is an emphasis on teaching children Hindu values in addition to the academic curricu-lum. For instance, Kalpana Saxena told me that children are taught to touch their teachers' feet when they arrive and leave school and are strongly encouraged to do the same to their parents at home. Muslim students must do this in school, but are told that if they cannot do this at home, they must demonstrate respect for their parents by saying "salam."[5] Additionally all students, including Muslim ones, have a required half-hour prayer session during which they must memorize and recite several Hindu prayers including the *gayatri mantra*, an ancient hymn from the Ṛg Veda, a sacred Hindu text. Indeed, as I accompanied Kalpana on her supervisory rounds of the schools under her jurisdic-tion, I witnessed what these children were being taught about Hinduism. At the Dakshinpuri School, when Kalpana asked a boy in the fifth stan-dard to name the seven sages of the Hindu pantheon, he rattled them off without any hesitation. At a one-room school in Madangir for nursery and kindergarten children, the teachers asked them to recite the *gayatri mantra* to show Kalpana that they had memorized it. Although, at the time, I could not have done this, the children had no problem reciting it.

Although these children belong to different castes and even different religions, the organization is clearly committed to teaching them Hindu prayers, practices, and values. The daily performance of prayers and other Hindu rituals enables the reiteration of Hindu nationalist con-structions of the subject and can be conceptualized as a "*stylized repetition of acts*" that produces the "illusion" of this very subjectivity (Butler 1999:

179, original emphasis). For instance, the movement as a whole encourages all its members to learn the *gayatri mantra* in order to construct a unified Hindu subject that transcends caste and sectarian divisions. This is interesting since knowledge of the *gayatri mantra* was traditionally limited to upper-caste Hindus. At the sacred thread ceremony of a Brahmin boy through which he attains his "twice born" status, the *gayatri mantra* is whispered into his ear, in some cases under a white cloth, to prevent others from hearing.[6] This example highlights the esoteric quality of the hymn, an attribute that the Hindu nationalist movement is deliberately altering by encouraging people of all castes to recite it. Indeed, making the hymn ubiquitous is part of a larger strategy to expand the movement's base by eliminating divisions in the Hindu community along caste lines. The movement's claim that everyone should know the *gayatri mantra* is also indicative of the desire to embrace what Nandini called a "Vedic" Hindu identity, which through such hymns can reflect and also create a common identity and culture for all Hindus regardless of caste. Yet, it is important to note that this desire to find symbols of unity and to do outreach work among lower-caste communities did not entail endorsing special reservations in government jobs and in schools for people of lower castes to help them overcome social and economic disadvantages.

In addition to teaching Hindu prayers and practices, there is a heavy emphasis on the moral development of these students. Class bias is a hidden subtext in comments about the need for moral improvement, since most of the teachers came from lower-middle-class backgrounds while the students were clearly from poor families in slums and resettlement areas. As she took me around the Dakshinpuri School, Kalpana told me that teachers have to train students not to swear and use the bad language that they learn at home. There were also several allusions to the criminal background of the students. The most notable was during a visit to a school situated on the outskirts of a slum called Azad Camp in Badarpur. The school consisted of two rooms one of which housed the kindergarten class and the other the first and second standards. The courtyard outside—partly covered with a metal roof under which two groups of children sat on the ground facing opposite directions—housed the third and fourth standards. Asha, one of three teachers at the school, was in charge of these two classes. Kalpana informed me that Asha's purse had been stolen with a thousand rupees in it. She had no doubt that one of the children in the school had stolen it, and was certain that Asha, although she would not admit to this, knew who the culprit was. Revealing her attitude toward the slum dwellers to whose service she had devoted her life, Kalpana said, "she is scared to say anything because with these slum people you never know. They might come and attack her or something. So she is not saying anything out of fear."

In her attempt to resolve the issue, Kalpana told the students that they should learn to give and not only to take, before asking them where the purse had gone. While most of the children said that they had not taken it, a group of boys sitting at the back claimed that a student who was not present that day had taken it. Asha immediately said the boy was innocent, and so Kalpana was forced to drop the issue. However, before she did this she emphasized that it was wrong to steal from others. She also said that if a child their age was stealing money, the only explanation for this was that the child was involved in disreputable activities like gambling or marbles. She returned to the issue later in her lecture when she was instructing students to treat each other as siblings. She told them that Asha was like an elder sister, and they had been wrong to steal from her.

I found this incident interesting for many reasons, one of which was Kalpana's firm belief that the thief was a student at the school, despite denials from Asha and other students. Even more intriguing was the explanation for why children might be forced to steal from others. Rather than recognizing the severe structural inequalities affecting the lives of these impoverished slum dwellers, Kalpana suggests that the only reason for stealing would be that they were engaging in immoral activities. For Kalpana, as for others in the organization, Sewa Bharati's task is to cleanse these children and their communities of such immoral and criminal tendencies, and Asha's misfortune provided a perfect teaching moment.

Leela Fernandes argues that "a politics of distinction" is central to maintaining the identity of the "new middle class" in India (2006: 139). She argues, "the internal uncertainties and instability of the new middle class are, in effect, managed through the reproduction of sociospatial distance from the urban poor and working classes." Fernandes shows how class divisions are reproduced through spatial separations in urban areas as well as through consumption practices and moral discourses. Kalpana's lecture to the class can be understood as a distinguishing practice that, in effect, reproduces the class divisions between her and the students. There were other instances in which this distinction was clearly, and uncomfortably, asserted. For instance, at the Azad Camp school, Kalpana called a little boy up to the front of the class and asked him whether he had washed his hands and face that morning. Although he said he had, Kalpana remained unconvinced and instructed the little boy to wash his hands and face before coming to school every morning and to bathe every day. Another time, while visiting a day care center (*balvadi*) for children of stonecutters in Lal Kuan, Kalpana called a little girl to the front of the class. She asked her why she had not combed her hair that morning. When the girl responded that she had combed her hair, Kalpana held out strands of the child's hair for the teacher and me to see, and asked, "then why is your hair looking so bad?" The girl said nothing and Kalpana sent her back to her place after telling her that she should ask her mother to apply some oil and comb it nicely every day before sending her to school. The child looked embarrassed and I felt terrible for her. Her hair was rough with blonde streaks indicating mal-nourishment and, even if her mother could afford to put oil in her hair, I wondered if it would have really made any difference.

I do not think Kalpana intended to humiliate these children. In fact, she spoke to them very lovingly and gently. Her attitude to them, and to the adults of these communities, reflected the patronage relationships characteristic of hierarchical organizations. While the attitude was humiliating, the individuals she came across did not challenge it, per-haps because they were familiar with similar responses from middle-class/upper-caste people they encountered in their daily lives. Sewa Bharati sees its task as teaching slum dwellers and other poor people to better themselves, not just economically and socially, but also morally. This paternalistic attitude toward the subjects of social work, along with the desire to teach them values such as "cleanliness, temperance, hard work, sexual restraint, and . . . love of family," has also been docu-mented by Karin Rosemblatt in her work on the alliances created by the popular front in Chile (Rosemblatt 2000: 3–4). Class hierarchies are embedded in these practices and attitudes and, in the instances described above, are reproduced in Kalpana's interactions with school children.

Despite these attitudes toward the urban poor, Sewa Bharati schools are often the only schools that are conveniently located for those in these slums or resettlement areas. Although some schools, like one that I visited in Lal Kuan, are more like tutorial classes for students who already attend overcrowded government schools, most Sewa Bharati schools provide a valuable alternative to government schools at a very low cost. The schools are highly subsidized by the organization. In schools in neighborhoods in which families are slightly better off, such as the Dakshinpuri school, students paid between fifty and sixty rupees per month in 1999. In contrast, the one-room school in Madangir and the day care center in Lal Kuan only charged twenty-five rupees. Special arrangements are made to accommodate children who cannot afford to pay any fees. In some schools, like the one in Madangir, only the teacher had a copy of the textbook and taught children from it. While maintain-ing flexibility in fee structure and course material, Sewa Bharati was insistent that all students wear uniforms to school consisting of a white shirt and grey shorts/skirt. Kalpana said that although uniforms did cost the parents money, it was important that children wore them since they clearly marked the school as a separate space from home and, consequently, made a difference in the child's attitude and behavior in school. Thus uniforms were one of many disciplinary mechanisms that not only enforced order, but also symbolized hierarchies and appropriate behavior.

Children were not the only targets of disciplinary mechanisms. Teachers were also disciplined in ways that reinforced the hierarchical divisions between Kalpana, the school supervisor, from a middle-class neighborhood, and the teachers, who were often from the low-income neighborhoods in which the schools were situated. Kalpana's rounds usually involved visiting different schools and centers and ensuring that the teachers and facilitators were doing their job properly. This was useful for me as I got to see not only the quality of education the students were receiving, but also how Kalpana interacted with and disciplined the teachers. In order to check on the quality of instruction, Kalpana would ask students questions about the curriculum that was supposed to have been covered or ask to see their notebooks. I was usually quite impressed by how much students knew. At the one-room school at Madangir, in addition to reciting the *gayatri mantra* and English rhymes like "Johnny, Johnny. Yes Papa!" and "One, Two, Buckle my shoe," the younger children knew their alphabets in English and Hindi, while the older students were also able to spell words like "balloon" and recite their tables till four. Kalpana was satisfied with the work of the teachers at this school, one of whom turned out to be her sister-in-law (*devrani*).[7]

However, when teachers failed to live up to Kalpana's expectations she would reprimand them in front of the students, an act that served to establish her own authority and also to diminish the teacher in front of her class. At the day care center at Lal Kuan she reprimanded the teacher when she examined the students' notebooks to discover that they had been writing alphabets rather than drawing patterns as required by the curriculum. She dismissed the teacher's explanation that she was responding to parents' expectations, saying that children could not be taught to write alphabets until they had learned to control the pencil with their fingers. After we left the center, Kalpana told me that Sewa Bharati hired the teacher because she had been recently widowed and needed the money, but she did not think she was smart enough for the job. She said that the problem with places like Lal Kuan was that they were often forced to hire teachers locally even if they had only a limited education because nobody else was willing to come there.

In their study of workers in the government Anganwadi program, James Ferguson and Akhil Gupta (2002) discuss similar mechanisms of surveillance and discipline deployed by supervisors, who are usually not local, on the workers, who are almost always local. They argue that the "rituals of surveillance" functioned to "*represent* and to *embody* state hierarchy and encompassment" (2002: 985, original emphasis). In Sewa Bharati, these rituals of surveillance, including public reprimands when teachers failed to live up to expectations, both represented the deeply hierarchical organization of Hindu nationalism, and embodied the encompassment of the local by this transnational movement. The example above also demonstrates one of the reasons why Sewa Bharati is so successful at drawing people into the movement. By reaching out to destitute widows and giving them much-needed income, the organization commands loyalty from those it has helped. This loyalty, which I will return to later, reinforces the hierarchical relationships between teachers and their supervisors, and can also be seen as a "ritual of encompassment" that brings individuals and local communities into the movement.

Sewa Bharati also runs vocational training programs such as sewing classes, *bhajan mandalis* (devotional song sessions), and monthly *havans* (fire sacrifices), to reach out to adults in these communities. At the adult outreach centers, women are taught valuable skills and also Hindu nationalist versions of religion and culture. For example, young women who attend sewing classes are lectured on a range of issues from family planning to appropriate behavior toward their husbands and their families. For instance, Kalpana told me that young women are given advice on how to interact with their mothers-in-law. She informed me that whenever she talked about family planning at these centers, young women would ask her about sterilization programs. She is able to direct these women to Sewa Bharati's contacts in various hospitals to perform the operation. They also run health clinics through which they check for diseases like tuberculosis, which, according to Kalpana, was widespread in urban slums. Ideally, in the Indian context, these services would be provided by the welfare state. Sewa Bharati's activities not only testify to the failure of the state to take care of all its citizens, but also become a way to insert the Hindu nationalist movement into the realm of the state.

I accompanied Kalpana to several *bhajan mandalis* organized for women by Sewa Bharati, and discovered how these spaces are used to disseminate the movement's ideas. During one such session, Kalpana and I joined a group of women who belonged to a Sewa Bharati sewing class. The women who had gathered there sang various *bhajans* (devotional songs) and I clapped along—not knowing any words. After a while Kalpana stopped the women and said she had some things to say about *bhakti* (devotion). She asked them why they attended these *bhajan mandalis*. The women gave various responses including that these enabled them to experience peace of mind and fulfilled their desire to be closer to god. Kalpana said that to be a true devotee one did not have to attend a *bhajan mandali.* She said: if your husband (*pati-dev*) is sick you should not run off to show your devotion to god. Instead you should serve your husband and in that act will demonstrate your devotion to god. This interpretation of *bhakti* and the use of the term *pati-dev* (husband-god), underscore the *pativrata* discourse in many upper-caste communities, which suggests that a woman's duty is to worship her husband. It is an ideology that resonates with many in the movement and implies that it is a woman's duty, her *stri dharma*, to serve her husband. The assertion that a woman can demonstrate her *bhakti* by performing her *stri dharma* and serving her husband also recalls the argument in the Bhagavad Gita that a devotee can show his/her devotion to Krishna simply by performing his/her duty as an act of sacrifice to Krishna and with no expectation of reward.

Bhajan mandalis are held throughout India as part of various *bhakti* movements and become a means through which the devotee is able to get closer to the god of whom s/he is a *bhakt.* While the poetry and music associated with *bhakti* movements often embody a critique of orthodox Hindu practice, caste hierarchies, and ritualism (Davis 1995: 40; Hawley and Juergensmeyer 2004), this is not always the case (Fuller 1992: 174). Indeed, Kalpana's interpretation of *bhakti* reinforces orthodox Hindu ideas about women's roles in the family. It reinforces the gender hierarchies of orthodox Hindus rather than the challenge to these hierarchies presented by *bhakti* poets like Mirabai (Hawley and Juergensmeyer 2004).[8] Kalpana's words clearly reinforce the role women are expected to play in the Hindu nation by drawing on a very conservative understanding of *bhakti.* The incident illustrates the upper-caste ideological basis of Hindu nationalism, emphasizes the centrality of texts like the Bhagavad Gita, and underscores the importance of performing one's duty and upholding the moral order of Hindu nationalism.

In addition to schooling women on how to conduct themselves, the *bhajan mandalis* can be understood as practices through which the Hindu nation is crafted in ways that transcend caste and sectarian divisions within communities. This became clear to me as I analyzed the performance structure of these sessions. Urban *bhajan mandalis* often have a certain performance structure in which there is one leader and a group of devotees who follow him/her and in which songs to a particular god are sung in a prescribed order (see Singer 1966). In contrast, the ones organized by the movement tend to be very loosely defined, like those Susan Wadley has described in a rural context where the only instrument used is a drum (see Wadley n.d.). The *bhajan mandalis* I attended were very similar to the ones Wadley describes, except for two things. First, different castes were represented in the group, while in Wadley's example the women present were Brahmin. Second, the lead singers would sing a couple of lines that would then be sung by the group as a whole, while in Wadley's example the participants sang together.

Bhajan mandalis, as many have argued, have often served to reinforce structural divisions rather than erase them (Hancock 1999; Fuller 1992; A. Singh 1976). This was noticeably not the case in the Sewa Bharati *bhajan mandalis* I attended. At these, anyone who knows a *bhajan* can sing it, regardless of which god it is sung in praise of. Not all those present will know the song, which is why the women who know it will sing a line and wait for it to be repeated by the group at large. As a result, there is no single leader at these *bhajan mandalis*. These differences are very critical to what the movement is trying to achieve through the organization of these events. For one, this performance structure gives everyone a chance to be the leader of a song, thus freeing the session from the structure and hierarchy that might characterize *bhajan mandalis* in their traditional performance contexts. More important, these strategies allow the movement to appeal to people who might be devotees of a variety of different gods. In this context the *bhajan mandalis* become a practice through which the movement not only constructs a unified Hindu subject, but also reinvents Hinduism as a single tradition that transcends the sectarian divisions that would normally be significant for many of those gathered.

Through the schools, vocational training classes, and *bhajan mandalis* described in this section, I became acutely aware of Sewa Bharati's extensive networks in slums and resettlement areas. Kalpana worked tirelessly in these neighborhoods, learning about the lives of women she encountered and helping them out in times of need. Because of her networking skills, the bonds between the women and Kalpana were extremely strong. She also expected and asked for their help and support when she needed it. The result was a mass base of support to be called into action when needed. I discovered this when I attended the rally to protest the pope's visit to India. During the rally, while everyone traveled from Badarpur in south Delhi to Karol Bagh in central Delhi in a procession of tempos, I noticed that children dressed up as Ram and Sita and other characters from the Ramayana occupied several of these tempos. I was informed that the children were from several of the Sewa Bharati schools in South Delhi. Indeed, as mentioned earlier, many of the adults were women who either worked for the movement or were affiliated with it through cultural and vocational training centers. Although they do not necessarily subscribe to the movement's politics, they live in the areas where Sewa Bharati works and come because of their connection with Sewa Bharati or with people like Kalpana who have made such a difference in their lives. This suggests that when required the movement calls upon those it assists in times of need to perform their obligations toward the nation (see Yuval-Davis 1997).

The Sewa Bharati schools and vocational centers become important places for the organization to disseminate the values, ideology and beliefs of Hindu nationalism. The schools in particular are places where Sewa Bharati women come in contact with people who may not sub-scribe to Hindu nationalist ideology and politics. By reaching out to Hin-dus and non-Hindus alike who attend the schools and vocational training camps in areas that have been neglected by the state and private agencies, and toning down the rhetoric of Hindu nationalism, women activists are able to present the benevolent aspect of the movement. At these venues, the Hindu nationalist movement is no longer the vehicle of an overt cultural chauvinism, but rather, paternalistically reaches out to all the poor: Hindu and non-Hindu. Kalpana's efforts to instill moral-ity and values such as cleanliness (which she clearly thought were lack-ing in these students) along with Hindu values and practices are also part of an attempt to govern the conduct and shape the subjectivity of the nation's citizens. The use of religious traditions and practices to con-struct the nation was particularly apparent in a series of events described below, organized to assist and honor widows of the Kargil War.

Capitalizing on Kargil

Here I examine a series of events organized by various wings of the Hindu nationalist movement, to honor and raise money for the families of soldiers who had died in the Kargil War. Sadhvi Rithambara's speech, discussed earlier, was delivered at one such event at the Constitutional Club on Rafi Marg (street) in New Delhi. In this section I discuss aspects of this and other events that focused on the widows of the Kargil War. Events organized to collect financial contributions for war widows and to recognize their sacrifice for the nation, provided an opportunity to construct the nation but also to shape subjectivity in ways conducive to Hindu nationalist politics. In particular, I analyze how religious imagery and practices are mobilized to construct this image of the nation and female subjectivity. I begin my examination by describing a fire sacrifice (*yajna*) organized by the VHP at the Constitutional Club as part of an event to raise money for war widows immediately prior to Rithamabara's speech. The Kargil *yajna* was one of several *yajnas* and *havans* organized by the movement throughout Delhi.

On a hot July afternoon in New Delhi, I attended the Vishwa Hindu

Parishad Fire Sacrifice for National Safety held under a canopy outside the annex to the Constitutional Club. I walked into the Constitutional Club behind a group of boys dressed in saffron *kurtas* and white *dhotis*[9] who had just alighted from a bus and were proceeding in single file toward the canopy alternatively shouting "Bharat Mata ki jai" (victory/ hail to Mother India) and "jai Shri Ram"[10] (victory/hail to Lord Ram). As I entered the canopy, the boys joined several others seated on red cotton rugs laid out on the floor. The *yajna* was already in progress and, in the midst of the young boys who were reciting Sanskrit *shlokhas* (verses), I saw eight men, later joined by two more, seated around a metal container that enclosed the fire. Later, Aditya Trivedi told me that the men around the fire included the head of the Rashtriya Sikh Sangh (National Sikh Organization), a Sikh gentleman from the Gurudwara Committee,[11] the head of the VHP cow protection movement, a former lieutenant general of the army, a former colonel of the army, a BJP representative, and two priests. They were surrounded by approximately two hundred people, of whom about six including myself were women; the majority were young boys from schools in Delhi run by or partly funded by the VHP.

We were later told by the master of ceremonies that one of the *mantras* (prayers) of the *yajna* was identical to one performed for Ram before his battle with Ravana, the demon king who abducts Ram's wife Sita in the Ramayana.[12] This statement was clearly an attempt to link the Kargil War to the battle against immorality in the Ramayana and indicates the moral stakes in the battle between India and Pakistan. The connection suggested not only that Pakistan was immoral—like Ravana—but also that the Indian soldiers who had been killed were fighting (like Ram) on the side of *dharma*. The statement illustrates how the VHP uses religious traditions to construct subjectivity—of both the Hindu nation and Pakistan. The performance of the ancient Vedic ritual of the *yajna* itself was interesting not only because it exemplified the VHP's efforts to infuse Hindu values in society, but also in the way it reconstructed Hinduism to unify this *dharmic* Hindu nation. Some comparison between the ancient ritual and the VHP *yajna* in the modern context is necessary here to draw out the significance of this performance.

A *yajna* is a fire sacrifice associated with Vedic Hinduism, in which offerings of clarified butter and other substances are made into a sacred fire. While fire itself represents the god Agni, it is also the vehicle for the transmission of these offerings from one world to the next. The Vedic fire sacrifice was performed on behalf of a male sacrificer (*yaja- mana*) who pays for the ritual and is its main beneficiary, although others seated around the sacred fire benefit indirectly (Jamison 1996: 30). Importantly, Stephanie Jamison asserts that these rituals were not per-

formed "purely for social or public ends" (30). Not only must the sacrificer be a householder, but his wife must be present and participate in
the ritual. Jamison argues that in the case of multiple sacrificers, each
must have a wife, or someone playing that role, present at the ritual (31–
32). In the Vedic sacrifice no non-Hindus would have been permitted
within the purified sacred space of the altar. Even in the modern reen-
actment of an ancient sacrifice in the documentary *Altar of Fire* (1976),
the cameraman hired to film the *yajna* was a Brahmin (Staal 1983). The
film shows the complex calculations involved in constructing the altar
modeled with clay using the exact measurements of the sacrificer.

In contrast, the *yajna* for the martyrs of Kargil was performed for specifically public/social ends, and the sacrificers were male members of
the movement who did not have their wives present. Two of those present were Sikh, not Hindu. As in the religious context, the persons offering the oblations and performing the sacrifice were Brahmins, but they
shared the sacred space of the altar with non-Hindu sacrificers who did
not have their wives present. The fire was contained in metal rather than
clay, and the space was not consecrated but hired from the Constitutional Club in Delhi through which anyone might pass.

I stress these differences not to suggest that the movement was not
performing an "authentic" *yajna*. Indeed, householders all over the
country perform smaller scale *yajna* that do not meet the complex speci-
fications of the ancient Vedic rite. My point here is to examine the specific ends met by the VHP's particular reinvention of this ancient ritual,
which was, following Talal Asad (1983), ineluctably linked to the sociopolitical context in which it was performed. The inclusion of Sikhs, the
indifference to caste, and the very public ends for which the ritual was
performed reveal the VHP's efforts to construct a national identity and
culture that can appeal to Hindus across caste and sectarian divisions,
and embrace Buddhists, Jains, and Sikhs, all of whom the movement
considers Hindu. Indeed a Samiti prayer describes members of these
religions as "children of goddess Bharat Mata"—drawing a primordial
link between the cartography of India that forms the body of the goddess and those belonging to religions that can claim to have been
founded within this territory. Decades ago Victor Turner argued that we
must pay attention to the transformative power of ritual symbols and
examine the ways they can become a "switchpoint of social action"
(Turner 1975: 80). The VHP fire sacrifice was one such potential switchpoint through which new understandings of community were created.

The performance of the ritual in a context in which both Sikhs and
Hindus were the sacrificers enabled and indeed produced a unified
national identity of the two religious groups as children of Bharat Mata.
Judith Butler (1993) argues that the ontology of the subject is produced

through performative acts that "cite" a particular construction of reality, of the world. Ritual performance is one such repetitive act that cites a particular construction of the world. In the case of this *yajna*, the ritual performance—and the events that followed it—cites a particularly Hindu nationalist construction of the world. This is a world in which Hindus are primordially linked to the territory of India as children of the goddess Bharat Mata, where "Hindu" is not just a religious identity but an ethnic marker that includes Sikhs and others who are also understood to be the goddess's children, and one in which Hindus have a privileged claim to the cartography of the nation. While none of this is explicitly mentioned, it is cited throughout the performance, infusing it with meaning and producing the very ontology of the Hindu nation and its subjects in the process.

Immediately following the fire sacrifice was an event to raise money for and honor widows of the Kargil War. This event was held in an air-conditioned auditorium adjacent to the canopy. Two framed photographs of uniformed Indian army soldiers who had died in the war were placed on an altar on the right-hand side of the stage. The program began after Sadhvi Rithambara and VHP leader Ashok Singhal lit a lamp placed in front of these photographs and made an offering of flowers to them. This was followed by speeches about the "tragedy" at Kargil, including the one delivered by Sadhvi Rithambara that I discussed earlier. One young man recited an incendiary poem that reflected the Hindu nationalist preoccupation with masculinity. Portraying the Kargil War as a battle for masculinity, he said: "you took our gestures of peace as weakness / but it is you who have lost your manhood." The speeches and poetry were followed by a ceremony to honor the families of the soldiers during which their wives and parents were invited to join the dignitaries on stage.

The first to be honored was a young widow dressed in a midnight blue synthetic *shalwar kamiz*,[13] who ascended the stage as the auditorium resonated with cries of "Bharat Mata ki jai." She was instructed to offer flowers to the photographs before heading toward Sadhvi Rithambara, who gently placed a white shawl on her shoulders and kept an arm around her while Ashok Singhal handed her a trophy. As the twenty-two-year-old widow, later introduced to me as Rinku, sadly accepted her trophy, an elderly gentleman sitting next to me wiped his eyes and with a trembling voice broke the silence by saying, "He Ram" (Oh Lord). Singhal then called for a moment of silence, followed by a recitation of the *gayatri mantra* in which most people in the audience participated. This ritual was repeated several times as widows and families followed Rinku's steps to accept their awards. The scene was deeply moving and several, including Sadhvi Rithambara, were struggling to check their emotions. The ceremony concluded with an announcement of the financial contributions of various wings of the movement for the families and recognition of the collections made from the audience during the event. While the event was designed to honor the soldiers' families and raise money for them, it also enabled the movement to harness national affect and emotion toward its own agenda. The moving scenes infused Hindu nationalist constructions of the war and the nation with an added poignancy. The speeches and poems explicated the suffering of these families in ways strongly connected to Hindu nationalist politics and rhetoric about the nation and its "enemies." The event as a whole provided an opportunity to reproduce the normative constructions of the movement to all those gathered.

The notion of sacrifice, of the soldiers and of the widows, was absolutely central to the emotive force of the event and inextricably linked to the efforts of the movement to shape male and female subjectivity. This became particularly apparent to me when I accompanied Urvashi, Rinku, and Rinku's mother-in-law to another event to honor the "martyrs" of Kargil, held at the Shri Sanathan Dharma Mandir (temple) in Janakpuri. After an uncomfortable hour-long journey from Dakshinpuri Extension in South Delhi to the western part of the city, during which the four of us had been crammed into an autorickshaw, we entered a large hall with a stage set up at the front of the room and mats laid out on the floor on which people were already sitting. On the wall above the stage was a large pop-out plaster impression of Krishna in his chariot taking Arjuna to battle. Just below this was a banner, in Hindi, announcing the event as one to honor the "martyrs" of Kargil. As in the previous event, there was an altar with photographs of the dead soldiers being honored. After a former lieutenant general (also present at the *yajna*) delivered a slide show constructing an account of the Kargil War, most of the event consisted of performances by school children in Janakpuri that focused on the idea of sacrifice for the nation. For example, a large group of children enrolled in a school run by Mahila Shakti in the Janakpuri slums sat in two neat rows on either side of the altar to sing a song in the soldiers' honor. The words of the song suggested that the soldiers had sacrificed their lives to awaken the nation to the threat at the border: "salam un javanon ko jo kho gaye / watan ko jaga kar jo khud so gaye" (we salute those soldiers we have lost / those who woke up our nation and then went to sleep).

Yet not only were the soldiers' sacrifices highlighted at this event, so were those of widows like Rinku who had been invited to attend. To conclude the event, each widow/mother was called onto the stage, handed a trophy of Krishna leading Arjuna into battle, and given a certificate to honor her sacrifice by the head of the BJP's Mahila Morcha. Each certificate was read aloud to all those gathered. The certificate mentioned when the soldier had enlisted, his rank, the number of battles he had fought in Kargil, and how he died. At the end of each certificate were the following words repeated for each soldier: "you have drunk mother's milk and have held up your duty to the sisters who have tied *rakhis*[14] on your wrist, and as such we know that your martyrdom will be valued by each one of us." The conscious reiteration of words and actions at this ceremony constructed the subjectivity of the soldiers and their families in very particular ways. The soldiers are martyrs who have died defending *dharma*, but also to protect their "sisters" from the "enemy" at the border—an image that recalls a normative gendered construction of both the nation and its violation in Hindu nationalist discourse. While men are honored for upholding *dharma* and dutifully protecting women from dishonor—which they are bound to do for any woman who ties a *rakhi* on their wrist—women are celebrated for sacrificing their husbands and sons for the nation.

Interestingly, in contexts where the ideology of *pativrata* is prevalent, widows are generally considered inauspicious and at least partly responsible for the death of their husbands. Married women perform several rituals and fasts for the health and well-being of their husbands. Female chastity is also linked to the welfare of men, and therefore, Lindsey Harlan asserts, "if her husband pre-deceases her, she may be suspected of unfaithfulness, in thought if not in deed" (Harlan 1995: 218; see also Wadley 1995; Courtright 1995; Lamb 2000: 217). In this case the movement uses the Kargil event to reconfigure widowhood. Although drawing on traditional constructions of female sacrifice and power, in this case their husbands' deaths are perceived as female sacrifice rather than lack of sacrifice. Most important, the ability to sacrifice their husbands for the nation makes them auspicious and elevates them to mothers/goddesses of the nation, a construction evident when each widow is greeted by cheers of "Bharat Mata ki jai" as she ascends the stage. For all those present at this event the subjectivity of the soldier and the widow are constructed in ways that glorify their death/loss as a moral sacrifice for the Hindu nation.

The speeches, songs, and award ceremony were also vehicles through which the movement shaped the perception of those gathered, not just of soldiers and widows, but also of the nation and the war itself. The strategic indexing of religious imagery and figures from the Mahabharata was central to this reconstruction of identity and culture. The plaster impression on the wall as well as the trophies depicting Krishna leading Arjuna to battle clearly suggested that this war—like the one described in the Bhagavad Gita—was a battle for *dharma*. The fratricidal battle between the Kauravas and the Pandavas in the Gita becomes the key to understand the battle between Pakistan and India. The duty of the Indian soldier to uphold *dharma* by fighting against Pakistan and defending India's borders is eloquently expressed through the story of the Gita, so familiar to Hindus that an image is sufficient to recall the entire dialogue. Through the image of Krishna driving Arjuna's chariot into battle, Arjuna's devotion to god is conflated with the soldier's devotion to the nation and projects the battle as one in which the very moral order of the world is at stake. Indeed this skillful interweaving of religious stories and imagery is central to understanding how Hindu nationalists shape the imagination, politics, emotions, and subjectivity of those present at such events.

It is also important to recognize here that these events occurred during an election campaign in which the incumbent BJP was attempting to rise above criticism of its conduct in the Kargil War. In this context, while the BJP articulated the Kargil War in secular terms as the leader of a secular coalition government and as an electoral party forced to abide by the rules of the Election Commission, the other wings of Hindu nationalism, unhampered by these limitations, were able to ensure that religious imagery about the Kargil War and the role of the BJP as the leader of a moral Hindu order saturated the public sphere. Redrawing the war as an epic battle against immorality led by the BJP through the successful infusion of religious imagery in the public sphere ensured the electoral victory of the BJP coalition (which had been floundering) in 1999 as an immediate aftermath of the Kargil War.

Conclusion

Social work is a key expansionary strategy of the Hindu nationalist movement through which it reproduces the normative constructions of the movement, reaches out to new audiences, and governs their conduct in ways that are conducive to achieving its goals. Whether assisting the urban poor in government hospitals, providing education to slum dwellers marginalized and neglected by the state, or raising funds for war widows in need of financial assistance, Hindu nationalist women activists are deeply involved in shaping the subjectivity of those they encounter and disseminating normative constructions of nation, culture, and identity that serve the goals of the movement. Even as they reach out to those in need, they shape their conduct by instilling morals, values, and religious ideas that are inseparable from the movement's ideological objectives. Those individuals that the movement encounters in government hospitals, Sewa Bharati schools, or cultural events to raise funds for Kargil widows may never vote for the BJP, officially join the movement, or embrace its politics and goals. However, it is clear that events and activities organized to assist the needy provide venues for the movement to come into contact with and disseminate its ideas to people who are not necessarily part of its usual support base. Instead of their usual expressions of Hindu chauvinism, Hindu nationalist activists use practices and discourses that present the movement as a benevolent body that is guided by religious morals and values, and assists and provides for those in need. Through the appropriation of traditions, stories, and practices that are sacred to Hindus, women activists suggest that Hindu nationalism is a religious movement with a *dharmic* charter, rather than a political movement with a Hindu chauvinistic one.

Jean Comaroff and John Comaroff have argued that unlike ideology, which is clearly visible, hegemonic power "hides itself in the forms of everyday life" (Comaroff and Comaroff 1991: 22). In this chapter we see the ways in which the hegemonic power of Hindu nationalism is hidden in "everyday life" through lectures in schools and at cultural events, through disciplinary mechanisms in schools and hospitals, and indeed through the acts of public assistance I described. The infusion of religious ideas and rituals at these sites is a particularly powerful way to naturalize ideas of the Hindu nation and to shape the attitudes and duties of men and women toward this nation in ways that are inseparable from the cultural politics of Hindu nationalism. Indeed, these hidden mechanisms through which the movement exerts power over individuals, shaping their behavior, attitudes, and conduct, are critical to understanding the expansionary power of the movement in India. While overt ideological statements might resonate with those who are susceptible to such ideas or already embrace them, the everyday acts described here articulate diverse groups and interests with the movement's objectives and are central to its ability to extend its base.

The movement capitalizes on the shrinking welfare state in increasingly neoliberal India, to position itself as the "protector and provider" of the urban poor. As Hindu nationalist organizations position themselves to become what Ferguson and Gupta (2002: 994) call "horizontal contemporaries" of the neoliberal state, it is also important to think further about their existing relationship to the "state." In 1999, as women in various wings of the movement positioned this transnational movement as a "horizontal contemporary" of the state, the BJP was leading the national government of India and as such constituted the state. Indeed, several scholars have argued, the state should not be viewed in opposition to or above society.[15] Discussing the "inordinately dispersed structure of governance and sovereignty" in India, Thomas Hansen argues that social movements and political parties in the country operate both within and beyond the boundaries of the state (2005: 191). This is particularly so in the case of Hindu nationalism where, during the

2002 pogrom against Muslims in Gujarat, the BJP state actively enabled violence by Hindu nationalists at the grassroots level (Hansen 2005: 182). The dispersal of governance that Hansen describes in the context of the Gujarat violence, which is also revealed through the work conducted by the movement as it provides public assistance as a "horizontal contemporary" of the state, is absolutely critical to understanding the expansionary power of Hindu nationalism in contemporary India.

While the expansionary mechanisms described here extend the reach of the movement in modern India, by attracting diverse individuals they also create pluralism within the Hindu nationalist movement. Indeed, the Hindu nationalist movement's ability to accommodate diverging perspectives has enabled its dominance in India. Yet, this does not mean that the movement equally values all voices, opinions, and acts. In fact, only those words and deeds that reiterate the normative constructions of Hindu nationalism are valued. When individuals transgress Hindu nationalism by not only failing to reproduce its normative constructions, but also performing the norms of other ideological systems, their acts are not condoned by the movement. Rather, their acts are considered dissonant and are disciplined, marginalized, or silenced by members of the Hindu nationalist movement. I now turn my attention to looking at dissonance and to examining the ways that women activists attempted to discipline and regulate such acts.

Chapter 5
Fun, Games, and Deadly Politics

Payal invited me to attend a three-day Samiti *shivir* (camp) that she was organizing from December 24 to 26 in Delhi. Unlike the weekly *shakhas* held throughout Delhi for local girls and women, these training camps are intensive immersion courses for those who want a deeper association with the movement. The *shivirs* can be anywhere between three days and two weeks long and cater to those who have already been exposed to the movement and are often regular attendees of *shakhas*. Although all the participants of the *shivir* I attended were from Delhi, the longer *shivirs* usually draw individuals from different regions of the country. These training camps typically include two types of activities: the *baudhik* sessions that focus on intellectual development, and the *sharirik* sessions that focus on enhancing physical strength and dexterity. The *baudhik* sessions intersperse periods of lecture and discussion with storytelling sessions and modules during which participants are taught to memorize prayers, patriotic and devotional songs, and also Hindu nationalist songs written by the ideologues of the movement. The *sharirik* sessions include the study of military commands, rigorous exercise, endurance training, yoga, and games.[1] I analyze these activities in the context of the *shivir* that I attended to illustrate how Samiti activists disseminate the movement's constructions of history and culture to new recruits, how they incorporate young girls into the disciplinary regimes of the organization, and also how they train them to be competitive, aggressive, and violent.

By shaping the minds and bodies of new recruits and orienting them toward the cultural politics of the movement, *shivirs* become central sites for the exercise of Hindu nationalist governmentality. The camps typically include a broad spectrum of individuals with varying levels of knowledge about and commitment to the movement. By interspersing lectures that overtly transmit the movement's ideology with more subtle mechanisms such as songs, prayers, and games, Samiti activists attempt to draw diverse individuals into the movement's embrace and school them to embody its values and discipline even if they are not convinced by its vision. Indeed, these *shivirs* are powerful sites for recruiting indi-

viduals into the movement, if not through ideological compulsion then
by appealing to their enjoyment of the fun and games and through the
bonds that form among members of the group. The physical and intellectual training is central to shaping the subjectivity of new recruits and
disseminating the values, commitments, and politics of the movement.
However, by attempting to draw diverse individuals into its membership,
the Samiti also open up venues for challenges and dissonance within its
ranks.

Operating in a diverse ideological field, Samiti activists attempt to
articulate this diversity with the goals of the movement. However, such
articulation is never complete in any discursive formation, and the possibilities for challenge are ever present (Laclau and Mouffe 1985: 105–7).
Ernesto Laclau and Chantal Mouffe (1985) assert that while "discourse
is constituted as an attempt to dominate the field of discursivity, to arrest
the flow of differences, to construct a centre" (112), it is always "sub-
verted by a field of discursivity which overflows it" (113). For a discourse
like Hindu nationalism to dominate the sociopolitical landscape of modern India, it must not only attempt to "dominate the field of discursivity" by articulating diverse identities, positions, and sentiments with its
own goals, but also it must continuously reinstate itself in this social
field.

Yet, as Judith Butler has argued, "That no social formation can
endure without becoming reinstated, and that every reinstatement puts
the 'structure' in question at risk, suggests that the possibility of its own
undoing is at once the condition of possibility of the structure itself"
(1997: 14). The lectures, songs, prayers, exercise drills, and games
described here are opportunities for Samiti activists to reinstate the ideology of the movement and to draw diverse individuals into the movement in the process of this reinstatement. Yet there is no guarantee that
this ideology will be reinstated, because it is contingent on the actions
of individuals who are drawn from all walks of life and are influenced by
multiple and competing ideological systems. Through a close examination of events, interactions, and conversations that occurred during this
three day training camp, I illustrate the ways in which Samiti activists
and all those who participated in the camp reproduced the movement's
ideology and also occasionally questioned, transgressed, and challenged
it. I analyze the ways in which leaders attempt to discipline or neutralize
dissonance, and, in so doing, to reaffirm the normative order of the
movement.

The Rashtra Sevika Samiti Training Camp

While *shakhas* are held regularly in colonies throughout Delhi and are
open to anyone interested in attending them, *shivirs* are residential

training camps held over a longer period, are much more intense, and are required for those girls and women who want to run their own *shakhas*. The *shivir* that I attended was held in the compound of a Hindu nationalist school in Delhi, then closed for the winter holidays. The school compound itself was situated within a larger compound that held the offices for various wings of the movement, as well as some limited residential facilities. We were not permitted to leave the school compound, and nobody except the various Hindu nationalists who came to talk to us was allowed into the compound for the three days of the camp. Immediately inside the gate of the school was an open area about the size of a tennis court, surrounded on three sides by the two-story school building. Most of the camp activities described here took place in this area or in the three classrooms that had been converted into living/learning areas situated just off the open area. Two classrooms were converted into dormitory style sleeping areas in which all the participants slept on thin cotton mattresses provided by the Samiti. The third classroom was the *baudhik* room in which we gathered for the lectures as well as to pray, learn songs, and listen to stories. The *shakhas* were held in the compound outside. Bathing facilities were situated near the entrance of the compound and included a long, partly covered area with faucets along the walls that provided cold water. Most of the participants did not bathe during the camp, either because it was too cold to bathe in cold water in December in Delhi or because of the lack of privacy.

The *shivir* followed a strict timetable, repeated daily, which divided the day up into *baudhik* and *sharirik* sessions. To provide a sense of the intensity of these camps, I have reproduced in Table 1. the timetable given to us during the three-day training camp that I attended. Although everyone present knew I was a researcher, I was also expected to be a full participant in all the activities at the training camp. As one of two adult women being trained along with a group of energetic teenage girls, I found the program mentally and physically exhausting and was also acutely aware of being supervised and controlled by the camp leaders almost constantly throughout the camp. However, before I describe the various activities and the disciplinary mechanisms in the camp, I would like to introduce the cast of characters who participated in the camp with me, either as fellow trainees or as teachers or supervisors.

The camp had been organized by Payal, one of a small group of Rashtra Sevika Samiti women who, as a *pracharika*, has chosen to be celibate and devote her life to the movement. Commenting on the small number of *pracharikas* in contrast to the thousands of RSS male *pracharaks*, Payal explained that this was because it was more acceptable for men to reject the life of a householder and devote themselves to a cause. *Pracharaks* and *pracharikas* are volunteers who, for the most part, are not paid a sal-

Table 1. *Shivir* Timetable

Jagran (wake up)	5 a.m.
Pratah Smaran (morning prayer)	5:45 a.m.
Yogasan (yoga)	5:45–6:15 a.m.
Pratah shakha (morning *shakha*)	6:15–8:00 a.m.
Nashta aur snan (breakfast and bath)	8:00–9.30 a.m.
Prarthana, geet abhyas (prayer and song lesson)	9.30–10.30 a.m.
Break	10.30–10.45 a.m.
Baudhik (intellectual session)	10.45 a.m.–12.30 p.m.
Bhojan (lunch)	12.30–1.30 p.m.
Vishranti (rest)	1.30–2.30 p.m.
Charcha (discussion)	2.30–3.45 p.m.
Tea	3.45–4.30 p.m.
Sayam shakha (evening *shakha*)	4.30–6.30 p.m.
Sayam smaran aur bhajan (evening prayer and songs)	6.45–7.45 p.m.
Bhojan (dinner)	8:00–9:00 p.m.
Manoranjak karyakram (entertainment programme)	9:00–10:00 p.m.
Vande mataram (hail to motherland, a patriotic song)	10:00 p.m.
Dip visarjan (lights out)	10.15 pm

ary by the movement, although they are provided with food, shelter, a travel allowance, and, in some cases, a small stipend. As I have mentioned before, Payal is in charge of supervising the running of *shakhas* throughout Delhi, a job that she loves. She told me that although many have told her to join politics because she now has such a large base of supporters, she prefers to do this work for the movement. Payal was in charge of both organizing and running the *shivir*, and managed to exude energy and enthusiasm throughout the *shivir* despite being the first to wake up in the morning and the last to retire at night.

Working directly under Payal were two teachers: Ruchika, a young woman in her early twenties, and Maya, fifteen. Both Ruchika and Maya had previously attended a fifteen-day training camp, which made them eligible to teach the rest of us. Maya ran a weekly *shakha* in South Delhi. Ruchika did not run her own *shakha* but enjoyed being involved in the movement. Attending the camp had not been easy for her because her parents, who are not members of the movement, had not wanted her to go. They had eventually relented after a fight, which as it turned out was almost in vain. Although Payal had told us to arrive at four o'clock, when Ruchika arrived at the school (forty minutes after me) there was nobody there and the armed guard at the gate had not been informed of the event. Her father, who had come to drop her off, was extremely unhappy at the situation, and was ready to take her back home when Payal finally arrived. Even after Payal confirmed that the camp was indeed taking place and that the other participants would be arriving shortly, Ruchika's father seemed extremely reluctant to leave her with two young women in the gathering dusk. That night, after pleading with Payal for permission to leave the school compound, I accompanied Ruchika to the nearby public telephone so that she could reassure her parents that the others had arrived. Even so, she was worried that her mother would send her father back to collect her.

At about six o'clock, a tempo arrived full of people from various parts of Delhi. Maya arrived on the tempo with her two sisters and her mother, all of whom are part of the movement. Maya was in tenth grade and had brought her "best friends" Gauri and Nita. Maya's younger sister Radhika, in the seventh grade, had also brought her "best friend" Leela. The girls had come with their mother, a member of the Samiti, and their three-year-old sister. The girls were very friendly and energetic and quite curious about me, asking me about my work and testing my knowledge of western pop culture. As we were talking, Gauri, who had the most questions for me, told me that she had only agreed to attend the camp because Maya had asked her to. The first night, after the lights were turned out, the five girls stayed up chatting about Salman Khan and Sharukh Khan, two leading male actors in the Hindi film industry, and boys. Gauri teased Maya, accusing her friend of having a crush on her brother.

While clearly normal conversation for teenage girls, these discussions would have drawn the ire of the elder members of the Samiti had they been there to overhear them, since female sexuality is only considered appropriate within the sanctified space of marriage. Here I am not suggesting that Hindu nationalist women do not violate sexual norms of the movement in their everyday lives. Indeed, if Vimla's gossip about fellow women activists is any indication, it is clear that Hindu nationalist women not only do have affairs, but also are aware of sexual transgressions in the movement. However, while members of the movement might have to make allowances for the transgressions of adults to maintain their sizeable base, this does not mean that they do not make every attempt to discipline female subjects, particularly impressionable young girls, into following sexual norms. Indeed, the above conversation would have prompted Samiti elders to discipline Gauri and Maya precisely because they recognize that these teenage Delhi girls inhabit worlds that are influenced by ideological systems in which such relationships are permissible.

Also in the tempo was a college student called Anshu, completing the final year of her bachelor's degree in commerce by correspondence, and two college-age friends, Divya and Bina, in their first year at Aurobindo College in Delhi. Divya's mother, a long-time member of the Samiti, was also at the camp, but along with all the other older women she was there in a supportive capacity. The older women attended the lectures and discussions but did not take part in anything else since they were responsible for cooking and keeping a maternal eye on things. Divya and Bina were very close friends who stuck to each other throughout the camp, and consciously separated themselves from the rest of the group. While everyone else wore *shalwar kamiz,* they wore trousers with shirts and were criticized by Payal for not wearing Indian clothes. Both were consistently late for everything and were regularly reprimanded for being tardy or for talking to each other when they were supposed to be paying attention to something else. Indeed, they were often reprimanded and disciplined by Payal and the other teachers, in ways that illustrated how dissonance can in fact sometimes serve to reinstate the norm (Butler 1999: 135).

It was only during game time that they really became part of the group and seemed to enjoy themselves. Bina told me that she only agreed to attend the *shivir* because Divya was going. She confided that she did not like what was being said about Muslims and Christians and wished that they had only the games and not the *baudhik* sessions. Bina and I were among the few who were consistently "bad" at learning the various Sanskrit *shlokas* (verses) and Hindi songs we were expected to memorize. She, like me, was basically mouthing words of songs we were supposed to have learned—pretending to know the words. When we played *antakshri*[2] of patriotic songs the first night, neither she nor Divya had anything to contribute. Although they consistently failed to meet Payal's expectations, the younger girls were quite impressed with Divya and Bina. Indeed, when the news broke that Bina rode a scooter around Delhi, all the girls began to whisper excitedly about this to one another. The freedom to ride a scooter unaccompanied around Delhi was not something most of these middle-caste/class girls had.

In addition to the returning members (the five older women, Payal, Maya, and Ruchika), there were twenty-one of us participating in the training. The ages ranged from twelve to about thirty. The only adult women participating were Rajani, a mother of four whose youngest son had accompanied her to the camp, and myself. Although I had been told by an RSS *pracharak* who had come to help the women set up camp that two doctoral students from Jawaharlal Nehru University in Delhi were also going to attend, these individuals never showed up. Led by Payal, Maya, and Ruchika, all of us participated together in the physical drills and games, lectures and discussions, and song and prayer learning sessions. Below I discuss these activities in some detail to examine how the ideology of the movement is reproduced and ingrained in the minds and bodies of the participants.

Ideology at Work

We spent approximately three hours a day listening to lectures delivered by various leaders of the movement during the *baudhik* and *charcha* sessions. Although the *charcha* sessions were supposed to be discussions, these also ended up being lectures with a few questions thrown out for discussion. In fact, what characterized these two sessions was the *lack* of discussion permitted within the "participation frameworks" set in place to structure relationships within the group (Goodwin 1990, cited in Schwartzman 1995: 248). Instead, these sessions were used to convey the movement's constructions of nation, culture, history, and gender to the group of trainees through a series of lectures. Below I discuss excerpts from two lectures delivered during the *baudhik* sessions, in order to provide a sense of what the movement seeks to convey to the participants in these camps.[3] Central to both lectures are themes that are critical to the Hindu nationalist movement and have already been discussed: that Hindu culture is threatened by Muslims and Christians, and that the values associated with Islam and with Christianity/westernization threaten the honor and sanctity of Hindu society.

Yashodha Mehta, a *karyavahika* (worker) of the Delhi wing of the Samiti, accompanied by her ten-year-old son, dropped by the venue for a couple of hours to deliver the first lecture. Senior to all those in the room, Yashoda sat on a chair at the front, facing the rest of us, who had been instructed to sit in neat rows on *daris* on the floor. After introductions, during which we were specifically asked about the level of training we had completed in the organization (*varg*), we were told to demonstrate our learning by singing a song we had memorized that morning—*Hindu jage, desh jage* (Hindus awake, nation awake). After an uncomfortable few minutes during which I mouthed the words to a song that most others seemed to have committed to memory, Yashodha said that she was going to speak on the subject of national security (*rashtra suraksha*). Below are excerpts from her lecture:

Raksha (protection) is something we do for ourselves while *suraksha* (security) is something we give to others. Our *rashtra* (nation) is the Hindu nation, while *rashtriya* is how we should think of our nation. We should be patriotic. That is what it means to be *rashtriya*. *Rashtriyata* is *desh prem*, the feeling of love for our nation. This is how we should understand our duty of providing *desh prem*, the feeling of love for our nation. This is how we should understand our duty of providing *rashtra suraksha*. But how does one do this? We need to be concerned about two things—internal security and external security.

The army is responsible for external security. However, we are all responsible for internal security. This includes the *raksha* (protection) of our culture, our values, and our nation. We are all responsible for this. Internal security depends upon the political realm, the intellectual realm, and the social realm. We can't have security unless we ensure the progress of the social realm. It is our responsibility to beware of intruders (*ghuspeti*). A *ghuspeti* is a person who comes to live in our midst and learns our weaknesses and having learned these, goes to live in the weakest parts of the country and creates discord between sections. These intruders include missionaries and Muslims who have come to live with us. Christians have begun to spread throughout society. They have succeeded because we have ignored these sections of society by forgetting our own values of *seva* (service). The other threat to our nation's security is smuggling—whether of arms or other commodities.

The third thing is our educational system. We all stress the importance of learning English. The blame must be placed on our society that lays so much emphasis on English. It is fine to learn English but we must have equal mastery over Hindi. The fourth thing is television. It is fine to watch television as long as you develop your own perspective on what is being presented. It is parents who need to teach their children this perspective so that when they see the corrupt images of the west on television they do not think that these are correct. One mother complained to me about boys Eve-teasing[4] her daughter. I asked her some questions and found out that she had permitted her daughter to go out at seven thirty in the evening in a miniskirt. I asked her: if you allow your daughter to do this then what else do you expect? The mother answered that she had told her daughter not to go out dressed like this but her daughter did not listen to her. But this was not the child's fault. It was the mother's fault. If she had taught her daughter the right values in the beginning this situation would never have arisen.

Yashodha raises several issues that reiterate Hindu nationalist norms and argues that it is the responsibility of every patriotic Hindu to uphold these values. She conflates Hindu/Hindi/India in her construction of national culture, consciously marginalizing religious and linguistic diversity in the country. All Hindus must demonstrate their patriotism, their love for the nation, by protecting the culture and values of the Indian/Hindu nation, what Yashodha calls "internal security." She focuses specifically on the threat presented by "intruders" who have surreptitiously infiltrated Indian/Hindu society. Capitalizing on the hysteria about "intruders" in the aftermath of the Kargil War in 1999, she labels Christian missionaries and Muslims "intruders" who engage in antinational activities under the guise of helping the poor. She emphasizes that all Hindus must perform their duty toward the nation by helping the poor and by raising their children with the right values.

It is no accident that a mother-daughter relationship is used to underscore the importance of imparting values to children, not only because all those gathered were young girls and women, but also because Hindu nationalists hold women responsible for disseminating Hindu values, traditions, and culture to the next generation. In Yashodha's example, the mother is to blame for her daughter's behavior. Suggesting that the girl had invited this attention through her westernized behavior (clothing, going out in the evening), Yashodha does not blame men for "Eve-teasing" her. The idea that it is a woman's responsibility to embody and maintain national culture and purity and deflect the influences of the west in Indian society is widely held, and used, by Hindu nationalists. Indeed, even as they pursued a policy of economic liberalization, the BJP-led government was extremely keen to project, in highly gendered ways, a commitment to "traditional" moral values (Fernandes 2006: 160–61). Not only are these values entrenched in a "tradition" invented in the process of crafting national culture (Hobsbawm 1983), but also this celebration of Hindu "tradition" is highly selective. Since nationalism is inherently a modernist project and Hindu nationalism is keen to present itself as a movement capable of taking over the reins of the Indian state in the modern world, it is perhaps not surprising that they have publicly opposed Hindu "traditions" such as dowry, the caste system, and widow immolation (*sati*). Some Hindu nationalists defended what they saw as "Hindu tradition" after Roop Kanwar's *sati* in Rajasthan in 1987 (see Hawley 1994; A. Basu 1995: 167–68), but this position was not commonly encountered once they achieved electoral success. When I asked Rajesh, a senior member of the VHP, what he thought of *sati*, he quoted the following lines from the poet Maithilisharan Gupt:

> Whether ancient or new, stop traditions that are bad
> Become wise and show the cleverness of a swan
> The idea that only what is ancient is good is not written
> The system should be according to the conditions.[5]

Using the poet's language, Rajesh argued that culture must keep pace with the times, and suggests that customs that may have been meaningful in one context are not always appropriate for the contemporary world.

Several of these themes were reiterated in a lecture delivered by Rukmini, a middle-aged Samiti *pracharika*, whose reputation as a strict disciplinarian who instituted harsh punishments to those who disobeyed her had already been conveyed to us by those who had attended previous *shivirs*. As she entered the room, a hush fell over the group, and all the participants, including Divya and Bina who usually had to be told to stop talking or playing the fool, paid attention. Although building on themes I have already discussed, Rukmini's lecture was particularly interesting to me because it was one of the few occasions in which leaders of the movement were challenged in these formal settings. This challenge came while Rukmini was lecturing about the superiority of Hindu *dharma* over other ways of conducting life:

> The Hindu *dharma* is a way of life (*jivan padati*). Hindus bathe every day while Muslims only bathe on *juma* (Friday). Muslims spit in the kitchen. This is not the Hindu *padati* (way). Why is there all this noise over the millennium? This is

not the Hindu millennium. Our twenty first century has already begun. In the Hindu *padati* sex[6] is only after marriage, which, in accordance with the Hindu way of life, is after eighteen years of age. Look at Mary. She was unmarried and gave birth at thirteen years. While biologically a girl can give birth at thirteen it is against the Hindu way to do this. Things like *sati* are new. It happened when Muslim invasions got worse. *Sati* custom was invented at this time.

At this point, one of the girls interrupted. Recalling a story from the Mahabharata, she said that when Pandu, the father of the Pandavas, died, his wife Madri jumped on his funeral pyre to punish herself for his death. Indeed, in this ancient epic, Pandu was doomed to die if he approached either of his wives with desire. Although he lived celibately for many years with his wives, he died the moment that he was unable to resist his desire for his wife Madri. Madri, burdened with guilt, ascended her husband's funeral pyre. By recalling this story, the girl raised an important counterpoint to Rukmini's suggestion that *sati* was invented to protect women from dishonor during "Muslim invasions," since the Mahabharata clearly predates the period Rukmini is referring to (eleventh century C.E.). However, unable or unwilling to engage in a discussion about the issue, Rukmini just said "yes" and continued with her lecture. Here Rukmini's suggestion that *sati* is not part of Hindu tradition and Rajesh's insistence that Hindu tradition needs to change with the times clearly contradict the views articulated by Hindu nationalist leaders, including Vijayradhe Scindia, after the Roop Kanwar incident (A. Basu 1995: 167–68). Their attempts are best understood as part of the ongoing project by various Hindu nationalist organizations to fashion a modern national Hinduism that resonates with the goals of the Hindu nationalist movement.

Rukmini elaborated at length on the dangers presented by Christianity and Islam to Hindu society in order to situate the importance of Samiti *shakhas*. Recounting many of the themes discussed earlier, Rukmini asserted that missionaries used schools and social work as fronts for converting innocents, and blamed Hindus for not having done enough to prevent conversions from the fold. Then she argued:

To prevent conversions we need to have an organization with *shakhas*. If we bring one woman in the fold we will correct ten families. So it is important to strengthen the organization. The aim of the Catholic Church is to have a church on every street, a bible in every house, and one Christian girl in every family. Asha Sharma has told me to bring up the fact that in Connaught Place, Santa Claus was giving thirty-rupee gifts to children.[7] To stop this from happening, you must be strong and fight with teachers who try to convert you. Muslims too, according to a plan, convert one-*lakh* girls to Islam every year.[8] Many of these girls are just kidnapped and forced to convert. Christianity teaches women to be free. In Islam men can have four wives. This is not the case with Hinduism, because *Hindutva* requires you to control your sexual urges.

Delivered the day after Christmas, it is not surprising that Rukmini's lecture focused on Hindu nationalist representations of Christians to the group. Yet, whether discussing Christianity or Islam, both lectures portray a Hindu nation persecuted by "foreign" religions. Christians and Muslims are consistently depicted as "foreigners" or "intruders" alien to Hindu India. These religions allegedly threaten the sanctity of Hindu society by introducing immoral practices. While Hindu nationalists associate Christians with sexual freedom, they suggest that Muslims, by permitting polygamy, cannot control their sexual urges. Rukmini's lecture is particularly insistent on the need for Hindus to organize to protect the Hindu nation against such onslaughts and infuse Hindu morality and culture into the social world. Although here she is underscoring the importance of the organizational work undertaken by the Rashtra Sevika Samiti through *shakhas*, it is important to recognize that the views presented by Rukmini and others during the camp are not idiosyncratic of the speakers or the organization, but rather are normative constructions regularly reproduced by activists in multiple wings of the movement. Indeed, these views build on Hindu fears and chauvinism that extend well beyond the Hindu nationalist movement and derive their validity from their hegemonic hold over the broader political community (Comaroff and Comaroff 1991: 24).

However, hegemonic or not, one should not assume that the ideas presented by Hindu nationalist leaders at these training camps went uncontested. The girl who questioned Rukmini's claim that practices like *sati* were responses to Muslim invasions was contesting key ideas in Hindu nationalist discourse. Most important, she was questioning the image of Hinduism as an ancient and unproblematic tradition and contesting the narrative that such practices only emerged as a consequence of a corrupting and invasive foreign presence. By pointing to Madri's act, the girl suggests to the contrary that institutions like *sati* can be traced to ancient traditions of Hinduism that predate Islam. In doing so, she transgresses normative constructions of the movement and represents a dissonant voice that performs other norms. In this public setting, Rukmini quickly silenced this dissonant view by dismissing the girl and continuing with her lecture. However, this was not the only dissonant view voiced during the *shivir*. As I mentioned earlier, Bina told me that she did not appreciate Samiti views on Christians and Muslims. Gauri actually confronted Rukmini after lunch, and told her that she disagreed with what she had said about Christians and Muslims. In this less public setting, Rukmini tried to reason with her and sway her from her dissonant position, but Gauri remained unconvinced. After Rukmini left, a visibly upset Gauri vented to her friends Maya and Nita, who listened intently. Maya, a *shivir* teacher and budding ideologue, was now a sympathetic ear in a different and oppositional discourse.

Such dissonant voices, which transgress the normative constructions of the movement, are indicative of the limited ability of Hindu nationalists to determine the opinions and views of its members. Recruiting diverse individuals into the movement in order to expand their base, Hindu nationalists encounter women and girls like Bina and Gauri who are influenced by other ways of being and, consequently, transgress Hindu nationalism by performing other norms. While Bina and Gauri only attended the event because their friends were going to be there, and it is possible that they may choose not to attend any further *shakhas* or *shivirs* (though, as we shall see, I have reason to believe otherwise), they are important influences on their "best friends" (Divya and Maya), who remain committed to the movement but may be affected by these dissonant views. That Hindu nationalist activists were quick to silence, seclude, or discipline such dissonant voices illustrates their awareness of the threat that such voices pose. At the same time, it is also important to recognize that the participants, even those who took an oppositional stance in the incidents described above, thoroughly enjoyed other aspects of the training camp that were more subtly coded with ideological messages. Next, I examine the songs, stories, physical drills, and games that were all encoded with the movement's ideological vision and yet were more acceptable to the participants.

Entertaining Nationalism: Songs, Stories, and Girl-Talk

While the lecture and discussion sections discussed above occupied us for three hours a day, we spent several hours each day learning and reciting prayers and songs, listening to stories about historical and mythical figures, participating in competitive games, and performing various drills to improve strength and stamina. These activities, all of which fall under the rubric of what some theorists call "play," were also key sites through which the movement disseminated its vision and affected and shaped subjectivity. While I discuss the physical drills and games in the next section, here I analyze the songs and stories, as well as the activities we engaged in during "free time," which included casual chatter and the "entertainment programs" every evening. Through this analysis I will show how such "play" becomes a critical site for reproducing Hindu nationalist norms.

While singing songs, learning prayers, and engaging in indoor games during the entertainment program might appear not to carry the same ideological weight as lectures and discussions, such activities are deeply imbued with nationalist ideology and, in being intricately bound up with pleasure, fun, and entertainment, can be effective tools to recruit new members. Indeed, several scholars have argued that we should not separate "pleasure and purpose" (Alter 1994: 557), or "play" from "work," since work is often "an element of play" (Turner 1982: 31). Social and cultural ideologies are often embedded in forms of play, and songs, stories, and games have often been used as tools to cultivate and groom subjects and disseminate values, morals, norms, forms of subjectivity, and hierarchies in various contexts.[9]

While pleasure is important to understanding the effectiveness of play, we must also recognize the performative power of play as a means of creating new forms of order and power. As in the rituals and *bhajan mandalis* discussed earlier, the forms of play examined here construct new forms of community among those gathered. As performances, these occur at particular times and places and are affected by those who participate in them. Performance can lead to ideas and meanings being redefined, recreated, and reinterpreted, and therefore does not simply reflect, but can "transform social structures," what Richard Bauman (using Raymond Williams) calls the "emergent" aspect of verbal performance (Bauman 1977: 45, 48). Since performance is dependent on those who participate in it, there is always a potential for challenge and subversion. For these very reasons, it is often subject to supervision, manipulation, and control. In the forms of play discussed below, I examine the ideological messages being disseminated, the regulatory and disciplinary structures in place to ensure their reproduction and the ways participants challenged and transgressed these messages.

I begin by examining the hour-long entertainment program held every night, during which we were supposedly permitted to engage in any group activity to entertain ourselves. The first night, under the strict supervision of Payal and the older women, we played *antakshri* using patriotic songs. A very popular game in India, in *antakshri* one team sings a few lines of a song (usually from a Hindi film) and challenges the other team to find a song that begins with the last letter of the word they ended with. On the second night, Payal put Maya and Ruchika in charge of the program, since she and the older women were busy with Rukmini, who had only just arrived. When Ruchika suggested we play *antakshri* with patriotic songs, there were several protests from girls in the room. While they had not protested in front of Payal the previous night, they had a different relationship with Maya and, by extension, Ruchika, and therefore felt free to challenge their authority. When someone suggested playing *antakshri* using film songs, both Maya and Ruchika argued that since Hindi film songs did not have the right moral tone for the camp we could not do this. Several girls in the room, including Maya's two friends Nita and Gauri, were upset and began to complain vociferously. Ultimately, Maya, relenting to peer pressure, compromised on playing charades with Hindi movie titles. As the game got underway, everyone began to have fun and there was much shouting and laughter. All of a sudden, Payal walked in and the room fell silent. With a raised voice she told us that we should stop playing this game immediately. She angrily said that we were at the camp to learn good cultural values and morals, not those taught in Hindi films. Then, ignoring Ruchika's loud protests that this had not been her idea, Payal asked Maya and Ruchika to step outside and, as Ruchika later informed me, gave them a thorough scolding for allowing things to get out of hand.

Although theoretically we could choose to entertain ourselves in any group activity, this incident reveals the ways our choices were governed and, when they did not conform to Hindu nationalist expectations, firmly disciplined. Playing charades with Hindi movie titles transgressed Hindu nationalist norms by failing to reiterate them and evoking a different ideological universe. Therefore we were disciplined, a process that clarified the norms, morals, and values all the participants were expected to uphold during the training camp. It also clearly marked the hierarchy among the participants. Payal, the one responsible for disciplining the others, was undoubtedly at the top of this hierarchy. When she ordered Maya and Ruchika out of the room, she also made their position above the rest of us very apparent. Being disciplined and observing hierarchies is a central aspect of the training imparted to students at these camps. This is apparent not only in this incident, but also on any number of other occasions when we were physically moved around until positioned in neat rows, reprimanded for being late or talking out of turn, lectured on keeping our shoes in neat rows outside the door, and instructed to maintain order, neatness, and cleanliness in our sleeping and learning areas.

While it could be argued that the entertainment program organized by the Samiti would undoubtedly carry certain prescriptions, Payal also monitored our "free time" between sessions and often joined casual banter between girls to insert her own ideas and agenda. For example, one morning Payal joined Ruchika, Gauri, Maya, Nita, Radhika, Leela, and myself as we sat around our room chatting after breakfast while a few were bathing and others were getting dressed. Payal shifted the conversation to Valentine's Day,[10] asserting that it was really about friendship. She said that society had become so dirty (*gandi*) that it had corrupted the real meaning behind the day, and made it about boys and girls and love. Gauri interjected saying that she tied friendship bands on all her friends on Valentine's Day. Payal responded by arguing that it was meaningless to recognize friendship only on one day of the year. What about the rest of the year, she asked the group? Asserting that Valentine's Day was a "western" festival that had been brought to India, she skillfully directed the conversation to emphasize how we should be wary of such practices in the same way that we should be wary of the missionaries coming from the "west" and converting Hindus.

Masterfully controlling what began as casual chitchat between girls, Payal shifted the discussion to issues that are key to Hindu nationalist ideology and politics. Rather than lecturing to the girls about the dangers of conversion or the moral inferiority of "western" customs like Valentine's Day, she joined in "girl-talk" and inserts these views as her contribution to the conversation. Rather than confronting them with an authoritative voice, she mingled with them and joins the banter. Unlike Rukmini, who authoritatively argued with Gauri, Payal tried to present her arguments in a less confrontational way, one that did not raise Gauri's hackles or draw her ire. Such conversations are an important way of reiterating the cultural politics of the movement, and disseminating them to those who might challenge or contest them in a more authoritative setting.

The stories that were told to us at the camp, as well as the songs we were taught to sing, were more obviously encoded with Hindu nationalist ideologies. Relating folklore about Hindu heroes is a key way in which the Samiti conveys its ideology in *shivirs*, and this training camp provided several opportunities for storytelling. In one instance, a Hindu nationalist *sadhvi* related a story about the Mughal emperor Akbar. The story was one I had heard from other members of the movement, and I have discussed other versions of it earlier. The *sadhvi* related it in the context of a longer lecture about the place of Hinduism and Hindu womanhood:

This was a *bazaar* only for women. A rule made by Akbar. He used to dress himself and his courtiers as women and go and then try to trick the women into going with him. Once while this was going on Rana Pratap's niece was there and Akbar managed to get her to follow him. However, she was too clever for him. Kiran *mai* attacked him with a dagger like Durga with one foot on his chest. Akbar begged for forgiveness calling her *ma* (mother). She forgave him but made him promise to stop the Mina *bazaar*. Character is everything. Girls should aspire to be Savitri and Ansuya and Sita.

The *sadhvi* concluded her talk by saying, "Do you like it if someone comes and curses your mother? We should feel the same way about Bharat Mata and be ready to fight for her. These *shivirs* are very important because they are for all Hindus and cement society together."

At an obvious level this story about Akbar vilifies the Muslim emperor as a lustful and immoral king preying on his innocent Hindu subjects, a construction of Muslims that, as I suggested earlier, is one of the organizing principles of Hindu nationalist historiography. Equally important, however, is the statement it makes about Hindu womanhood. Particularly important to the agenda of the Samiti, it is able to construct an image of a strong and virtuous Hindu woman in the figure of Kiran *mai*, who is able to defend herself and her virtue from defilement by the lustful king. Kiran *mai* is no ordinary woman. As Rana Pratap's niece she is linked not only to a legendary warrior but also to the Rajput community, a Hindu warrior caste celebrated for its bravery. Key to this discussion is the construction of motherhood. Kiran *mai* forgives Akbar when he refers to her as "mother," reflecting an idea held by many in the movement that forgiveness is one of the key virtues of motherhood. Additionally, the exemplary womanhood demonstrated by Kiran *mai* makes her like the goddess Durga, battling demons to uphold *dharma*. Also implicit is the idea that virtuous women who uphold morality and are pure, chaste, self-sacrificing, and forgiving are like goddesses. The *sadhvi* uses the story to suggest that women like Kiran *mai*, Sita, and Savitri embody ideal Hindu subjectivity and should be role models for Hindu women today.

For the *sadhvi*, these are women who protected their "character" and remained virtuous and self-sacrificing in the face of adversity. Savitri was willing to sacrifice her own life to protect her husband, which reflects her virtue and bravery. Saturated with the ideology of *pativrata*, her example becomes a way for the Samiti to teach those gathered the importance of being self-sacrificing and brave. Sita, Ram's wife in the Ramayana, represents the ideal woman of orthodox Hinduism, suffering all the hardships of exile in the forest because the proper place of a woman is by her husband's side. Although Ravana kidnaps her, she maintains her chastity and purity by living in his garden rather than his home, and remains steadfastly devoted to her husband. This story conveys values that are central to the ways the Samiti hopes to shape Hindu female subjectivity. Importantly, such ideals are not expressed in the form of a pedantic lecture, but rather in the form of a familiar story, much less disagreeable to teenage girls.

The songs too were important vehicles for the dissemination of ideology, reproducing as they did norms that are critical to Hindu nationalist discourse. We were required to memorize the songs, and then demonstrate our progress by standing up individually to sing them alone. Since I was the worst at learning the lyrics, followed closely by Bina, I spent many uncomfortable moments feeling very much like the class dunce. The fact that, despite this, I still remember the tunes and a few lines from the songs, but need to refer to my fieldnotes for the content of the lectures, testifies to the efficacy of the songs as tools for disseminating Hindu nationalist ideas, and the efforts taken to ensure that we memorized them. Below I provide a rough translation (rather than a poetic one) of the second verse and the chorus of one of the songs we were made to write out and then memorize in the song and prayer learning class every morning:

Chorus: Hindus awake! Nation awake!
             Self-respect and determination awake
             Hindus awake! Nation awake!
             Self-respect and determination awake
             The true *dharma's* victory will be imminent
Stanza 2:   Love will awake between friends
             The stream of one blood will awake
             It is one nation and one culture
             It is one nation and one culture
             Our duty to ourselves must awake.[11]

Dharma, as I have suggested earlier, can refer to duty, religion, as well as the moral order of the world. Here, the chorus repeatedly asserts that the "true *dharma*" will be victorious, when Hindus "awake" and strive to establish this moral order. For Hindu nationalists, this moral order is one in which a primordial Hindu nation, linked by blood, love, culture, morality, and religion, can be established in India. Contained in a catchy, if repetitive tune, the lyrics suggest that it is the duty of an already existent nation of Hindus to wake up from a state of passivity to one of self-respect and self-determination. This is a nation marked, as the next verse claims, by the awakening of the god Ram (legendary for his sense of duty) in every one of its members. The song does not dwell on tensions between Muslims and Hindus, or the dangers of Christian proselytizing. However, it manages to convey the righteousness and morality of the Hindu nation and its natural claim to the territory of India. Its power rests in its ability to reiterate the claims of the Hindu nation without recourse to vilification of an "other."

While Hindu nationalist values and constructions of subjectivity are clearly coded into these songs and stories, we must not presume that all those gathered necessarily embraced these ideas. In fact, since several girls challenged Hindu nationalist ideas in other contexts, we should not assume a "correspondence between encoding and decoding" here either (Hall 1980:135; see also Mankekar 1999: 255). However, apart from Bina and myself, most of the girls were quite enthusiastic about learning and singing these songs as well as listening to the stories that were related. As each of us sang these songs, practiced the lyrics, or recited the prayers that were taught, we enabled the reiteration of Hindu nationalist ideas, and "cited" the discursive norms that produced them (Butler 1993: 13). Our repetitive performative acts reproduced, and therefore sustained, Hindu nationalist ideology during the camp.

"First It Was All Fun and Games": Games and Drills at the Samiti Training Camp

For the Samiti, the ideal female subject should be chaste, pure, and self-sacrificing, but also brave, strong, capable of participating in the struggle for a Hindu nation, and, if necessary, like Kiran *mai*, of upholding *dharma* with violence. Consequently, improving stamina and learning to be physically fit through lessons in yoga, physical exercises and drills, and a variety of games is an important part of the Samiti training camp. Apart from increasing the stamina and physical fitness of the participants, the drills, exercises, and games are clearly tools through which girls and young women, like their male counterparts in the RSS, are trained to discipline their bodies and learn to be competitive, aggressive, and obedient. Here I describe some of the activities that were part of the *sharirik* (physical) training that we received in the camp, to analyze the ways in which they were ingrained with the ideological imperatives of Hindu nationalism.

Each morning before breakfast we spent half an hour doing yoga, before spending almost two hours learning and performing physical exercises and drills during the morning *shakha*. It was bitterly cold when we assembled in the compound and, although it was dark and foggy, having shivered through yoga on the cold cement floor inside the classroom, I was glad to participate in the strenuous physical workout. We ran around the compound, performed various exercises, and did a painful number of sit-ups before being ordered to stand in neat rows, an arms-length on all sides from each other, to learn various military commands. As Payal called out the Hindi commands and sternly corrected errors, we repeatedly stood at attention, at ease, performed right and left turns, until we could follow the commands in perfect unison with our eyes closed. Like the physical drills we had been performing, these military commands ingrained discipline, order, and obedience into our very bodies until we could follow Payal's orders with little thought.

Describing similar physical drills and commands at male *shakhas* run by the RSS, Joseph Alter has argued that despite a claim to indigenousness, these sessions are western in origin and are designed to teach discipline and obedience to hierarchy (1994: 565–67). Alter describes the RSS *shakha* as a "regimen of coordination where consciousness is being choreographed for its collective effort" (568). Indeed, like the male *shakhas* he describes, the morning exercises at the Samiti *shakha* were calculated to teach the girls to obey the commands of their leader and, as importantly, to coordinate perfectly with the movements of others so that the whole group was acting "as one body" (565). Nicely complementing the efforts of camp leaders to instill discipline and order in other contexts, the physical drills trained participants to obey the hierarchies of the organization and to discipline their bodies to act in unison with others in reaching the goals of the Hindu nationalist movement.

According to Payal, a major lesson in the *sharirik* sessions is to improve mental focus and concentration. At a *shakha* I had attended in September with Payal, she said to those gathered: "Concentration and the ability to pay attention is important in all our lives and in almost every task we do. So it is important that we all learn this." While clearly embedded in the physical drills described above, this lesson was an important part of many of the games that were played during the camp as well. Yet, unlike the drills, many games were also characterized by the lack of order and discipline, and focused instead on inculcating other qualities in the participants. The physically strenuous games improved stamina and strength while also training participants to be competitive, aggressive, and even violent. They were also subtly coded with Hindu nationalist values and visions of the world and became important vehicles for disseminating these to the participants. Games have often been used to transmit ideological messages and to shape and define subjectivity in various contexts. Arjun Appadurai (1997) illustrates how the British used cricket to convey the values and ideology of the Victorian elite, not only to the English working classes, but also to their colonial subjects. Yet, while the game provided a space for fashioning the colonial subject in the delicacies of sportsmanship, fair play, team spirit, and emotional control, it also became the ground of contestation that ultimately overturned the Victorian values that it embodied (1997: 92, 107). In what follows, I describe a number of games that we played during the *shivir* to examine some of the values and qualities they tried to inculcate in the participants. Yet, as forms of play that are less subject to control, I will also analyze the ways in which they provided arenas for contestation even as they shaped and recruited subjects into the Hindu nation.

Murgi (chicken). In this game the participants were divided into two teams. Each had to stand in rows facing each other with a gap of about six feet between the rows. Each person was given a number that reflected her position in the row (see Figure 1). Thus number 1 in team A was the first person in the row and team B had a person across the gap with the same number. Payal would call out a number chosen randomly and then the two people (one from each team) with that number had to come into the gap hopping on one foot with both hands behind their backs holding up the other foot. The idea was to see which of the *murgis* (chickens) could knock the other one off balance so that she was forced to put the other foot down.

Team A:	1	2	3	4	5	6
	X	X	X	X	X	X

GAP

Team B:	X	X	X	X	X	X
	1	2	3	4	5	6

Figure 1. Murgi.

Tanks. Here the participants got into groups of five and formed a tight circle holding on to the people next to them with their arms around each other's waist. There were about five or six groups. When Payal blew on her whistle all the groups (each, a tank) hurled themselves at the others with the objective of making the other groups fall or break up. The team/tank left intact and standing at the end was the winner. This game could become very rough. Maya hurt herself quite badly in this game. Her big toe nail came off and her toe was bandaged for the rest of the *shivir.* However she still continued to participate in some of the more peaceful games and in the morning *shakha* the next day.[12]

Kisan aur lomdi (the farmer and the fox). In this game the participants were made to stand in a large circle. One person was made the farmer and the other was the fox. The object was for the farmer to catch the fox. If the fox was caught then she became the farmer and had to chase the new fox (the former farmer). At any point in the chase the fox could tap the shoulder (usually it ended up being more like a shove) of anyone in the circle and make her the fox instead. The farmer would have to keep running until she caught the fox. If she could not catch the fox then Payal would ask the fox to allow herself to be caught so that the farmer could rest. The chase was around the circle, and often entailed weaving in between the girls standing in the circle.[13]

Tota aur pinjra (the parrot and the cage). In this game the participants had to get into groups of three. Each group of three had to stand in their group but also structurally in a larger circle (see Figure 2). Two of them formed the cage by holding hands, and the third—the parrot—stood in the middle. One person was made the catcher and another was made an un-caged parrot. The catcher ran around and through the circle trying

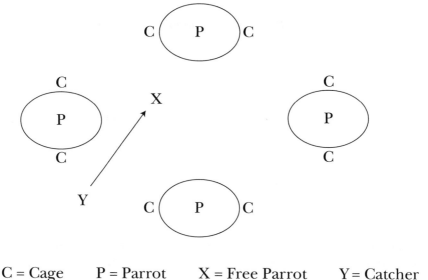

C = Cage   P = Parrot   X = Free Parrot   Y = Catcher

Figure 2. Tota aur Pinjra.

to catch the parrot. The parrot could either run or enter into any of the cages to escape. At this point the parrot already in the cage would have to leave it and start running. If the parrot was caught, then she became the catcher and the catcher became the parrot and could escape into one of the cages. This was a fast paced game and, like the previous game, entailed a good deal of fast running and a great deal of quick turning. One girl, who was unfortunately not very fast or dexterous, ended up being the catcher for so long that she fainted from exhaustion.

Number-making game. In this game all the participants were made to run around in a circle. When Payal called a number everyone had to quickly stop running and join up in groups of that number. Those who couldn't were out.[14]

Jai *Shivaji.* In this game the participants had to run around in a circle. Payal stood in the center of the circle and would call out "*jai* Shivaji," and we would have to answer "*jai* Bhavani." Meanwhile Payal called out the pace of our running by calling out in Hindi "one two, one two." The pace of our running depended on the speed at which she said this. If she said "*jai* Bhavani" instead of "*jai* Shivaji," then we would have to respond with "*jai* Shivaji" and run in the opposite direction. Likewise, if she now said "*jai* Shivaji" we would have to change direction. This was the only game played during the morning *shakha* after we had spent a considerable amount of time learning military commands.

Jai Shivaji was designed to improve endurance while maintaining mental focus so that we could obey commands instantaneously. Like the physical drills, this game disciplined participants to obey commands and follow them in unison with others so as to act as one body (Alter 1994). Indeed, since we were all running in a circle, if a single individual was late in following a command the whole group would end up collapsing on one another. Moreover, the game acts as an important mnemonic device that indexes a past and a present for the Hindu nation. Shivaji of course is revered by Hindu nationalists and held up as a role model today because they believe that he struggled against Muslim rule to found the Hindu nation. The Hindu goddess Bhavani was his family deity and allegedly a motivating force for Shivaji. By using their names in place of military commands, the game alludes to these characters, and in so doing indexes a construction of the past and present that is central to the movement without explicitly talking or lecturing on them. The game becomes a subtle way to reiterate this history and cite the ideology that grounds it, without challenge from those (Divya, Bina, Gauri) who might have otherwise objected to this construction of the past.

There are other ways in which these drills and games reflect the ideology and goals of the movement. For instance, many of them have their counterparts, and perhaps even their origins, in the west. However they appear on the *shakha* program in their indigenous guise. Since a major goal of the Samiti, and Hindu nationalism more generally, is to celebrate Hindu culture and denounce and eschew western influences, it is no coincidence that the girls are playing games with Indian names and characters and learning drills to Hindi commands (see also Alter 1994: 567). The Samiti is also committed to the belief that Hindu women have become weak and need to be trained physically and mentally to defend the culture, values, and territory of the Hindu nation. As a result many of these games are extremely strenuous and build strength, stamina, and endurance. Indeed, then in my mid-twenties, I was exhausted from running around with teenagers during the games. Girls who were not physically fit were also exhausted, and, as I mentioned, one actually fainted during a game.

In addition to strength and stamina, the games also train participants to be competitive, aggressive, and violent. The games described here are very rough, aggressive, and competitive games in which the participants took great pleasure in pushing and shoving their opponents during the excitement. The game "tanks" is particularly aggressive, and the participants were very enthusiastic about charging with as much speed as possible without breaking the circle and hurling themselves at the other tanks to knock them over or break them up. This would result in people being knocked over, stomped upon, and crushed by the attacking tank. Indeed, as with Maya, sometimes girls got hurt while playing. Through such games, the Samiti teaches girls to be aggressive and violent, qualities that are central to Hindu nationalism but are often neglected in the upbringing of middle-class and middle-caste Hindu girls. Instead of training these girls to be docile, they are encouraged to fight and win even if it means beating down or hurting others. Games like "tanks" also teach them that the power to win often lies in the cohesion of the group. In this game, the tank that was able to withstand assaults and ultimately emerged victorious was the one in which participants overcame individual boundaries, held onto each other most closely, and were able to act in perfect unison.

What is also interesting about the rough and aggressive nature of these games is the way they contrast with the order and discipline required of participants during the rest of the camp. The game sessions become an opportunity for participants to break away from the rules that structure their interactions with others in the normal course of the camp and express behaviors and emotions that, although limited by a new set of rules, would not have been acceptable outside this context (see Sutton-Smith 2001). While discipline, obedience, and hierarchy were emphasized throughout the camp, the games provided an arena where participants were able to exert power over others and even, on occasion, challenge hierarchies.[15] They were also occasions when the group was at its most cohesive, since the energy and excitement of the game brought participants together regardless of the ideological, class, ethnic, and other distinctions that existed in other contexts. While these differences were not erased, they were suppressed in favor of group identity, enabling communitas, however momentarily (Turner 1969).

For instance, Bina and Divya, who had consciously stuck together and had maintained their distance from the other participants throughout the camp, were enthusiastically part of the group during these games. It was the only time that they really interacted with the other members and were extremely good at the games. Although visibly reluctant to listen to the lectures or participate in the prayers and songs, Bina was so drawn into the games that she pleaded—unsuccessfully—with Payal to continue playing them after the *shakha*. The games provided a moment when Bina and Divya were able to transcend their ideological differences from the rest of the group, and focus on group identity in their determination to ensure the success of their team. The ability to render these differences unimportant, even momentarily in the excitement of the game, is powerful enough to permit the recognition of one's membership in a larger community and, to adapt Victor Turner's analysis of ritual symbols to these games, can potentially be transformative moments (Turner 1969).

Yet this sense of community did not necessarily include the leaders of the Samiti who were organizing the camp and in fact the games sometimes provided occasions to emphasize the differences between "us" and "them" as well as opportunities to challenge their authority. For example, when Payal joined in some of the games, the girls were particularly competitive with her, although they never managed to get her out or catch her. While the Samiti's goal was to create a community organized by hierarchical relationships, the participants challenged the existence of this hierarchy in play by trying to defeat Payal. Apart from the enthusiastic manner in which she was chased, the participants would also gleefully cheer the catcher on (much more than in other cases) when she happened to be chasing Payal. While participants in the camp almost never challenged Payal in other contexts and appeared to accept her authority over them, this example illustrates how they used the unruly context of the game to subtly challenge the hierarchy she had instituted throughout the camp.

None of the participants seemed aware of the subtle ideological messages encoded into the games, although they had objected to them in other contexts. As I mentioned above, even Divya and Bina, who had kept their distance from other participants and constantly misbehaved during the camp by talking during lectures or being tardy, thoroughly enjoyed the games. Indeed, Bina told me that, although she had disliked the sentiments expressed about Muslims and Christians in *baudhik* sessions, she had enjoyed the games and wished they had only played games throughout the camp. Interestingly, despite her aversion to the movement's ideology, Bina agreed to attend a festival that Payal was organizing in mid-January, *makar sankranti*,[16] in which good food and lots of fun games were promised. Bina's example suggests that games become an important means through which new members are recruited, particularly in a context where participants are influenced by multiple ideological systems that compete with and sometimes contest Hindu nationalism. Although Bina is clearly influenced by alternative ideological systems and challenges the movement in word and deed, she is still drawn to the movement because of her relationship with Divya and because of the fun she had during game time. This is in fact a strategy through which the movement tries to gradually entice individuals into its networks. For instance, Sneha, who had attended her first *shivir* when she was ten years old and began working with Durga Vahini when she was fifteen, told me: "First it was all fun and games. Then when I was older I started listening more carefully to the *baudhik* lectures and understood the importance of what was being said."

Conclusion

The *shivirs* become important arenas to disseminate the culture, history, politics, and values of the Hindu nationalist movement as well as to shape subjects in ways that are conducive to the goals of the movement. While lectures and discussions are direct ways of conveying these ideas, the songs, stories, physical drills, and games are more subtly coded with the ideological prescriptions of the movement. Indeed, the stories and songs are particularly useful tools to disseminate these ideas because they are able to convey Hindu nationalist constructions of history, politics, and morality without raising the hackles of those who might otherwise disagree with them. Yet, as I have argued, each time we listened to a story or participated in reciting Hindu nationalist prayers and songs, we provided an opportunity for the movement to reproduce its ideology through our actions and words.

The camp not only provided a space for the dissemination and reproduction of Hindu nationalist ideology, but also created a powerful arena to shape the subjectivity of the participants. While lectures, discussions, stories, and songs disseminated constructions of the ideal female subject, the disciplinary measures in the camp tried to instill these constructions of subjectivity in each individual. Organizational hierarchy and discipline were instilled through instructions and surveillance of conduct throughout the camp, and were also apparent during the physical drills. Participants were literally trained to embody aggression, competitiveness, and violence through the games played during the camp. The goal of this training was to create female subjects who are not only aware of the cultural politics of the movement, but also physically and mentally strong enough to participate in the political struggles of Hindu nationalism.

The games in particular were powerful ways in which to recruit subjects who were otherwise opposed to Hindu nationalist ideas. Although Bina and Gauri voiced their disagreement with the Samiti's construction of Muslim and Christian subjectivity, they were enthusiastic about attending a subsequent Samiti event because they had thoroughly enjoyed hanging out with their friends and playing games during the camp. The example shows how the Samiti draws individuals into its embrace for a multiplicity of reasons to expand the base of Hindu nationalism. Some may join because they are drawn by its constructions of culture and history, while others join because of existing relationships with members of the Samiti, or because of the opportunities it provides for playing games that are pleasurable and which allow them to cultivate qualities like aggression that may not be permissible in everyday life.

Allowing for such diversity is an essential expansionary tactic of Hindu nationalism in the diverse ideological landscapes of postcolonial India. However, in drawing individuals into the movement for myriad reasons, even when they might disagree with its ideology and politics and when they subvert its rules and hierarchies through recalcitrant behavior, the movement also creates a space within its ranks for dissonant subjects who transgress the normative constructions of the movement. Just as Hindu nationalist ideology is reproduced through the performative acts of individual members of the movement, it can also be destabilized by the acts of dissonant subjects who fail to uphold the ideological expectations of the movement or who overtly challenge them in word or deed. Next, I examine these dissonant subjects of Hindu nationalism to theorize some of the complexities of nationalist allegiance and belonging in the modern world.

Chapter 6
Acceptable Transgressions

I arrived at Jamuna Sinha's house in northwest Delhi feeling quite light-headed and was extremely relieved when she offered me a cup of tea. I had just spent ninety minutes in an autorickshaw in morning rush hour traffic in Delhi, trying vainly to avoid inhaling the exhaust from the DTC bus crawling along beside me. As I sat down next to Jamuna on the brown synthetic velvet sofa in her living room, I was conscious of how disheveled I looked with my dusty windblown hair, crushed handloom *shalwar kamiz*, and wrinkled *dupatta* (scarf), which I had scrunched up and used as an air filter during the journey. Looking neat and clean in her nylon sari, she turned to her husband, who was reading the newspaper at the other end of the room, and asked him to make tea for me. He got up immediately, and I could hear him bustling around in the adjoining kitchen preparing tea as I talked to Jamuna about Durga Vahini and Matri Shakti activities in Delhi. After handing me tea and placing a plate of biscuits on the coffee table in front of us, he quietly went back to the chair where he had been sitting and resumed perusing the paper. As I continued my conversation with Jamuna, I couldn't help thinking about how much this scene challenged my own stereotypes about Hindu nationalist women.

Having read widely about normative constructions of womanhood in the Hindu nationalist movement, I was well aware of the roles that women were expected to play in the movement and in their families. Deeply influenced by *pativrata* ideology, these constructions suggest that women must be chaste and pure while remaining subservient to their husbands and serving their every need. I had not expected to find a middle-class Haryanavi *jat* woman sitting on a sofa and ordering her husband to make tea, a task usually performed by women of her community and sociopolitical location.[1] While this reversal of roles forced me to recognize my own stereotypes, it also sparked my interest in learning about the extent to which Hindu nationalist women actually conform to the movement's normative expectations in everyday life. As the months crept by and women let me into their homes, lives, and stories, I became increasingly aware of the multiple ways in which women covertly or overtly transgressed and sometimes vocally challenged Hindu nationalist rules and expectations as they negotiated the complex ideological and political mosaics surrounding them to craft their own lives and selves. Here I focus on such dissonant subjects, those who transgress Hindu nationalist norms and invoke those of other ideological systems. Indeed, their acts were seen as dissonant by others in the movement who diligently strove to disseminate its normative constructions and, as the examples of Gauri and Bina at the *shivir* indicate, disciplined dissent.

Here I would like to reiterate that I am not singling out these individuals because I think they are unique. Individuals are not automatons of bounded cultural systems, can be influenced by multiple ideologies available in any cultural formation, and often act in ways that do not conform to dominant expectations. Instead, I label them dissonant subjects with the knowledge that many Hindu nationalists have probably engaged in dissonant acts at one time or another. I do this to draw attention to behaviors that do not conform to the normative expectations of the movement, so that we can see Hindu nationalist women as complex subjects and make this very complexity a point of analysis. While much has been written about the normative constructions of Hindu nationalism, here I draw attention to dissonant subjects for what they might reveal about the expansionary tactics of the Hindu nationalist movement in contemporary India.

Why do Hindu nationalist women engage in dissonant acts? Culture of course is not a bounded totality but can best be understood as an open field containing several different strains and possibilities. Hindu nationalist culture is no exception. As I have shown, Hindu nationalist ideology, like all cultural ideologies (see Ahearn 2001: 120), is not internally consistent and contains discrepancies and ambiguities. Sometimes women cannot live up to the norms and become dissonant subjects simply because of the competing demands and expectations within the ideology itself. For instance, women are expected to be self-sacrificing mothers, strong leaders, committed workers, and devoted wives. Both Sita, the ideal *pativrata,* and goddess Durga, the armed and independent slayer of demons, are held up as role models for Hindu womanhood. On occasion, these roles can challenge each other, and therefore women fail some of these expectations as they fulfill others. According to Judith Butler, this expectation "to signify a multiplicity of guarantees in response to a variety of different demands all at once" results in failures and generates the possibility of dissonance within ideological systems (Butler 1999: 185). Thus dissonant acts should not be understood to emanate from a "transcendental subject" or a free will somehow disengaged from the larger social and cultural contexts in which they are performed, but rather as possibilities present in all ideological systems (Butler 1999: 185; Ahearn 2001: 115).

In addition to competing expectations within the movement itself, it is important to recognize that Hindu nationalist women do not have a "unitary consciousness" (Mankekar 1999: 17), but rather can be drawn to multiple and competing discursive systems in modern India. Indeed, the social worlds of Hindu nationalist women are marked by multiple ideologies or "systems of representation" (Hall 1985: 104) that compete with and sometimes challenge Hindu nationalist ideological prescriptions. For example, even as they lectured on the importance of containing sexuality within marriage or respecting parental authority in deciding marital alliances, many women loved watching and discussing Hindi movies about love and forbidden relationships between men and women. Additionally, the complexities and difficulties of their own lives sometimes made it impossible for them to uphold Hindu nationalist expectations in everyday life. Influenced by multiple and competing ideological systems, faced with inconsistencies and ambiguities within Hindu nationalism, and forced to contend with the contingencies of everyday life, Hindu nationalist women sometimes transgressed the ideological prescriptions of the movement and performed other norms.

I have already examined the centrality of women's acts to the production and reproduction of Hindu nationalist ideology. Indeed, I have shown that it is through such everyday acts that Hindu nationalist ideology exists in the world. However, although women activists diligently reiterate Hindu nationalist norms as they use religion, history, politics, and social work to recruit new members, appealing to diverse individuals does result in a plurality of positions within the movement. While many of these positions are consistent with one of the diverging tendencies within Hindu nationalist ideology, occasionally they are dissonant in that they challenge or transgress Hindu nationalist norms and cite others. Here I focus on women's dissonant acts because they reveal the compromises the movement must make to ensure its dominance on the sociopolitical landscape of modern India. It is precisely the movement's ability to accept dissonant subjects within its embrace, even when it disapproves of their acts, which grounds its expansionary potential. Their acts may be hidden from public view so that they do not compete with the normative constructions that women activists reproduce in their everyday work for the movement. However, the fact that dissonant subjects continue to be embraced by the movement illustrates how Hindu nationalists' compromise on ideological purity in their everyday struggle for dominance in contemporary India.

Women, Family, and Nation in Hindu Nationalism

What are the normative constructions of Hindu womanhood against which women's actions and words can be read as transgressive? I have already discussed various different roles that women can play in the Hindu nationalist movement. Some of the most powerful women in the movement are the renouncers, celibate religious ascetics who perceive their involvement as a higher spiritual path through which to perform their devotion to god/goddess/nation. Others like Payal have chosen to be *pracharikas*, celibate women who have forsaken householders' obligations to devote their lives to the movement. As Hindu women living very public lives outside natal/marital bounds, they must maintain strict celibacy to signal their morality and protect their honor. By far the majority of Hindu nationalist women are married and participate in their capacity as mothers and wives in a household. For married women, sexuality must be strictly contained within the family for the purpose of reproducing the Hindu nation. These three constructions of womanhood reproduce the same normative understanding of the place of women's sexuality. For the renouncers and the *pracharikas*, female sexuality must not be expressed at all, while for householders it must be contained within the institution of marriage and for the purpose of reproduction. As we shall see, the notion of family is central to containing female sexuality and consequently to maintaining the sanctity of Hindu nationalist society.

Family has been an important metaphor in Indian nationalism since the colonial period, when it provided a model for the roles men and women would play in the nation (Visweswaran 1994). Gandhi famously claimed, "the doctrine of *satyagraha* [the struggle for truth] is not new: it is merely an extension of domestic life into the political" (cited in Visweswaran 1994: 57). This articulation of familial relations with political struggle, Kamala Visweswaran argues, also enabled a reproduction of unequal relations of power and authority within the home onto the landscape of nationalist politics (58). Yet, even as it circumscribed women's roles in the nationalist movement, the metaphor of family also opened up spaces for women in the public sphere to which they might not have had access, particularly if they were from middle-/upper-class/caste communities. The same is true of Hindu nationalist women today, many of whom come from families that practiced some form of veiling or seclusion of women in the past. Today, due to this metonymy of family and nation (Mankekar 1999) wherein the Hindu nation itself is imagined as an extended family, women activists are able to access the public sphere, and also to shape and influence it in powerful ways as they conduct their work for the movement.

The idiom of kinship ensures the sanctity of Hindu society, since it posits that the relationships between men and women in the movement are analogous to familial ties. It suggests that women can serve and fight for the Hindu nation because Hindu women have a duty not only to their immediate family but also to all those brothers, fathers, and sons who belong to the extended family of the Hindu nation. For a movement that garners support by proclaiming its dedication to public morality, the importance of demonstrating its own sanctity by reinterpreting relations between its male and female members within the socially sanctioned idiom of kinship cannot be emphasized enough. Indeed, the familial metaphor facilitates a subtle contrast between a moral Hindu nation and an immoral westernized public that it seeks to reform. The metaphor was central to Aditya's description of the women's wing of the VHP (in English):

The women's wing is considered as a sister's or mother's wing not as a friends circle unlike other organizations with western thinking. . . . In western thinking they do not think of women as sisters, mothers, or daughters. They consider women as friends. Because in Hindu thinking the question of a lady friend does not arise, to keep the sacredness in the relations between men and women we see women as sisters, daughters, or mothers. In our thinking women and men's friendship is not considered good.

Aditya argues that the notion of friendship between men and women is inherently western and also immoral since it potentially enables the expression of sexuality outside marriage. Vimla made a similar argument in the interview about the alleged immorality of Christians, in which she claimed that in Hinduism girls are not allowed to "wander around with strangers." According to Vimla, relationships between men and women that are unprotected by kinship are highly immoral. As a Hindu nationalist activist, Vimla interacts on a daily basis with men who are not members of her biological family, so it is particularly important for these individuals to be scripted into the movement as family—as brothers, uncles, or sons. As mothers, sisters, or daughters, women are unambiguously defined as family and also drafted into roles that determine how men should treat them and interact with them. Not only are men required to interact with them in socially prescribed ways, but also women's presentations of self must resonate with the social selves constructed for them by the movement. They must contain sexuality strictly within the marital contract, avoid premarital or extramarital relationships, avoid friendships with men, and dress, talk, and behave in ways consistent with their subject positions within the movement.

Much of the work that women's wings like Matri Shakti and the Samiti engage in builds upon these familial subject positions. Mirroring their roles in the family, Hindu women are viewed as the guardians of Hindu nationalist traditions, values, morals, and ideology whose primary responsibility is to cultivate these ideas in their children.[2] The Rashtra Sevika Samiti handbook declares, "Women are the foundation pillars of the nation taking into account their capacity to mould the family in either way."[3] Here the family is seen as the basic unit of the nation, and therefore the place where social and ideological reform must be initiated. Since women, as mothers, are centrally involved in reforming not just their children but also the Hindu nation, they must be taught to inculcate values that are conducive to the movement's vision and ideals. Writing about the "new" woman of Hindu nationalism, Tanika Sarkar asserts, "as mothers of the future leaders of the community, women needed to be taught the lessons and the intentions of the new politics, so that they could convey them to the children at home" (T. Sarkar 1998: 91). The centrality of women to the well-being of the nation is also emphasized in the Rashtra Sevika Samiti Handbook:

Woman is a common bond of affection and attachment in a family, in her capacity as a daughter, a sister, a wife and a mother. The family, society automatically becomes weak and feeble, when this bond looses its grip and power. It is, therefore, utterly necessary to make women strong physically, mentally, intellectually and spiritually also, so that she can get correct and coordinating outlook regarding her duties towards the family and society and create a deep sense of devotion and pride for nation, religion and culture. With this motive in mind Rashtra Sevika Samiti started functioning.[4]

Men and women in other wings of the movement echo this sentiment as well. As Aditya put it, "when we [VHP] train a man we train one man. When we train a girl we train a full family. When a girl gets proper training—*sanskar*—she can impress a full family whether as a sister, daughter, wife or daughter-in-law." The *sanskar* Aditya refers to is of course steeped in Hindu nationalist ideology, and it is the duty of women to impress these ideas on their children and other members of the family. Yet in each of these statements it is clear that women's power and authority within the movement are rooted in how well they conform to the roles of mother, daughter and sister and in upholding the patriarchal values of Hindu nationalism.

These roles also enable women to participate in the struggle for a Hindu India in more violent ways. The author of the handbook posits, "A Hindu woman is an eternal mother a symbol of love, sacrifice, dedication, fearlessness, sanctity and devotion. The tenderhearted woman becomes bold and aggressive if time demands." While the story of Jijabai is used to show women how they can inspire their children to fight for the Hindu nation, other models of womanhood, such as the legendary

Jhansi ki Rani (queen of Jhansi), are used to suggest that women must take up arms and participate in this battle themselves. For example, Payal informed me that Jhansi ki Rani fought valiantly against the British not only to prevent her territory from being conquered, but also to defend the Hindu nation. Similarly, Hindu nationalists often relate stories of ordinary women who engage in violent action in defense of the Hindu nation. An elderly VHP member spoke with pride about the women in his community at the time of partition, when his own village in Sialkot (now Pakistan) was under attack. He informed me that since the villagers had only three guns, they let the group come very close before shooting the leaders. Once the leaders died, the attackers began to run away, and the villagers chased them and threw hand grenades. He said proudly that the village women followed in their wake, carrying *trishuls* (tridents) and knives to stab and kill those who had only been wounded in the grenade attack.

In this example, women engage in violent acts in a supportive capacity, assisting men as loyal daughters, wives, and mothers, to finish what they started. Women are actively encouraged to perform their duty toward the nation while fulfilling their roles as mothers and wives. As Amrita Basu has argued, "The message they [Hindu nationalists] convey is that women can assume activist roles without violating the norms of Indian womanhood or ceasing to be dutiful wives and mothers" (A. Basu 1995: 179). In fact, although women can become *sadhvis* or *pracharikas*, in actual practice they are not encouraged to renounce their roles as wives and mothers. For instance, Aditya said (in English), "We don't encourage women not to marry in order to join the VHP and devote their lives to the VHP. We want them to work for the cause while remaining in the family system. She is then not an economic burden on the organization. It is easier for men to work in the social field without family but not so easy for a girl because of social atmosphere and some natural instincts."

What should be clear from this discussion is that situating women within the family is central to Hindu nationalist constructions of womanhood. While emphasizing women's roles as mothers and wives and their duty to tend the home and serve their husbands and families, when necessary the movement also interprets "home" and "family" to include the social networks of the Hindu nation. Thus Hindu nationalism while, on the one hand, restricting women's activities to being good mothers and wives, also provides a space, albeit a contested one, for women to move outside their homes and engage in activities outside the confines of their own biological families. As several scholars have shown, the use of motherhood to create a space for political activism is common to many social movements and nationalist ideologies.[5] This is because in most political communities, all citizens are not equal and the social construction of "difference" (on the basis of gender, race, ethnicity) often determines an individual's "access to entitlements and their capacity to exercise independent agency" (Yuval-Davis and Werbner 1999: 4, 5). In the context of Hindu nationalism, normative constructions of gender that associate women with motherhood lead to the construction of motherhood as the appropriate site for the exercise of female citizenship.

Ideological Inconsistencies

Many Hindu nationalist men and women articulated this idealized image of women as mothers shaping their children and the next generation of nationalist activists. Yet a closer examination of how men and women mobilized these constructions of female subjectivity in various discursive contexts suggests that rather than assuming ideological unity we need to pay attention to the inconsistencies within ideological systems. Hindu nationalist ideology should not be viewed as a unified discourse, since it is deeply affected by the interests, desires, and perspectives of those who articulate it. Rather than search for ideological purity somehow separable from the acts of those who articulate it, we need to refocus our attention on ideological practice and examine its multiple contours. Indeed, following Butler, this very practice creates the illusion of a preexisting ideology against which each act may be measured (1999: 179–80). Below I examine the multiple contours of Hindu nationalist ideology to reveal the inconsistencies and tensions that, in part, enable dissonant acts within the movement. These diverging perspectives, although structured by key Hindu nationalist norms, also reveal, in Paola Bacchetta's words, that "when women and men struggle for what they collectively call a 'Hindu nation' they do not necessarily have exactly the same entity in mind" (Bacchetta 1996: 127).

While most women in the movement were in agreement about the preeminent place of motherhood in women's lives, there was some disagreement on whether this construction of female subjectivity precluded them from engaging in activities considered part of the male domain. Indeed, amid nationwide discussions about whether there should be reservations for women in politics, several men and women I talked with articulated their own views on women's ability to participate in the political world. Aparna Pandit of the Delhi Samiti, responding to my question about the place of women in Indian society, said, "women are society's other half and they must be educated so that they can know of their rights and responsibilities. Wherever there are decision making bodies then women must have a say." She asserted that as mothers women should look after the home, but they must also contribute to society.

Some women passionately contested the claim that women should not participate in politics. In one instance, Vimla got into a heated argument with a male colleague from the VHP on the subject of reservations when he tried to convince her (and me) that women should stick to what they are good at (taking care of the home). Nivedita, a leader of the BJP Mahila Morcha, was adamant and accused the BJP and other political parties of being male-dominated. She angrily asserted that when the BJP does have women in committees or posts, they either put in "dumb women" or claim they cannot find good women to fill the posts. She told me that she supported a nationwide agitation that the Mahila Morcha was planning to challenge BJP discrimination against women. Nivedita crossly exclaimed: "women in the BJP are just used as show pieces for *dharnas* and *pradarshans* [sit-ins and demonstrations/ agitation]."

Both Nivedita and Vimla firmly believe that women and men are equally capable of succeeding in politics and that they should be provided with the means and opportunity to do so. In contrast, Aditya believed that women lacked the capacity to thrive in certain avenues of life. Explaining why he was overseeing women's activities in the VHP, he said (in English):

Despite claims that women are equal to men whenever they need to organize an event they need the help of men. . . . We say that women are not equal but rather superior to men. This does not mean they should do the same thing. Men cannot rear children as good as women can. So in this case women are superior to men. This business of 33% reservation[6] [for women] will not work in politics. Politics is a dirty game. Particularly in Indian politics when people want to climb the hierarchy they have to find some godfather. To placate that person they have to do so many things. With men those things are limited to financial or hard work or flattery and singing praises in the field. When women come into politics they can't always keep themselves in the running without compromising themselves. Now there are few women and they come up because of their own abilities. When there are many women in the field they will compete against each other and to get attention of seniors they may have to do some such things which are not looked upon well within our society. I think you get my point.

Aditya believes that while women are superior to men in their roles as mothers, they have poor organizational skills and are unsuited for the political world. The insinuation is that women will be morally compromised if they join politics in large numbers because they will have to use their bodies to gain the favor and attention of male politicians. This view was also articulated by women like Sita Mishra of the VHP. In these cases the construction of women as mothers of the nation, repositories of

Hindu nationalist traditions, morals, and culture, and responsible for disseminating these to the next generation, is precisely what precludes them from engaging in political activities. Since women bear the burden of maintaining honor and purity within the family and the community, and their actions and character reflect on the community at large, their morality must be strictly guarded.

Aditya's assertion that motherhood makes women superior to men is one that resonates with men and women throughout the movement. For instance, Sadhvi Rithambara contends, "God has given a mother such an elevated position. When people say, Sadhviji do something for women so that they can even get ahead of men, I say, you are a fool, for putting women on the same plane as men when they have been given a place that is even higher than that of gods" (Rithambara 1999: 52). This not uncommon view in Hindu nationalism builds on associations of women with goddesses in many Hindu traditions. For example, Jamuna told me that girls in Durga Vahini are called "Durgas," indicating their connection to this powerful goddess. The Samiti considers women "Bharatmata's daughters" with similar powers and qualities (Bacchetta 2002: 49). Unlike the victimized Bharat Mata constructed by the RSS, the Samiti views her as the Supreme Being and constructs her fiercely independent image from two ancient sacred texts, the Devi Mahatmaya and the Devi Bhagavata Purana (48–49). In the Devi Mahatmaya, the goddess, embodying uncontrolled *shakti*, is created from the bodies of the male gods as the only being powerful enough to defeat the buffalo demon. It is these stories that Rithambara is recalling in her statement that women have a position that is "higher" than that of the gods.

Yet to attain this elevated status, women must conform to Hindu nationalist constructions of female subjectivity. They must maintain their purity and morality and demonstrate their self-sacrificing nature as wives and mothers to gain the respect accorded to goddesses. This construction of women as self-sacrificing wives and mothers is also central to Hindu nationalist images of self and other. Responding directly to the Sadhvi's statement, Rajesh, a senior member of the Delhi VHP, said:

If you do a comparison between women's lives in Hinduism versus Christians and Muslims you will find that Hindu women are the most respected. Hindu women fast for their husbands and sons. They never fast for themselves. They don't ask for anything for themselves. This kind of attitude can only be found in Hindu women and that is why they are so respected. Sadhvi Rithambara is correct. All these statements about men and women being equal are all wrong because women are superior to men because of things like that and because of their roles as mothers. Muslim women are given no respect.

While echoing some of what Sadhvi Rithambara and Aditya had to say, Rajesh's words also reveal what else is at stake if women do not conform to Hindu nationalist constructions of female subjectivity. By being self-sacrificing and devoted mothers and wives, they not only attain an elevated position within the community, but also enable Hindu nationalists like Rajesh to assert the superiority of Hinduism over other religious traditions. Here women are clearly symbols of community honor and status. However, the respect they supposedly command among Hindus depends on how self-sacrificing they are, how well they suppress their own desires to serve the needs of their husbands and children, and how carefully they protect their own moral integrity.

There is in fact a great deal of overlap between these diverging perspectives on women's roles in the movement. While Nivedita and Vimla may fervently argue that there should be reservations for women in politics, they would not necessarily argue with Aditya, Sadhvi Rithambara, and Rajesh about women's status in Hinduism or about the preeminence of women's roles as mothers. Similarly, although Aditya might strongly oppose reservations for women, he is not critical of BJP women who already hold political posts. His argument is not against the participation of some women in traditionally male domains, but against appeals for greater representation. He and Rajesh use traditional constructions of female subjectivity to contest such claims for better representation that might threaten male authority in the movement. Each of these views is voiced openly in the movement and commands a substantial following among its membership. In this sense they represent different tendencies within Hindu nationalism and enable the movement to appeal to diverse audiences with varying views and aspirations. However, these tendencies are not dissonant, in that they do not transgress normative Hindu nationalist constructions of the national or gendered subject, but instead stretch their boundaries to be more inclusive.

This inclusion comes at a price, since it draws diverse individuals with multiple and competing interests and desires into the movement's embrace. Some individuals may find it impossible to reconcile the obligations of political office with those of being a good wife and mother. Others may believe that as "Durgas" or "Bharat Mata's daughters" they deserve to be respected by men and choose not to remain in marriages where they are disrespected or abused. Some individuals may be compelled by other ideological systems and may hold views that do in fact transgress or challenge Hindu nationalist norms. Citing possibilities offered in other ideological systems, they might act in ways that transgress the normative constructions of the Hindu nationalist movement and become dissonant subjects. Below I examine the lives and stories of women who transgress the moral and political prescriptions of the movement, and in so doing, become dissonant subjects within the Hindu nationalist movement.

Ruptured Moralities

As I have already indicated, most of the women I worked with in Delhi were North Indian, lower-middle/middle-class women belonging to the middle- and upper-caste groups. Many lived in Delhi Development Authority (DDA) apartments for low-income groups in south and west Delhi, although a few lived in houses in wealthy private housing colonies in south Delhi. All of them had some education, though not many had a college degree. Almost all came from Hindu nationalist families and had been encouraged by them to join the women's wings of the movement. Most of them came from families with fairly conservative ideas about the place of women in society and, had it not been for their participation in the movement, many of them would not have been permitted to work outside the home. With few exceptions, women had arranged marriages and came from families that believed that female sexuality must be contained within the institution of marriage. Many were deeply committed to Hindu nationalist constructions of female subjectivity and strove to embody these ideals.

Yet Hindu nationalist activists who engage in the urban public sphere in Delhi are familiar with diverse constructions of womanhood in India and abroad. As subjects formed amid multiple and competing ideological systems in the plural landscape of modern India, they were often drawn to other ways of being and knowing that directly or indirectly challenged Hindu nationalist ideals. Indeed, they sometimes felt caught between the normative expectations of their families and communities and their own desires. Hailed by complex and competing desires and needs and struggling with the contingencies of everyday life, women were not always able or willing to live up to Hindu nationalist expectations of female subjectivity. While committed to the movement, they did not always follow its prescriptions to make sense of their own lives and struggles. Below I relate the stories of women who transgress Hindu nationalist constructions of womanhood as they endeavor to surmount the compulsions and exigencies of daily life and to fulfill their own desires.

Rather than presume a pure ideological space against which certain acts are deemed transgressive, I think it is more instructive to examine how the temporality of practice complicates the contours of ideological systems. When women's discursive and non-discursive practices do not conform to any of the plural constructions of womanhood available within Hindu nationalism and instead invoke the norms of other ideological systems, they signal what I have been calling a transgression. Women in the movement are under great pressure to conform to Hindu nationalist constructions of Hindu womanhood, and are certainly compelled toward particular ways of being and knowing through the coercive power of its "compulsory system" (Butler 1999: 178). However, no ideological system is a "sutured totality," and therefore the subject can never be fully determined (Laclau and Mouffe 1985: 106, 115). Indeed, as individuals living in particular historical moments and swayed by multiple needs, desires, and demands in their everyday lives, women cannot and do not always inhabit Hindu nationalist norms. Instead they occasionally perform other norms, an act that reveals that they are complex subjects (rather than just hypocrites) whose actions are inflected by multiple ideologies. Their transgressions of the norm make them dissonant subjects who testify to the inability of Hindu nationalism to determine the subject even as it tries to regulate and direct the actions of its members toward a certain normative positions.

I often learned about these dissonant acts through women's stories about their own lives and those of their colleagues in the movement. These stories emerged during informal interactions, casual conversations, and intense gossip sessions over the course of the year. It is crucial to recognize that these narratives, influenced by women's awareness of my research interests and their perception of me (as westernized, independent, and "different"), were not innocent of agendas. Indeed, as linguistic anthropologists have argued, language is a "form of social action" that does not simply "reflect an already existing reality, it also helps to create that reality" (Ahearn 2001: 110–11). The stories women told me were tools through which they crafted their own lives and selves and also shaped my perception, and ultimately my representation, of who they were. Sarah Lamb has argued that, even when they may be inaccurate or have no "pragmatic outcome," the stories women tell us about their lives must be understood as "a mode of social action, a creative act of self making and culture making, through the telling of words" (Lamb 2001: 20, 21).

At the same time, while these stories are crucial to how *some* of my interlocutors wanted me to see them and others in the movement, I am also aware that discussing such acts could compromise their relationships with superiors, colleagues, and families. Following the lead of ethnographers working in violent political contexts who have gone beyond using pseudonyms to protect the identities of those they work with (Nordstrom 2004; Malkki 1995), when necessary I have created new names for old characters or simply not used names at all. Below I discuss the lives of Vasanti and Urvashi, both activists who are deeply committed to Hindu nationalism yet transgress some of its moral prescriptions in everyday life.

VASANTI'S STORY

In 1999, Vasanti, a VHP activist in her late twenties, had been married to a physically abusive man for eight years and had a son who was six and a daughter who was four. I met Vasanti less than a month after she left her husband and children following a particularly brutal episode. Although she missed her children terribly, she had left them with her husband, believing that he loved them and would provide for them better than she could on her stipend from the movement. Through her conduct, Vasanti transgressed the normative construction of Hindu womanhood as self-sacrificing wife and mother. She left her husband, deeming it unnecessary to remain in a situation that caused her emotional and physical pain. She also left her children, ironically, because of her own interpretation of what it meant to be self-sacrificing. She believed she had put their needs for a good life above her own desire to keep them with her.

Although here Vasanti violated the norms upheld by the movement, she agreed with much of what the movement had to say about society. She was committed to making India a Hindu nation and, like other Hindu nationalists, did feel that Christianity and Islam had threatened Hindu society and culture over the centuries through conversion and the introduction of "foreign" values. And, even as she transgressed the moral prescriptions of the movement in her own life, she upheld its constructions of gender in her work for the VHP. For instance, Vasanti applauded the morality of Hindu women who guard their virtue by remaining within the protective limits and authority of their natal/marital families. Yet in her own life she has escaped these very confines to live independently in a room provided for her by the movement. Although Vasanti may cite the Hindu nationalist subject in her discussions with others and publicly affirm the norm, in her own life she has transgressed and resisted its imperatives.[7] Vasanti—like other dissonant subjects in the Hindu nationalist movement—testifies to the complexities of subject formation in Indian modernity. She clearly recognized herself as a dissonant subject, since she once told me that I should focus my analysis of Hindu nationalist women on others who worked with her because she did not fit the norm.

Most of those who worked with Vasanti, including her superiors, knew about these circumstances, supported her publicly by providing her with shelter, food, and a stipend, and accepted her as a valued member of the VHP. Yet they clearly viewed her as a dissonant subject and reiterated normative constructions of Hindu womanhood when speaking about her with me. For instance, a female coworker and friend expressed her disapproval to me privately saying, "she should never have left her children." When I mentioned the physical abuse, she said: "she should have come to an agreement with her husband. She should have tried to explain to him that he should not beat her instead of leaving her children." She claimed not to understand how any mother could abandon her children, and said that that if Vasanti had to leave her husband, she should at least have taken her children with her. She made it very clear that Vasanti should have worked things out with her husband and should have compromised and stayed with him. These criticisms, particularly her transgression of the norms of motherhood, would resonate with many women in the movement.

While the women I worked with did not condone domestic abuse, such behavior is seen to arise from the corrupting influences of modernity, and the burden of reform rests with women rather than men. Separation and divorce are frowned upon and viewed as a "western" solution rather than one that adheres to "Hindu" values and commitments to family and children. Neera Gupta of the Samiti told me, as we were sitting in her house at her posh south Delhi address, "Mothers are people whose habit is to give and not to take." In a long conversation about how weak women had become, she argued that it was women's cowardice that enabled domestic abuse. She firmly asserted that women were responsible for teaching their children Hindu culture and values, and should prioritize their children's needs over their own. In abusive situations Neera insisted that women should not abandon their children but instead stand up for their beliefs and teach their husbands through their own moral example. Here Neera is echoing a normative construction of the ideal wife in Samiti discourses. Paola Bacchetta (1996) argues that in addition to being chaste, courageous, and faithful, the ideal wife, modeled on Ram's wife Sita in the Ramayana, is also expected to induce "a sense of duty in her husband" (154). She argues that the Samiti retools the concept of *pativrata*, to suggest that a woman must consider both husband and nation god and be devoted to both. Reiterating these Samiti norms for women's behavior, Neera told me that women needed to understand that marriage is about compromise and that they alone had the strength of forgiveness and tolerance to bear these problems and rise above them. Compelled by other ways of being, clearly Vasanti did not believe that such compromise was necessary. For other women like Urvashi, circumstances made compromise impossible.

Urvashi's Story

Although I had been to her house several times and met her two daughters and three grandchildren on several occasions, Urvashi had never talked to me about her husband. One afternoon in late November after she finished her work at the hospital, I insisted on giving Urvashi a ride home by autorickshaw because she complained of feeling dizzy. As the autorickshaw wound its way around a major commercial area in New Delhi, Urvashi pointed to a store and said, "that is our shop." Upon further questioning I discovered that the shop belonged to her husband's family. Not knowing what I was getting into, I responded conversationally that I had never met her husband. It was then, on the long dusty journey to her house, that Urvashi told me the distressing story of her marriage. She said that she had not left her husband, but that she had been made to leave (*nikal diya gaya*) by her father-in-law who had insisted that she live with her mother, only making occasional visits to her husband's home. Over the years, he had gradually abandoned her leaving her to fend for herself and her children financially, physically, and emotionally.

In her life narrative, as well as in her critique of other women, Urvashi manages to present herself as a virtuous Hindu woman even as she violates the norms of female subjectivity by living outside the protection of her husband's family and raising her children alone. She presents herself as struggling against all odds to be a good Hindu woman, to provide for her children, and to rear them in accordance with Hindu values and traditions. Although she was unable to be a devoted wife and daughter-in-law, Urvashi believes that she has been a good mother who never abandoned her children despite all the hardships in her life. She attributes her survival to her own hard work and the financial support she has received from the VHP over the years. Apart from the regular stipend she received from them, she had also been given money by the organization for things including the start-up costs of her son's canteen. She told me that the VHP was her family now. Yet despite the assistance and support she receives, her life has not been easy. We spent many afternoons discussing the difficulties of daily existence as she struggled to surmount her own personal and financial circumstances to find a suitable husband for her youngest daughter. Urvashi's youngest daughter was a vivacious young woman in her second year of college, who was educated, pretty, and self-assured. Very fond of both of them, I was deeply disturbed by Urvashi's tales of the dowry demands being asked of her. Yet, even as I advised her against marrying her daughter into a family that demanded dowry, I was deeply aware that as a single mother in a precarious social/moral and financial situation, it might have been difficult for Urvashi to do otherwise.

Despite the unusual circumstances of her marriage, Urvashi always upheld the normative Hindu nationalist constructions of female subjectivity while talking to me. Once, while discussing the breakup of a colleague's marriage, Urvashi asserted that the relationship would not have ended disastrously had the colleague married a man chosen by her parents from her own caste. Since I did not know about Urvashi's husband at this time, I interpreted this statement as simply her views on what she dismissively called "love marriages." In other conversations, Urvashi had been critical of women who had married for love, contending that such relationships violated Hindu traditions. However, after I learned that Urvashi's marriage had disintegrated despite the fact that it had been arranged by her parents with a man from her own caste community, I began to recognize the complex motivations underlying her conversations with me. As a lower-middle-class and middle-caste North Indian Hindu woman living outside her parents' home and unable to access the moral protection of her husband's home, Urvashi was in a difficult position. Although she was in her late forties when I met her in 1999, she was very young when she began to live on her own as a single mother working to make ends meet in Delhi, and deeply vulnerable to malicious gossip about her moral status. Her strict adherence to the normative constructions of Hindu nationalism, in addition to the moral protection that her work with the VHP provided, conferred a degree of propriety on her nontraditional life style. Working within the Hindu nationalist family, publicly voicing its normative constructions, critiquing women who violated these rules, and trying to adhere to community expectations for her own daughter enabled her to derive moral authority even as she failed to espouse the movement's norms for female conduct in her own life.

As scholars have shown, it is not unusual for women to uphold normative expectations publicly while challenging them privately, particularly when they begin to see that their own honor is vested in the system.[8] Indeed, Urvashi's moral status is, to some degree, contingent on the purity of the Hindu nationalist family with whom she works, a point that explains her critique of "love marriages" within and beyond the community. Even more important, in this case Urvashi was talking to me, an ethnographer she knew would represent the lives of women in the movement.[9] Her desire to influence my representation of Hindu nationalist women when I clearly knew about their transgressions may also have affected both her critique of others and her attempts to portray herself as an ideal Hindu woman struggling against the contingencies of everyday life to uphold the very norms that cast her as a dissonant subject.

While Urvashi and Vasanti transgressed the norms for female conduct by living outside the protection of their husband's home and neglecting their obligations toward their extended family (Urvashi) and children (Vasanti), other women violated Hindu nationalist expectations of female sexuality. I was party to gossip about the romantic liaisons of fellow activists. I was told that one woman who always made a point of projecting herself as the ideal Hindu nationalist subject was in fact living with a man who was not her husband. Another woman I worked with was allegedly having an extramarital affair, and was also accused of openly flirting with other men in her husband's presence. I want to emphasize that in both cases this was gossip I could not verify. It is important to note, however, that gossiping about affairs is itself a dissonant act since it fails to reiterate Hindu nationalist norms and invokes possibilities in other ideological systems. In some cases, women who were in fact having affairs took me into their confidence. I learned that, although their colleagues and superiors knew of some of these affairs, they were willing to look away as long as they were conducted with discretion and did not affect the public persona of the activists.

I am not suggesting here that there was any public approval by the movement of women's romantic liaisons. These women were clearly viewed as dissonant subjects by others in the movement. Indeed, Hindu nationalist women who gossiped about their colleagues' affairs usually expressed disapproval of such behavior. Although some of my interlocutors were accepting of courtship before marriage, they were less so of sex outside marriage. For example, Ela Dube asserted that, although her husband wanted her son to marry a Brahmin from his community, she was willing to let her son marry a woman of his choosing regardless of caste. Claiming that women are more liberal than men on such issues, she also contended that "love marriage" has existed for centuries. At the same time, Ela disapproves of sex outside marriage and told me she had been horrified to meet an unmarried girl at the All India Institute for Medical Sciences who was there to get a "Copper-T" (IUD) inserted.

Notwithstanding views like Ela's, members of the movement are well aware that some Hindu nationalist women do have affairs. What these examples reveal is that while Hindu nationalists may disapprove of dissonant acts, individuals who engage in them are not deemed entirely unacceptable to the movement as long as they hide their dissonance from public view. In fact while such conduct can rupture the moral image the movement might want to project, it is also under pressure to accept such transgressions in its expansionary movement across the sociopolitical landscape of the country. The stories above illustrate that there are myriad forces that intersect in the lives of individuals who support a movement (see Nash and Rojas 1992). Indeed, as Hindu nationalist women negotiate the plural topography of urban India, they are compelled by multiple ideological frameworks, succumb to competing desires, and are drawn to contradictory ways of being as they battle with the contingencies of daily life. The Hindu nationalist movement must make allowances for the gulf between discursive ideals and everyday practice and accept the transgressions of its membership to some degree, if it is to continue to recruit support from diverse audiences and mobilize a mass base.

Transgressing Nationalist Unity

Hindu nationalist constructions of female subjectivity are deeply influenced by North Indian and upper-caste prescriptions for women's role and conduct. Indeed from their inception, organizations like the RSS have been Brahmin-dominated. While of course Hindu nationalism has its supporters in South India and among lower-caste/class groups, it is predominantly an upper-/middle-caste/class movement that has been most successful in the central and northern states. This demographic profile has not deterred the movement from presenting itself as the true representative of Hindu India and reaching out to Hindus from all castes and all regions. Its success in incorporating Hindus into its political framework depends in large part on how well it crafts a unified national identity for the Hindu nation. Throughout this book I have examined the multiple strategies through which the movement crafts nationalist unity amid the plural landscapes of modern India. I have shown how Hindu nationalist activists use revisionist histories of the past and present to depict a Hindu nation under siege by "foreigners" (Muslims and Christians) who supposedly have denigrated Hindus in the past and threaten their security in the present and future. I have examined the ways in which religious identity, ideas, and ritual practices are used to construct a monolithic identity for the Hindu nation, as well as to craft a loyal Hindu subject willing to sacrifice him/herself to defend the nation. Many of these practices are directed at governing individuals to replace regional and caste subjectivities with a Hindu nationalist one.

This attempt to transcend caste and regional divisions and create a unified Hindu identity has been a central preoccupation of Hindu nationalists since the 1980s, when they were trying to build an electoral base amid the furor over the release of the Mandal Commission Report, which threatened to divide Hindus along caste lines. Indeed the various *rath yatras* (chariot processions) across multiple states in India, the attempt to generate Ram *bhakti* throughout India, and indeed the Ramjanmabhumi movement itself were all designed to craft a Hindu identity that would seemingly transcend these regional and caste-based divisions (see Davis 1996; Hasan 1996) even as they ultimately reinforced them. Caste in particular is of concern to the movement, which faces serious threats to its electoral base as well as its moral image from political groups and parties affiliated with lower-caste and dalit groups. Several women spoke of the efforts taken by various Hindu nationalist groups to unite Hindus across caste lines. Many women were deeply involved in these efforts, and yet many continued to observe caste prescriptions and practices in their own lives and allowed caste hierarchies to structure their interactions with others. Thus even as they upheld and actively disseminated a unified Hindu nationalist identity in public, they often transgressed its normative prescriptions in their own lives and interactions.

Urvashi often lectured to other women about transcending caste prescriptions even though she strictly followed them in her own life. She was insistent that her daughter marry a man from her own regionally specific caste community (*jati*). Marrying any Hindu, even if he belonged to the broader *varna* (class) category of *vaishyas* (traders) simply would not do. Urvashi got her daughter engaged to a young man with a tenth standard education who worked in a government office, a job with such generous perks (housing, pension) that it made him a "good catch" in the community. Subsequently, many of my conversations with Urvashi dwelt on the increasing dowry demands being made of her, all well beyond her means. Urvashi informed me that the groom's family had asked for a Bajaj scooter, a refrigerator, a color television, and a washing machine, in addition to fifty thousand rupees in cash. She asserted that although she does not like the concept of dowry, the groom's family would be shamed in the eyes of the caste community if she did not give the dowry requested.

Although these have become common in middle- and upper-class households, most of the women I worked with who come from Urvashi's lower-middle-class economic background could not afford washing machines or maids who would wash their clothes for them. Consumer goods such as washing machines can signify class status, and increasingly dowry demands have begun to reflect the changing lifestyle of what Leela Fernandes refers to as the "new middle class" (2006: 74). Owning such consumer goods provides a way to claim a higher class status and, particularly for those who occupy a marginal class position, to distinguish themselves from lower class groups (Fernandes 2006; Mankekar 1999). Urvashi knew that the groom's family was exploiting her own social and economic marginality to achieve a higher status for itself. Yet she wanted to uphold community expectations, admittedly because she did not want to shame the groom's family, but possibly also because she did not want to be perceived as anything less than middle-class or with any of the qualities middle-class groups often attribute to those with lower-class status.[10] These desires competed with the movement's projections of Hindu unity and led Urvashi to transgress Hindu nationalist prescriptions as she fulfilled her own desires for her daughter and protected her own position in her caste/class community.

While privately maintaining caste practices, many women actively participated in the movement's work to transcend caste divisions. On one occasion, Urvashi took me to a *kirtan* (devotional song session) organized at the home of a middle-class woman she identified as belonging to the *chamar* caste—a caste group of leatherworkers once considered "untouchable" by upper-caste Hindus. It was election season and the *kirtan* had been organized by Mandira Gupta, a member of the Mahila Morcha. Urvashi informed me that the BJP candidate's wife would visit the group at some point during the event. The *kirtan* was a means through which activists like Mandira and Urvashi attempted to craft an identity that transcended the caste differences among the women gathered. Almost all the women present belonged to middle-/upper-caste groups and yet were enthusiastically singing devotional songs in the home of a woman whose caste group has been discriminated against for centuries. They sat around a woman beating on a drum (*dholak*) singing songs to different deities and all partook of the *prasad* that had been prepared by the host and was distributed at the end of the *kirtan*. Through these acts the activists present crafted a unified identity that not only bolstered their claims to nation, but also enabled the BJP candidate's wife to appeal to caste groups that were not usually part of the party's base.

However, when Mandira, Urvashi, and I returned to Mandira's house in the same DDA Middle-Income Group colony with our large plates of *prasad*, I discovered that both of them privately resented the woman who had hosted the event. As we sat eating the assortment of sweets, savories, and the banana on our plates, Mandira and Urvashi began to gossip about how the "*chamar*" was trying to get above herself by serving such huge plates of *prasad*. It was clear in their conversation that class status and education did not change the fact that she was a *chamar* and therefore ranked lower than they did on the caste/moral hierarchy. Indeed, Mandira and Urvashi deployed their caste status to undermine any chance the woman had of using her class position to claim an equal social position. Thus, far from claiming the equality of all Hindus, these two Hindu nationalist activists privately believed that they were morally superior to the woman who had hosted the event because of their higher caste status. Although willing to disregard pollution rules that would have prevented them from eating the *prasad* cooked by a lower-caste woman, they were not prepared to relinquish their higher position in the hierarchy. They also expressed resentment of the rise of lower-caste groups in India by complaining vociferously that today *chamars* get all the benefits because of reservations for them in government jobs and universities while *baniyas* (trader caste) don't get anything. A male BJP activist sitting in the room with us responded jokingly that both of them should fill out forms saying that they were *chamars* and take advantage of the reservation system. Mandira was horrified by this suggestion: "Are you crazy? I have three daughters to marry. How can I do that?"

Mandira and Urvashi are willing to embrace the movement's commitment to reaching out to lower-caste groups in an attempt to mobilize more support for the movement, but clearly continue to hold prejudices and resentment against them. These cases reveal that, much as the leaders of the movement might want to create a pan-Hindu identity, its members often continue to perceive caste and other divisions between themselves and others. While here I focus on caste, there were other ethnic and regional prejudices that shaped the interactions among the women I worked with. On one occasion Ramani, a woman from Kerala who is currently a member of the Delhi Samiti, illustrated the regional prejudices and tensions that divide women in the movement. One day, frustrated by her attempts to get a group of women to sit in rows at a Samiti meeting, she said to me in Malayalam: "women from here [north India] can't understand what you mean even when you speak to them in their own language."

Women's transgressions in the movement must be situated within the plural context of modern India. They negotiate their identities in contexts marked by multiple systems of representation and multiple experiences of social, economic, political, cultural, and religious differences. While each of these women is active within the movement, Hindu nationalist ideology is not the only influence on their lives. In fact, for some of the women I met, Hindu nationalist ideology was not what initially brought them into the movement. While many of the women had joined the movement because their families (parents or husband) encouraged their involvement in the women's wings, some had joined for a host of different reasons. Nivedita's father-in-law had been a leader of the Indian National Congress,[11] but she joined the BJP because she was tired of Congress corruption and the sexual harassment she claimed women faced in the Congress Party. Although they were both members of the BJP and the VHP, Urvashi claimed that Mandira had only joined the VHP because "she is greedy for an election ticket" and knew she would be given preference because of her affiliation with the VHP. Other women, as I have already indicated, join the movement because of personal contacts with its members (Bina and Gauri) or because it gives them access to powerful political leaders (Priya). These examples suggest that women's initial involvement with the movement may have little to do with their commitment to Hindu nationalism, although many are receptive or become receptive over time to its politics. The movement accepts this diversity in its membership in order to mobilize support for Hindu nationalist politics and politicians. In so doing, it also enables and accepts dissonant subjects unwilling or unable to live up to its ideological expectations.

Unacceptable Transgressions

Living in worlds entangled with multiple ideological systems and compelled by competing desires and needs as they navigated the exigencies of daily existence, it is not surprising that many women transgressed the prescriptions of self advocated by the movement and became dissonant subjects. Although their acts were perceived as dissonant and were the focus of gossip and critique, their superiors and colleagues continued to support these women. In this sense their acts were acceptable transgressions as long as they were hidden from the public gaze and did not interfere with their work for the movement. Indeed, I have argued that many of these women continued to uphold ideal Hindu nationalist subjectivity in their public personas and in their interactions with new recruits, even as they violated these prescriptions in their own lives. Urvashi, for instance, is deeply committed to Hindu nationalism, including to the normative constructions she violates. Indeed she demonstrates through her example how important these constructions are in her life. Even so, due to circumstances in her life she becomes a dissonant subject. The VHP acceptance of Urvashi and willingness to continue to support her financially, illustrate how the organization embraces flexibility and compromises on ideological purity in order to keep her within their ranks.

However, although the movement must be willing to accept some of the transgressive practices of its members if it is to continue its expansionary movement across the plural landscape of India, it must also maintain its distinction to ensure its political survival. It must draw the line somewhere. Consequently, while the dissonant acts described so far were tolerated by the movement, there were others that were deemed unacceptable. Indeed, women went to great lengths to hide acts they suspected would be unacceptable. Here I briefly discuss two dissonant acts that fall into this category. Because of their clandestine nature these are isolated examples, and I can only speculate on what they might reveal about a political movement struggling to maintain a distinctive essence amid the pluralism that marks Indian modernity.

While many in the movement are willing to tolerate women's romantic transgressions even when they disapprove of them, not all love affairs are equally acceptable. Meena, for example, was having a highly clandes-tine affair with a Muslim man, and she told me several times that I was the only one who knew this story. I had no reason to doubt her when she insisted that she would have lost the support of the movement had her superiors found out about the affair. Meena believed her affair was an unacceptable transgression that had to remain hidden from her col-leagues and superiors. In Hindu nationalist discourse, national purity becomes pivotal to asserting the moral superiority of a nation that has been besieged, desecrated, and defiled by "foreign" invaders. These are signifying tropes upon which hinge an entire cultural politics that pits a beleaguered Hindu nation against a disreputable foreign invader. As I have argued, women's bodies are central to representing Hindu victim-ization as well as to claiming the superiority of Hindu culture and the nation. Meena's affair threatens this signification. Not only does she refuse to be the victimized subject of Muslim aggression, she willingly threatens the purity of the Hindu nation through her affair with a Mus-lim man.

The other transgressive act deemed unacceptable by the movement challenged the Hindu nation's heteronormative core. Heteronormati-vity is central to national ideologies in various parts of the world because it enables harnessing sexuality for the production and reproduction of the nation (see Yuval-Davis 1997). While celibate women can be accepted because they renounce sexuality altogether, homosexuality threatens the heteronormative order. One of my interlocutors told me that a young woman, who had worked for the movement for some years, had been thrown out without ceremony when people ascertained that she was attracted to women. I could not verify this information, but the hor-ror in my interlocutor's voice conveyed the unacceptability of homosex-uality among women in the movement. Indeed, Hindu nationalists eloquently conveyed the unacceptability of female homosexuality in the movement in their nationwide protests in 1999 over the Indian release of Deepa Mehta's film *Fire*, which depicts a sexual relationship between two daughters-in-law. Such incidents suggest that dissonant acts or images that threaten the heteronormative construction of the Hindu nationalist subject are unacceptable transgressions believed to defile the very core of the nation.

"Yeh to Sansar Hain. Hum Sab to Insan Hain"

"This is the way of the world. We are all human," said a young Hindu nationalist woman as we gossiped about two women in the movement who were having affairs. I had just remarked that I could not reconcile my conversations with these women with the knowledge that they were having affairs. Indeed, in separate conversations with me, they had discussed the moral degeneration of Hindu society and the need for women to uphold Hindu morality and eschew western influences. Yet, the woman asserted, we are only human and therefore fallible, forced to reconcile public/political ideals with the personal circumstances in which we find ourselves. These circumstances, as I have suggested throughout this book, are entrenched in the plural worlds of modern India and influenced by the daily struggles and competing needs and desires of individual women. Yet, even as these exigent circumstances might cause women to become dissonant subjects, it is critical to recognize that at other moments many of them do live up to the ideal and entirely endorse the politics and agendas of the movement. Urvashi, Vasanti, Jamuna, and the other women alluded to here work tirelessly in neighborhoods throughout Delhi to disseminate the ideology of the movement on the subject of religious conversion, on the need to establish India as a Hindu nation, and indeed on the subject of female morality. Many of these women believe fundamentally that India must be a Hindu nation and are willing to endorse the violence that they consider necessary to establishing the nation. And the movement is clearly willing to ignore their occasional romantic and political peccadilloes as long as they keep these out of public view and continue to do the work of the movement.

Dissonance within the movement is enabled not only by the existence of multiple ideologies in the plural worlds of modern India, but also by the expansionary strategies of Hindu nationalism itself. By recruiting individuals like Gauri and Bina, the movement is accepting individuals who are and may well continue to be dissonant subjects. Yet the multifaceted strategies through which the movement appeals to diverse groups and recruits new members are vital to expanding its base in contemporary India. While some individuals are drawn to the movement because of its constructions of history or current politics, others are seduced by the intimation that it is the sacred duty of Hindus to participate in the struggle to establish a Hindu nation. Some see Hindu nationalism as a means to political power, while others view the movement as source of support, engaging in state-like practices to provide for those most marginalized by the breakdown of the welfare state. While the movement attempts to govern its subjects and shape their conduct in ways that fulfill the goals of the movement, this is not always possible since it cannot fully determine the acts, desires, morals, and politics of its membership. Recruiting members amid the plural landscape of modern India, the Hindu nationalist movement deploys strategies that can generate dissonance within even as these very strategies underlie its dominance in the country. Since dissonant acts can challenge the normative order by validating other discourses and revealing the fault lines within, they may be quickly concealed from public view and rendered impotent by disapproval or condemnation. Yet, even as activists struggle to reiterate the normative constructions of the movement, their willingness to embrace dissonant subjects within their ranks has enabled the expansionary power of Hindu nationalism in modern India.

Notes

Introduction

1. All names in this book are pseudonyms, except when individuals were delivering public speeches or when their words and deeds were widely known or discussed in the media.

2. The Ramjanmabhumi temple literally means the temple on the birthplace of Ram, the Hindu god-king believed to be an incarnation of Lord Vishnu.

3. Sangh Parivar literally means Sangh Family, the cluster of organizations related to the Rashtriya Swayamsevak Sangh (RSS).

4. It is beyond the scope of this introduction to delve into the complex histories of these different organizations and their rise to power in postcolonial India. Excellent sources on the rise of Hindu nationalism include Hansen 1999; Jaffrelot 1999; Bhatt 2001.

5. Formed in 1925 by Keshav Baliram Hedgewar, the RSS is an all-male paramilitary organization in which many leaders of the Hindu nationalist movement, including those in the VHP and the BJP, got their start.

6. Formed in 1980, the BJP was fairly marginal until it embraced the Ramjanmabhumi movement, and Hindutva, in the late 1980s and early 1990s (Hansen 1999: 160–65). In its subsequent electoral successes it has transitioned from a central figure in the parliamentary opposition to forming the national government in coalition with other political parties from 1998 until 2004.

7. Sewa Bharati also runs programs in rural India.

8. See, for example, Hansen 1999; Jaffrelot 1999; Bhatt 2001; A. Basu 1995, 1996; Bacchetta 2004; Banerjee 2005; Rajagopal 2001; T. Sarkar 1995, 1998.

9. For instance, Joann Rogers and Jacqueline Litt 2004 argue that women are actively recruited into the World Church of the Creator, a Christian white supremacist organization, because their roles as mothers make them key to reproducing these ideas. Others have noted that gendered assumptions about women make them attractive to right-wing groups and violent political movements. Kathleen Blee notes that women are actively recruited by racist groups because they may be "less visible to outsiders," allow "better access to potential recruits," can recruit men in their families, and are "less legally vulnerable" (2002b: 102, 107). This has also been noted of women involved in political violence, particularly what is labeled "terrorism." Paige Whaley Eager argues that when women are chosen for suicide bombing missions, it may well be because *as women* they are less likely to be searched, may be less suspect, and may therefore—as in the case of the female Tamil Tiger who assassinated the Indian prime minister Rajiv Gandhi in 1991—get closer to their targets (2008: 194).

10. This trajectory resembles the way in which Hutu violence has been constructed as "native" violence against "settlers" in Rwanda (Mamdani 2001).

11. Building on George Mosse's work (1985) on the relationship between nationalism, sexuality, and respectability, Brackette Williams argues that in the nationalist ideologies of dominant groups the masculinity of those considered to belong to "inferior" races is often stereotyped to embody a "lack of control over their lower passions" and "lust for the 'pure' women of other races" (B. Williams 1996: 7).

12. There is a rich scholarship on religious violence in India. See, for instance, Das 2007; Appadurai 2006; Bacchetta 2004; Varshney 2003; T. Sarkar 2002; Hansen 2001; Banerjee 2000; Hansen 1999; C. Mahmood 1996; Kakar 1996; van der Veer 1994; Pandey 1990.

13. Similarly, Kathleen Blee has noted in the case of the U.S. white supremacist movement, that the construction of white women as "racial victims" is central to crafting a role for women in the movement that does not challenge patriarchy (2002: 116).

14. Authors who have analyzed women's agency in perpetuating communal violence include Bacchetta 1994, 1996, 2002, 2004; A. Basu 1995, 1998; Banerjee 1995, 2000, 2005; Jeffery and Basu 1998.

15. Scholars who have discussed the link between the global rise in violent conflagrations and the increasing structural inequalities produced by globalization in other parts of the world include Cockburn 2004: 43; Farmer 2005; Giles and Hyndman 2004: 302.

16. See Ahearn 2001: 120; Laclau and Mouffe 1985: 106, 115; Butler 1999: 185.

17. Several scholars have used the concept of hegemony, derived from Gramsci's cultural writings, to understand how postcolonial nationalisms grapple with this diversity and to theorize the intricate processes through which these nationalist activists articulate multiple identities and interests into their frameworks. See, for instance, Chatterjee 1986; Brow 1996; Mankekar 1999; Gupta 1998; Fox 1990a; B. Williams 1991.

18. Susie Tharu and Tejaswini Niranjana suggest that the ability of Hindu nationalists to articulate their agenda in terms of the humanist subject enables their hegemonic power (1999: 515).

19. My thoughts here have been informed by the work of Abu-Lughod 1986; Lamb 2000; Raheja and Gold 1994; and Scott 1990, among others.

20. Laclau and Mouffe argue that hegemony is not simply "an external relation between preconstituted social agents" but refers to "the very process of the discursive constitution of those agents" (1982: 100).

21. Butler borrows from Derrida the idea that a discursive structure requires repetitive performance in order to sustain its existence (Butler 1997: 13; Derrida 1988).

22. Butler is drawing on Michel Foucault's understanding of the regulatory power of discourse (see Foucault 1980b).

23. See, for instance, the full text of Advani's speech at an event organized by the Karachi Council on Foreign Relations, Economic Affairs, and Law, available on the BJP website at http://www.bjp.org/Press/june_0505.htm.

24. Interview, June 6, 2005, transcript at http://www.rediff.com/cms/print.jsp?docpath = //news/2005/jun/06i nter1.htm; see Noorani 2006.

25. In his excellent discussion, Jeffrey Sluka (1999: 11–13) cites, among others, Starn 1994; Taussig 1987; Scheper-Hughes 1995.

26. Other scholars who have sought to use ethnography to understand the motivations of individuals who join violent religious and social movements

include C. Mahmood 1996; Blee 2002; Deeb 2006. Scholars who have used interviews to engage with individuals involved in such movements include Juergensmeyer 2000 and Stern 2003.

27. The willingness of right wing women to talk to outsiders to further their own agendas has also been noted by Janny Groen and Anneike Kranenberg in their book on Muslim women in Holland involved with the Hofstad Network, a radical Islamic group (see Groen and Kranenberg forthcoming 2009).

28. On this point, look at the work of Blee 2002: 11 and Robben 1995.

29. Several feminist anthropologists have argued that we need to pay more attention to the politics of ethnography, including Mascia-Lees and Sharpe 2000; Visweswaran 1994; Behar 1993.

30. Although I have used pseudonyms throughout this ethnography, when possible I have chosen last names that preserve the integrity of both caste and regional affiliation to demonstrate the predominance of brahmins (Sharma, Dube) and vaishyas (Agarwal, Gupta) in the Hindu nationalist movement.

31. My thoughts here are informed by, among others, the work of Hefner 1998; Asad 1983, 1997; van der Veer 2002; Sunder Rajan 2003: 153.

Chapter 1. Everyday Histories

1. See http://www.indian-express.com/full_story.php?content_id = 1402 for the full text of the speech (*Indian Express*, April 24, 2002).

2. See, for example, Basu and Roy 2007; Jaffrelot 2007; Nussbaum 2007; Hansen 2005; Sarkar 2002; Mander 2002; Kumar and Bhaumik 2002.

3. See Appadurai 2006: 7, 74; Warren 1999: 231; Gourevitch 1998: 95.

4. Ann Grodzins Gold and Bhoju Ram Gujar (2002) have eloquently illustrated this in their study of the divergent memories of Rajasthani men and women they worked with.

5. At the time I conducted fieldwork, Usha Chati (Usha taiji) was the Pramukh Sanchalika of the Samiti. Pramila Medhe replaced her in July 2006. I use her real name here since this excerpt was from a speech at a public venue.

6. My thinking on these issues has been informed by, among others, Keesing 1983; Gold 2001; Visweswaran 1994.

7. She used the term *akhand Bharat* to refer to a pre-partition India that includes minimally what is today India, Pakistan, and Bangladesh, but can also include other areas such as Afghanistan. *Akhand Bharat* literally means undivided India (see Hansen 1999: 269).

8. Dalit is the term used by groups considered "untouchable" by upper-caste groups to refer to themselves. Although the Indian Constitution bans the practice of untouchability, Dalits continue to face discrimination by upper-caste Hindus. The term means "oppressed."

9. The saffron RSS flag was adopted in 1926 (Basu et al. 1993: 18). The RSS itself has very strong Maharashtrian roots—its early prayers were partly in Marathi (the language of Maharashtra) and the flag was said to have been Shivaji's symbol (18). Through these symbols we see an interesting and significant conflation of region (Maharashtra) with nation (Hindu India).

10. Several of the stories in this chapter are from Rashtra Sevika Samiti *shakha* guides, published every three months. They are teaching manuals used by the leaders of the *shakhas* to teach the women/girls who attend the training sessions, and provide a framework for each session. The pamphlets themselves are not handed out to the members. The pamphlets are about 20 pages (5 $\frac{1}{2}$ × 8

inches) and thus simply provide an outline for three months which the instructors must elaborate on. In actual performance the stories were added onto or changed to address specific issues the leaders wanted to communicate. However, as I was unable to tape the stories in their performance contexts, I have relied on the printed versions, which I have translated from the Hindi version.

11. Given the centralized Samiti command structure, I would imagine that similar stories are used in other parts of the country as well, particularly in Maharashtra, where Jijabai is an important figure in folklore and history.

12. For more on how stories embody historical memories see Gold and Gujar 2002. For more on how stories are used to transmit cultural ideals see Narayan 1989: 99–100.

13. Stathis Gourgouris uses the term "mythistory" to describe the process by which "historical order embraces the legendary" (1996: 11).

14. In 1999, Rajendra Singh (Rajju Bhaiya) was Sarsanghchalak of the RSS. He has since been replaced by K. Sudarshan.

15. Savarkar celebrates this "religious counter-aggression" (1971: 204) and speaks of how this "outburst of Hindu rage . . . resounded through town after town and village after village" (203).

16. In his essay "Effeminacy of the Inhabitants of Indostan," Robert Orme contends: "Breathing in the softest of climates; having so few real wants; and receiving even the luxuries of other nations with little labour, from the fertility of their own soil; the Indian must become the most effeminate inhabitant of the globe" (Orme 1974 [1782]: 306).

17. I am grateful to Sudipta Sen, who shared some of his unpublished work with me and introduced me to this idea.

18. The image that emerges in Orientalist histories is of a hypermasculine Muslim despot whose birth in a hot climate predisposes him to fall victim to the pleasures of the flesh For instance, Alexander Dow in his 1770 *History of Hindostan* (1973 [1770]: xx) writes: "In the silence which attends despotism, everything is dark and solemn. . . . Men indulge themselves under the veil of secrecy. . . . The enjoyment of the company of women is the chief object of life among the great; and when they retire into the sanctuary of the harem, they forget in a variety of charms, their precarious situations in the state. The necessary privacy enhances the indulgence; and the extreme sensibility, perhaps peculiar to the natives of a hot climate, carries pleasure to an excess which unmans the mind."

19. Here I am referring to cultural memory, what Marita Sturken describes as "a field of cultural negotiation through which different stories vie for a place in history" (1997: 1). It is precisely this cultural memory that Hindu nationalists seek to shape and dominate through their stories about Jijabai. There has been some interesting work on how nationalist movements tailor cultural memory to serve specific nationalist agendas. See, e.g., Agarwal 1995; Swedenberg 1995.

20. For more on this, see Wikan 1990.

21. She is referring to Nizam Osman Ali Khan, the Muslim ruler of Hyderabad state from 1911 until 1948. Despite the Nizam's desire that the princely state remain a sovereign entity after the partition of the subcontinent into India and Pakistan, Hyderabad was annexed into the Indian Union in 1948. He continued as governor of Hyderabad until 1956, when the state was divided along linguistic lines as part of Nehru's plan to divide India into linguistically based administrative units.

22. Neera probably means 1956.

23. The *mina bazaar* was a section in Akbar's fort in which the ladies of Akb-

ar's harem could make purchases from female vendors. No men except Akbar were permitted to attend.

24. Ramdhari Singh Dinkar (1908–74) was a poet who wrote in Hindi. Members of the Hindu nationalist movement often cite him.

25. See Menon and Bhasin 1998; Mazumdar 1994; Yuval-Davis 1997; Butalia 1998.

26. See Lamb 2000 for an excellent discussion of patrilineal constructions of kinship.

27. This theme of the goddess fighting for morality is central to many devotees. See, for instance, Wadley 2005, where Durga fights for Raja Nal against his enemies who are aided by Kali. Also see P. Ghosh 2003, where Durga secures Ram's victory over evil through her intervention in his battle against Ravana in the Ramayana.

28. M. G. Ranade asserts, "All accounts agree in describing Shivaji from his earliest youth as being intensely fond of hearing the old epics of Ramayana and Mahabharatha" (1900: 21).

29. Dadoji Khond Dev was appointed by Shivaji's father to be the governor of Pune (O'Hanlon 1985: 179, n.33).

30. Trivedi and Pandit are priestly castes; Agarwal and Gupta are merchant castes.

31. Sambhaji was Shivaji's brother.

32. Stewart Gordon asserts that luring his enemy away from the battle-grounds on the plains and into his own region was a key part of Shivaji's strategy because his own "superior knowledge of the local countryside" gave him a "strategic advantage" (1993: 190).

33. Gordon asserts that the Marathas, of whom Shivaji was one leader, were never really an empire or even a confederacy (1993: 178). In fact, through much of Maratha history, the primary organization was along the lines of smaller bands of armed forces controlled by a Deshmukh, appointed by land grants of several villages given to them by the Muslim Deccan Sultanates, who would collect revenue and protect their own interests, or when required the interests of the rulers, with these small armies (Gordon 1994: 195–96, 204). Shivaji came from one such line of Deshmukhs—the Bhonsles. Shivaji did fight against Muslim rulers. However, when captured by the Deccan Sultanate army, Shivaji joined their service (206).

Chapter 2. National Insecurities

1. See also Narula 1999: 31–32; Kim 2005: 160.

2. For more on violence against Christians in Gujarat, see *Times of India*, December 30, 1998, 1; December 31, 1998, 8. In January 1999 there was an attack against four missionaries in Allahabad, all of whom were seriously injured. For more on this incident, see *Times of India*, January 26, 1999, 11. Then, in an event that captured the attention of the international media, on January 22, Australian missionary Graham Staines and his two sons were shot to death and then burned while they were sleeping in a Jeep in Manoharpur village in Orissa. For more on this incident, see *Times of India*, January 25, 1999, 1, 3; *Indian Express*, February 28, 1999, 4. For more on Hindu nationalism and anti-Christian violence in Orissa, see A. Chatterji 2004. For more on attacks on churches in India, see *Times of India*, December 28, 1998, 1; December 29, 1998, 8.

3. See, for instance, Dirks 1996; Mazumdar 1994; P. Chatterjee 1989.

4. The older sections of the Vedas clearly focus on the performance of ritual sacrifices that were central to early Vedic Hinduism. In the Upanishads we see a shift away from performance of ritual to an examination of the philosophy behind it. They mark a turn to speculation about the nature of the supreme being (Brahman) and the relationship between the individual soul (*atma*) and Brahman. Reformists like Raja Ramohan Roy focused on the later part of the Vedic corpus to construct nationalist Hinduism.

5. This report, "The Untold Story of Hindukaran," dated January 4, 2006, can be found at www.pucl.org.

6. Syrian Catholics are 42 percent of the Christian population of Kerala, Orthodox Syrian/Jacobites 18 percent, and Latin Catholics 17 percent (Dempsey 2001: 7–8).

7. Unlike many other Hindu nationalists, Ela's dislike of missionaries does not include prejudice against Christians in general. She told me that she visits a church every Tuesday to feed people—mainly the elderly and lepers. Every Tuesday she cooks potatoes and *chappatis* (bread) by herself to take to the church. She does this on her own volition and not as a representative of the movement. Other Hindu nationalists are critical and argue that she should be helping Hindus, not Christians. Her response is that Hindus have plenty of people to help them while the elderly and infirm at the church have no one else.

8. The 1560–1812 Goan inquisition under Portuguese rule was directed at those considered "Christian heretics" as well as non-Christians including Hindus (Kim 2005:161).

9. In recent years, much has been written about the power of collective memory to mobilize communities for collective action (Oberoi 1992; Swedenberg 1995; Agarwal 1995). Ted Swedenberg has shown how historical memories become important justifications for action against the Israelis and for the consolidation of the Palestinian nation. Purshottam Agarwal, analyzing the mass rape of Muslim women in Surat at the hands of Hindu men, asserts that this has to be understood in the context of communal appropriation of public memory accompanied by the construction of history to justify such violence as political retribution (1995: 31–32).

10. See, for instance, P. Chatterjee 1989; Natarajan 1994; Yuval-Davis and Anthias 1989; Yuval-Davis 1997.

11. According to the 2001 census, 2.3 percent of the total population of India were Christian. The percentage of Christians, and therefore their visibility and political clout, varies considerably by state: Christians are 19 percent of the population of Kerala but in the majority in some northeastern states like Mizoram (87%), Meghalaya (70.3%), and Nagaland (90%). However, the population of Kerala is significantly higher than those of these northeastern states; the total number of Christians in Kerala is 6,057,427, compared to Meghalaya, 1,628,986; Nagaland, 1,790,349; and Mizoram, 772,809. The Christian population was 0.6 percent in Gujarat, where anti-Christian violence occurred in 1998–99; 2.4 percent in Orissa, where Graham Staines was murdered; and 0.9 percent in Delhi, where most of those I worked with resided (2001 census figures at http://www.censusindia.net/religiondata/.

12. Aditya is referring to those killed as a result of the various violent insurgencies in the northeastern states of Assam, Tripura, Nagaland, Manipur, and Meghalaya. This violence often endangers the lives of civilians because of the tactics used, including bombing trains and buses.

Chapter 3. Violent Dharma

Epigraph: Speech recorded at the Sri Mad Bhagavad Gita Gyan Yagya on August 22nd, 1999 by the author.

1. I use the real names of Sadhvi Rithambara, Sadhvi Shiva Saraswati, and Sadhvi Kamlesh Bharati in this chapter when analyzing speeches at public events.

2. In the speeches I recorded, Hindu nationalist female renouncers variously used *dharma* to refer to the moral order of the world, to duty, and to Hinduism in general. I have specified the meaning when it is not clear from the context.

3. It is important to recognize that renouncers are supposed to have transcended all identities—including gender. However, as Meena Khandelwal 2004 has argued, the social world often continues to view renouncers as having gender, caste, and other social identities. As I suggest later in this chapter, the dual perception of *sadhvis* as renouncers *and* women is crucial to their role in Hindu nationalist politics.

4. For excellent discussions of agency see Ahearn 2001 and Mahmood 2005.

5. Khandelwal relates the story of Queen Chudala who runs a kingdom and resides in wealth, power, and luxury. Yet, she is so detached from these as well as from the symbols of renunciation (living alone and avoiding possessions, luxuries, etc.) that she has already attained liberation (2004: 40–42).

6. It is important to note that not all renouncers would accept political activity as *seva*.

7. See, for instance, P. Chatterjee 1986; Minor 1986: 4; Flood 1996: 124.

8. See Yuval-Davis 1997; Menon and Bhasin 1998.

9. *Sindhur* is the red powder married women wear on their heads to symbolize their status. I have glossed *sindhuri* nights as "married nights" because Rithambara is referring to nights shared with their husbands as married women.

10. Purnima Mankekar has demonstrated how similar images of female sacrifice in popular culture appeal to female television viewers in India (Mankekar 1999: 259–88).

11. Khandelwal 2004 discusses the strategic use of femininity by female renouncers she worked with.

12. Islamabad, Rawalpindi, and Karachi are cities in Pakistan. Islamabad is the capital of Pakistan.

13. Mohammad Ali Jinnah was the leader of the Muslim League and of the Pakistan movement in colonial India. The movement sought to establish Pakistan as a separate state for Muslims, an idea that came to fruition on August 14, 1947.

14. Rithambara is referring to the conflict between India and Pakistan over the disputed territories of Kashmir.

15. At the time, Nawaz Sharif was prime minister of Pakistan. Later that year he was deposed in a coup staged by General Pervez Musharraf.

16. Gandhari is the wife of the blind king Dhritarashtra who is the father of the Kauravas.

17. In the Gita Krishna tells Arjuna, "Whatever you do—what you take, what you offer, what you give, what penances you perform—do as an offering to me Arjuna" (Bhagavad Gita 9.27).

18. Four stages in the life of all twice-born (upper-caste) men as laid out around the first century C.E. in the *Dharmashastras* include: *brahmacharya* (student), *grhasta* (householder), *vanaprastha* (forest dweller), *sanyasa* (renouncer).

19. She used the word "jungle" in her speech.

20. The *sudarshan chakra* is a sacred weapon associated with Vishnu. It is used by Krishna, an incarnation of Vishnu, in the Mahabharata.

21. Vaishnavas are devotees of the Hindu deity Vishnu. Krishna, is one of Vishnu's ten incarnations.

22. Krishna's sacred weapon, the *sudarshan chakra*, symbolizes the weapons that are necessary for this historical moment.

23. These idols "miraculously" appeared inside the mosque one night in 1949 and were widely seen by many in the movement as a divine sign that indeed the mosque stood on the birthplace of Ram. Anand Patwardhan, in his film *In the Name of God (Ram ke Nam* 1992), has interesting footage in which he interviews the Hindu priest attending to the idols inside the mosque, who admits to having been involved in planting them there in 1949.

24. Women VHP members I spoke to contradicted this statement by claiming to have been in Ayodhya at the time of the destruction of the mosque.

25. Ram uses an army of monkeys to destroy the demon king Ravana. Also, Hanuman, the monkey-god who plays a critical role in the defeat of Ravana, is said to be one of Ram's greatest devotees. The suggestion is that many associated the sight of monkeys on the roof of the mosque with a religious sign from god that indeed this was Ram's birthplace.

Chapter 4. Benevolent Hindus

1. The youngest woman was seventeen years old; many were under twenty-one. The lowest weight I recorded for a pregnant woman was 35 kg (77.4 lbs); many were under 40 kg (88.4 lbs).

2. Although she was speaking to me in Hindi she used the English word.

3. CBSE is an acronym for the Central Board for Secondary Education, a curriculum used in schools run by the national government throughout the country.

4. Resettlement colonies were created in an attempt to get rid of the slums in Delhi. Slum dwellers were relocated to these colonies, a classic example of spatialized class practices (see Fernandes 2006: 139). These efforts are particularly associated with Indira Gandhi's attempts to "clean up" the city prior to India's hosting of the Asian Games in Delhi.

5. Salam means peace in Arabic and Urdu and is used as a form of greeting by Muslims and others in India.

6. I am grateful to an anonymous reviewer for this detail. See also McGee 2004: 346.

7. The term *devrani* literally refers to the wife of one's husband's younger brother.

8. For more on the contradictory pulls of marriage and *bhakti* see Gold 1994; Harlan 1995; Kinsley 1981.

9. A *kurta* is a long tunic worn over pants in many parts of India by both men and women. A *dhoti* is a long piece of cloth that is wrapped around the waist and worn by men.

10. "Jai Shri Ram" was also used by members of the VHP to greet each other on an everyday basis. Thus instead of saying "hello" or "good morning" they would say "Jai Shri Ram" and would expect the same in response.

11. A Gurudwara is a Sikh house of worship.

12. I suspect this may have been the *aditya hridayam*, a powerful mantra given to Ram by Sage Agastya.

13. This is a North Indian dress consisting of a long tunic (*kurta*) worn over baggy pants.

14. *Rakhis* are colorful strings tied by sisters on their brothers' wrists to ask for their protection during the annual Hindu festival called Raksha Bandhan. In an interesting reinterpretation of this ritual, Durga Vahini and Matri Shakti women organized an event at the army hospital in Janakpuri to tie lotus shaped *rakhis* on the wrists of soldiers wounded at Kargil. The lotus is the electoral symbol of the BJP, which had just kicked off its 1999 election campaign.

15. My thoughts on the relationship between the state and the grassroots are informed by Hansen and Stepputat 2001; Fuller and Harris 2000; Gupta 1995.

Chapter 5. Fun, Games, and Deadly Politics

1. In the longer camps they include martial arts training as well as instruction in fighting with *lathis* (bamboo poles) and daggers.

2. *Antakshri* is a well-known game played throughout India, usually using songs from Hindi films. In the game, one team sings a few lines from a song. The other team then has to sing a song starting with the last letter of the previous song. A team loses if unable to think of a song starting with the letter assigned by the other team. During the camp we had to play *antakshri* using patriotic songs rather than Hindi film songs.

3. I was not permitted to use a tape recorder at the camp, so both excerpts are reconstructions based on jottings during the lectures.

4. The term Eve-teasing is used throughout India to refer to the harassment of women by men in the public realm. It can include catcalls and whistling but also includes lewd gestures, lewd comments and actual physical advances.

5. This is a rough translation of the Hindi verse recited by Rajeshji: Prachin ho ki navin, chodo rudiya jo ho buri / Bankar viveki tum dikhao, hans jaisi chaturi / Prachin batain hi bhali hain, yuh vichar alik hain / Jaisi avastha ho jahan, vaisi vyavastha thik hain

6. While her speech was delivered in Hindi she used the English word "sex."

7. Asha Sharma is head of the Delhi wing of the Rashtra Sevika Samiti. Connaught Place is a major commercial district in central Delhi.

8. One lakh is one hundred thousand.

9. See Sutton-Smith 1997: 106; Appadurai 1997; Alter 1994; Narayan 1989.

10. Various Hindu nationalist groups have criticized and demonstrated against Valentine's Day. For instance, in February 2001, the Shiv Sena led a raid into greeting card shops in Mumbai to destroy the Valentine's Day cards.

11. Hindu jage, desh jage, Svabhiman sankalp jage (2) / Satya dharma ki vijay sunishchit/ Bandhu bandhu me pyar jage/ Ek lahu ki dhar jage/ Ek desh hain, ek sanskriti (2) / Sva kartavya vichar jage.

12. The game was referred to by the English word "Tanks."

13. Two readers have suggested that this game is similar to "Duck Duck Goose" played in the United States.

14. As one reader has suggested, this game is similar to musical chairs.

15. Several theorists have argued that play provides a venue for challenging the hierarchies in everyday life, overturning or subverting power relationships, and, particularly for children, challenging the power adults exert over them

(see, e.g., McMahon and Sutton-Smith 1995; Sutton-Smith 1995; Goldstein 1995).

16. *Makar sankranti* is a harvest festival celebrated in many parts of North India. Harvest festivals are celebrated at the same time in other parts of India, such as *pongal* in Tamil Nadu and Andhra Pradesh and *lohri* in Punjab.

Chapter 6. Acceptable Transgressions

1. Jamuna and her husband are *jats,* a land-owning caste, and are from Haryana, a state that borders Delhi. According to one study of Haryanavi *jats* in Delhi, although women used to engage in agricultural labor in their village contexts, in the urban setting their mobility is often highly restricted to maintain purity and morality, they have limited education and decision-making power, and are often "raised conservatively" so that they can be married to families in rural Haryana (Khanna 2001: 46–49, 51).

2. See also T. Sarkar 1995, 1998; Bacchetta 1996, 2004; A. Basu 1995.

3. The book is available online at http://www.hindubooks.org/dynamic/ modules.php?name = Content&pa = showpage&pid = 1418&page = 2, from which the references below are taken. The handbook, used to teach new members about the organization, was among the many movement volumes Payal studied closely to gain seniority in the Samiti.

4. This quote can be found at the online version of this book at http:// www.hindubooks.org/dynamic/modules.php?name = Content&pa = showpage &pid = 1418&page = 2.

5. See, for instance, Werbner 1999; Yuval-Davis and Werbner 1999; Gonzalez and Kampwirth 2001; Kampwirth 2001; Yuval-Davis 1997.

6. In 1999 there was much debate within the BJP on the subject of reservations because the women were asking for a 33 percent reservation of seats and offices for women. This was part of a larger debate that was occurring within all political parties.

7. There is a wealth of feminist scholarship on the ways women subvert and resist dominant structures and discourses in contexts where public challenge could be detrimental (Abu-Lughod 1986; Radner 1993; Lamb 2000; Raheja and Gold 1994). Many of these build on James Scott's (1990) conceptualization of "hidden transcripts" and "everyday forms of resistance."

8. See Raheja and Gold 1994; Abu-Lughod 1986; Lamb 2000.

9. Anthropologists who have used the life history method have shown that our interlocutors often have their own agendas that inflect their words and shape their interactions with us (see Buechler and Buechler 1996; Keesing 1983; Lamb 2001).

10. Some middle-class Hindu nationalist activists conflated class with moral status in conversations with me. On one occasion Neera blamed the dual-career household for the degeneration of Hindu culture: "How can a child learn her culture if she is left with the *ayah* (nanny)? She will obviously learn the culture of the *gali* (street)." Asserting that only a mother can teach her child good values she asked, "how can you expect a child who has spent more time with the servants to learn anything about her culture?"

11. The Indian National Congress dominated the independence movement against the British and was transformed into the Congress Party after independence.

Glossary

adivasi (*ādivasi*): indigenous group
Akhand Bharat (*Akhand Bhārat*): undivided India
antakshri (*antākshri*): Indian game using songs
arti (*ārtī*): worship
ashramas (*āśramas*): the four stages of life for a Hindu
atma (*ātmā*): self
balvadi (*bālvādi*): children's day care
baniya (*baniyā*): merchant, trader caste
bansuri (*bāṇsurī*): flute
baudhik (*bauddhik*): intellectual
bazaar (*bāzār*): market
bhajan: devotional song
bhajan mandali (*bhajan maṇḍali*): devotional song session
bhakt: devotee
bhakti: devotion
Bharat (*Bhārat*): India
brahman: ultimate reality
brahmin (*brāhman*): priestly class
chamar (*chamār*): leatherworking caste once considered "untouchable" by upper caste Hindus
charcha (*ćarćā*): discussion
dari (*darī*): cotton rug
desh bhakt (*deś bhakt*): patriot
dharma: sacred duty, moral order, religion
dharna (*dharnā*): sit-in
dupatta (*dupaṭṭā*): scarf
ekal vidyalaya (*ekal vidyālay*): one-teacher school
ghuspeti (*ghus paiṭhi*): intruder
guru: teacher
havan: fire sacrifice
Hindutva: Hinduness
insan (*insān/insāni*): human
jati (*jāti*): caste
jhuggi: makeshift hut
kartritva (*kartṛitva*): agency, government
karyalaya (*kāryālaya*): office
karyavahika (*kāryavāhika*): worker
kirtan (*kīrtan*): devotional song session
kshatriya: warrior class
kunwari (*kuṇwārī*): virgin, unmarried

lakh (*lākh*): hundred thousand
lathi (*lāṭhī*): bamboo staff
mandir: temple
mantra: hymn
masjid: mosque
matritva (*mātṛtva*): enlightened motherhood
moksha (*moksh*): liberation from *samsara*
namaste: greeting
netritva (*netṛtva*): leadership
parda: veil
parivar (*parivār*): family
paschimi sabhyata (*paśćimī sabhyatā*): western manners; westernization
pativrata (*pativratā*): woman who worships her husband
pracharak (*praćārak*): unmarried, celibate male volunteer
pracharika (*praćārika*): unmarried, celibate female volunteer
pradarshan (*pradarśan*): demonstration/ agitation
prasad (*prasād*): blessed food
pravachan (*pravacan*): religious lecture
puja (*pūjā*): worship
puri-aloo (*pūrī-ālū*): fried bread and potatoes
raj (*rāj*): rule
rajya (*rājya*): kingdom
raksha (*rakshā*): safety
rashtra (*rāshṭra*): nation
rath yatra (*rath yātrā*): chariot procession
sadhvi (*sādhvī*): female renouncer
saheli (*sahelī*): female friend
samsara (*samsāra*): cycle of birth, death, and rebirth, the world
sansar (*sansār*): the world
sanskar (*saṇskār*): to polish or perfect
sati (*satī*): widow burning
seva (*sevā*): service
shakha (*śākhā*): branch
shakti, (*śakti*): female creative principle, strength
shalwar kamiz (*shalwār qamiṣ*): Long tunic worn over loose pants
sharirik (*śārīrik*): physical
shivir (*śivir*): camp
shloka (*śloka*): Sanskrit verse
shuddhi (*śuddhi*): purification
stri dharma (*strī dharma*): woman's duty
sudarshan chakra (*sudarśan ćakra*): Krishna's sacred weapon
suraksha (*suraksha*): security
surya namaskar (*sūrya namaskār*): salutation to the sun
trishul: trident
vaishya (*vaiśya*): merchant, trader class
Vaishnava: devotee of the Hindu deity Vishnu
vanavasi (*vana-vāsī*): forest dweller
varna (*varṇa*): social class
yajna: fire sacrifice

Bibliography

Abu-Lughod, Lila
1986   *Veiled Sentiments: Honor and Poetry in a Bedouin Society*. Berkeley: University of California Press.
Advani, Lal Krishna
2005a   Interview with Hamid Mir, Geo TV.
2005b   Speech Delivered at Karachi Council on Foreign Relations, Economic Affairs, & Law.
Agarwal, Purshottam
1995   Surat, Sarvarkar and Draupadi: Legitimizing Rape as a Political Weapon. In *Women and the Hindu Right: A Collection of Essays*, ed. Tanika Sarkar and Urvashi Butalia. 29–57. New Delhi: Kali for Women.
Ahearn, Laura M
2001   Language and Agency. *Annual Review of Anthropology* 30: 109–37.
Alonso, Ana Maria
1988   The Effects of Truth: Representations of the Past and the Imagining of Community. *Journal of Historical Sociology* 1(1): 33–57.
1994   The Politics of Space, Time, and Substance: State Formation, Nationalism, and Ethnicity. *Annual Review of Anthropology* 23: 379–405.
Alter, Joseph
1994   Somatic Nationalism: Indian Wrestling and Militant Hinduism. *Modern Asian Studies* 28 (3): 557–88.
Anderson, Benedict
1983   *Imagined Communities: Reflections on the Origin and Spread of Nationalism*. London: Verso.
Appadurai, Arjun
1997   *Modernity at Large: Cultural Dimensions of Globalization*. New Delhi: Oxford University Press.
2006   *Fear of Small Numbers: An Essay on the Geography of Anger*. Durham, N.C.: Duke University Press.
Asad, Talal
1983   Anthropological Conceptions of Religion: Reflections on Geertz. *Man* 18 (2): 237–59.
1997   Europe Against Islam: Islam in Europe. *Muslim World* 87: 183–95.
Baber, Zaheer
2000   Religious Nationalism, Violence and the Hindutva Movement in India. *Dialectical Anthropology* 25: 61–76.
Bacchetta, Paola
1994   "All Our Goddesses Are Armed": Religion, Resistance and Revenge in the Life of a Militant Hindu Nationalist Woman. In *Against All Odds: Essays on Women, Religion and Development from India and Pakistan*, ed.

Kamla Bhasin, Ritu Menon, and Nighat Said Khan. 132–56. New Delhi: Kali for Women.

1996   Hindu Nationalist Women as Ideologues: The Sangh, the Samiti and Differential Concepts of the Hindu Nation. In *Embodied Violence: Communalising Women's Sexuality in South Asia*, ed. Kumari Jayawardena and Malathi de Alwis. 126–67. New Delhi: Kali for Women.

2002   Hindu Nationalist Women Imagine Spatialities/ Imagine Themselves: Reflections on Gender-Supplemental-Agency. In *Right-Wing Women: From Conservatives to Extremists Around the World*, ed. Paola Bacchetta and Margaret Power. 43–56. New York: Routledge.

2004   *Gender in the Hindu Nation: RSS Women as Ideologues*. New Delhi: Women Unlimited.

Bacchetta, Paola and Margaret Power
2002   Introduction. In *Right-Wing Women: From Conservatives to Extremists Around the World*, ed. Paola Bacchetta and Margaret Power. 1–15. New York: Routledge.

Bakhtin, Mikhail
1981   *The Dialogic Imagination: Four Essays*. Trans. Michael Holquist. Austin: University of Texas Press.

Banerjee, Sikata
1995   Hindu Nationalism and the Construction of Women: The Shiv Sena Organizes Women in Bombay. In *Women and the Hindu Right: A Collection of Essays*, ed. Tanika Sarkar and Urvashi Butalia. 216–32. New Delhi: Kali for Women.

2000   *Warriors in Politics: Hindu Nationalism, Violence, and the Shiv Sena in India*. Boulder, Colo.: Westview Press.

2005   *Make Me a Man! Masculinity, Hinduism, and Nationalism in India*. Albany: State University of New York Press.

Barsamian, David
2000   *Eqbal Ahmad: Confronting Empire: Interviews with David Barsamian*. Cambridge, Mass.: South End Press.

Basu, Amrita
1995   Feminism Inverted: The Gendered Imagery and Real Women of Hindu Nationalism. In *Women and the Hindu Right: A Collection of Essays*, ed. Tanika Sarkar and Urvashi Butalia. 158–80. New Delhi: Kali for Women.

1996   Mass Mobilization or Elite Conspiracy? The Puzzle of Hindu Nationalism. In *Contesting the Nation: Religion, Community, and the Politics of Democracy in India*, ed. David Ludden. 55–80. Philadelphia: University of Pennsylvania Press.

1998   Hindu Women's Activism in India and the Questions It Raises. In *Appropriating Gender: Women's Activism and Politicized Religion in South Asia*, ed. Patricia Jeffery and Amrita Basu. 1–14. New York: Routledge.

Basu, Amrita and Srirupa Roy
2007   Beyond Exceptionalism: Violence and Democracy in India. In *Violence and Democracy in India*, ed. Amrita Basu and Srirupa Roy. 1–35. Calcutta: Seagull Books.

Basu, Tapan, Pradip Datta, Sumit Sarkar, Tanika Sarkar, and Sambuddha Sen
1993   *Khaki Shorts and Saffron Flags: A Critique of the Hindu Right*. Tracts for the Times 1. New Delhi: Orient Longman.

Bauman, Richard
1977   *Verbal Art as Performance*. Rowley, Mass.: Newbury House.

Behar, Ruth
1993   *Translated Woman: Crossing the Border with Esperanza's Story*. Boston: Beacon Press.
Bernard, H. Russell
1994   *Research Methods in Anthropology: Qualitative and Quantitative Approaches*. Thousand Oaks, Calif.: Sage.
Bénéï, Véronique
2000   Teaching Nationalism in Maharashtra Schools. In *The Everyday State and Society in Modern India*, ed. C. J. Fuller and Véronique Bénéï. 194–221. New Delhi: Social Science Press.
Bhatt, Chetan
2001   *Hindu Nationalism: Origins, Ideologies, and Modern Myths*. Oxford: Berg Press.
Blee, Kathleen M.
2002a   *Inside Organized Racism: Women in the Hate Movement*. Berkeley: University of California Press.
2002b   The Gendered Organization of Hate: Women in the U.S. Ku Klux Klan. In *Right Wing Women: From Conservatives to Extremists Around the World*, ed. Paola Bacchetta and Margaret Power. 101–14. New York: Routledge.
Bloch, Maurice
1974   Symbols, Song, Dance and Features of Articulation: Is Religion an Extreme Form of Traditional Authority? *European Journal of Sociology* 15: 55–81.
Bose, Sugata and Ayesha Jalal
1999   *Modern South Asia: History, Culture, Political, Economy*. London: Routledge.
Brass, Paul
1994   *The Politics of India Since Independence*. 2nd ed. New Cambridge History of India IV.1. Cambridge: Cambridge University Press.
Brow, James
1996   *Demons and Development: The Struggle for Community in a Sri Lankan Village*. New York: Oxford University Press.
Buechler, Hans and Judith-Marie Buechler
1996   *The World of Sofia Velasquez: The Life of a Bolivian Market Vendor*. New York: Columbia University Press.
Butalia, Urvashi
1998   *The Other Side of Silence: Voices from the Partition of India*. New Delhi: Penguin.
Butler, Judith
1993   *Bodies That Matter: On the Discursive Limits of "Sex"*. New York: Routledge.
1997   Further Reflections on Conversations of Our Time. *Diacritics* 27 (1): 13–15.
1999   *Gender Trouble: Feminism and the Subversion of Identity*. New York: Routledge.
2004   *Precarious Life: The Powers of Mourning and Violence*. London: Verso.
Chakrabarty, Dipesh
1997   The Time of History and the Times of Gods. In *The Politics of Culture in the Shadow of Capital*, ed. Lisa Lowe and David Lloyd. 35–60. Durham, N.C.: Duke University Press.
Chatterjee, Partha
1986   *Nationalist Thought and the Colonial World: A Derivative Discourse*. Minneapolis: University of Minnesota Press.
1989   Colonialism, Nationalism, and Colonized Women: The Contest in India. *American Ethnologist* 16 (4): 622–33.

1993   *The Nation and Its Fragments: Colonial and Postcolonial Histories.* New Delhi: Oxford University Press.

Clifford, James
1988   On Ethnographic Authority. In *The Predicament of Culture: Twentieth-Century Ethnography, Literature and Art.* 21–54. Cambridge, Mass.: Harvard University Press.

Chatterji, Angana P.
2004   The Biopolitics of Hindu Nationalism: Mournings. *Cultural Dynamics* 16 (2/3): 319–72.

Clifford, James and George E. Marcus
1986   *Writing Culture: The Poetics and Politics of Ethnography.* Berkeley: University of California Press.

Cockburn, Cynthia
2004   The Continuum of Violence: A Gender Perspective on War and Peace. In *Sites of Violence: Gender and Conflict Zones,* ed. Wenona Mary Giles and Jennifer Hyndman. 24–44. Berkeley: University of California Press.

Cohn, Bernard S.
1988   The Census, Social Structure and Objectification in South Asia. In Bernard S. Cohn, *An Anthropologist Among Historians and Other Essays.* New Delhi: Oxford University Press.

Comaroff, Jean
1983   *Body of Power, Spirit of Resistance: The Culture and History of a South African People.* Chicago: University of Chicago Press.

Comaroff, Jean and John Comaroff
1991   *Of Revelation and Revolution.* Vol. 1, *Christianity, Colonialism, and Consciousness in South Africa.* Chicago: University of Chicago Press.

Courtright, Paul B.
1995   Sati, Sacrifice, and Marriage: The Modernity of Tradition. In *From the Margins of Hindu Marriage: Essays on Gender, Religion, and Culture,* ed. Lindsey Harlan and Paul B. Courtright. 184–203. New York: Oxford University Press.

Das, Veena
2007   *Life and Words: Violence and the Descent into the Ordinary.* Berkeley: University of California Press.

Davis, Richard H.
1995   Introduction: A Brief History of Religions in India. In *Religions of India in Practice,* ed. Donald S. Lopez. 3–54. Princeton, N.J.: Princeton University Press.

1996   The Iconography of Rama's Chariot. In *Contesting the Nation: Religion, Community, and the Politics of Democracy in India,* ed. David Ludden. 27–54. Philadelphia: University of Pennsylvania Press.

Deeb, Lara
2006   *An Enchanted Modern: Gender and Public Piety in Shi'i Lebanon.* Princeton, N.J.: Princeton University Press.

Dempsey, Corinne
2001   *Kerala Christian Sainthood: Collisions of Culture and Worldview in South India.* New York: Oxford University Press.

Derrida, Jacques
1988   Signature, Event, Context. In Derrida, *Limited Inc,* ed. Gerald Graff. Evanston, Ill.: Northwestern University Press.

Dirks, Nicholas B
1992   Castes of Mind. In *Imperial Fantasies and Postcolonial Histories.* Representations 37. 56–78. Berkeley: University of California Press.
1996   The Conversion of Caste: Location, Translation, and Appropriation. In *Conversion to Modernities: The Globalization of Christianity*, ed. Peter van der Veer. 115–36. New York: Routledge.
Douglas, Mary
1966   *Purity and Danger: An Analysis of Concepts of Pollution and Taboo.* New York: Praeger.
Dow, Alexander
1973 [1770]   *The History of Hindostan.* New Delhi: Today and Tomorrow's Printers and Publishers.
Eager, Paige Whaley
2008   *From Freedom Fighters to Terrorists: Women and Political Violence.* Aldershot: Ashgate.
Eaton, Richard
1984   Conversion to Christianity Among the Nagas: 1876–1971. *Indian Economic and Social History Review* 21 (1): 17–19.
1993   *The Rise of Islam and the Bengal Frontier, 1204–1760.* Berkeley: University of California Press.
Elder, Joseph
1990   Some Roots and Branches of Hindu Monasticism. In *Monastic Life in the Christian and Hindu Traditions: A Comparative Study*, ed. Austin B. Creel and Vasudha Narayanan. 1–36. Lewiston, N.Y.: Edwin Mellen.
Farmer, Paul
2005   *Pathologies of Power: Health, Human Rights, and the New War on the Poor.* Berkeley: University of California Press.
Ferguson, James
1990   *The Anti-Politics Machine: Development, Depoliticization, and Bureaucratic Power in Lesotho.* Cambridge: Cambridge University Press.
Ferguson, James and Akhil Gupta
1992   Beyond "Culture": Space, Identity, and the Politics of Difference. *Cultural Anthropology* 7 (1): 6–24.
2002   Spatializing States: Toward an Ethnography of Neoliberal Governmentality. *American Ethnologist* 29 (4): 981–1002.
Fernandes, Leela
2006   *India's New Middle Class: Democratic Politics in an Era of Economic Reform.* Minneapolis: University of Minnesota Press.
Flood, Gavin
1996   *An Introduction to Hinduism.* Cambridge: Cambridge University Press.
Foucault, Michel
1977   Nietzsche, Genealogy, History. In *Language, Counter-Memory, Practice: Selected Essays and Interviews.* Ed. Donald F. Bouchard, trans. Donald F. Bouchard and Sherry Simon. Ithaca, N.Y.: Cornell University Press.
1980a   Two Lectures. In *Power/Knowledge: Selected Interviews and Other Writings, 1972–77.* Ed. Colin Gordon, trans. Colin Gordon et al. 78–108. New York: Pantheon.
1980b   *The History of Sexuality.* Vol. 1, *An Introduction.* Trans. Robert Hurley. New York: Vintage.
1988   Technologies of the Self. In *Technologies of the Self: A Seminar with Michel Foucault.* Ed. Luther H. Martin, Huck Gutman, and Patrick H. Hutton. Amherst: University of Massachussetts Press.

2003   *The Essential Foucault.* Ed. Paul Rabinow and Nikolas Rose. New York: New Press.

Fox, Richard G.

1990a   Introduction. In *Nationalist Ideologies and the Production of National Cultures,* ed. Richard Fox. 1–14. American Ethnological Society Monograph Series 2. Washington, D.C.: American Anthropological Association.

1990b   Hindu Nationalism in the Making, or the Rise of the Hindian. In *Nationalist Ideologies and the Production of National Cultures,* ed. Richard G. Fox. 63–79. American Ethnological Society Monograph Series 2. Washington, D.C.: American Anthropological Association.

1996   Gandhi and Feminized Nationalism in India. In *Women Out of Place: The Gender of Agency and the Race of Nationality,* ed. Brackette F. Williams. New York: Routledge.

Fuller, C. J.

1992   *The Camphor Flame: Popular Hinduism and Society in India.* Princeton, N.J.: Princeton University Press.

Ganguly, Sumit

2001   *Conflict Unending: India-Pakistan Tensions Since 1947.* New York: Columbia University Press.

Ghosh, Bishnupriya

2002   Queering Hindutva: Unruly Bodies and Pleasures in Sadhavi Rithambara's Performances. *In Right Wing Women: From Conservatives to Extremists Around the World,* ed. Paola Bacchetta and Margaret Power. 259–72. New York: Routledge.

Ghosh, Pika

2003   Unrolling a Narrative Scroll: Artistic Practice and Identity in Late Nineteenth Century Bengal. *Journal of Asian Studies* 62 (3): 835–71.

Giles, Wenona and Jennifer Hyndman

2004   New Directions for Feminist Research and Politics. In *Sites of Violence: Gender and Conflict Zones,* ed. Wenona Giles and Jennifer Hyndman. 301–15. Berkeley: University of California Press.

Gokhale, Nithin and Ajith Pillai

1999   The War That Should Never Have Been. Cover Story. *Outlook Magazine* (September 6): 20–27.

Gold, Ann Grodzins

1992   *A Carnival of Parting: The Tales of King Bharthari and King Gopi Chand as Sung and Told by Madhu Natisar Nath of Ghatiyali, Rajasthan.* Berkeley: University of California Press.

1994   Devotional Power or Dangerous Magic? The Jungli Rani's Case. In *Listen to the Heron's Words: Reimagining Gender and Kinship in North India,* ed. Gloria Goodwin Raheja and Ann Grodzins Gold. 149–63. Berkeley: University of California Press.

2001   Shared Blessings as Ethnographic Practice. *Method and Theory in the Study of Religion* 13 (1): 34–49.

Gold, Ann Grodzins and Bhoju Ram Gujar

2002   *In the Time of Trees and Sorrows: Nature, Power and Memory in Rajasthan.* Durham, N.C.: Duke University Press.

Goldstein, Jeffrey

1995   Aggressive Toy Play. In *The Future of Play Theory,* ed. Anthony D. Pellegrini. 127–50. Albany: State University of New York Press.

Gonzalez, Victoria and Karen Kampwirth

2001   Introduction. In *Radical Women in Latin America: Left and Right,* ed. Victoria Gonzalez and Karen Kampwirth. 1–28. University Park: Pennsylvania State University Press.

Goodwin, Marjorie H.
1990   *He-Said-She-Said: Talk as Social Organization Among Black Children.* Bloomington: Indiana University Press.

Gopal, Sarvepalli
1991   *Anatomy of a Confrontation: The Babri Masjid-Ramjanmabhumi Issue.* New Delhi: Viking.

Gordon, Stewart
1993   *The Marathas 1600–1818.* Vol. 4. London: Cambridge University Press.
1994   *Marathas, Marauders, and State Formation in Eighteenth Century India.* New Delhi: Oxford University Press.

Gourevitch, Phillip
1998   *We Wish to Inform You That Tomorrow We Will Be Killed with Our Families: Stories from Rwanda.* New York: Picador.

Gourgouris, Stathis
1996   *Dream Nation: Enlightenment, Colonization, and the Institution of Modern Greece.* Stanford, Calif.: Stanford University Press.

Gramsci, Antonio
1971   *Selections from the Prison Notebooks.* London: Lawrence and Wishart.

Grewal, O. P. and K. L. Tuteja
1990   Communalism and Fundamentalism: A Dangerous Form of Anti-Democratic Politics. *Economic and Political Weekly* 25 (47), November 24, 1990.

Groen, Janny and Annieke Kranenberg
        Strijdsters van Allah: Radicale moslima's en het Hofstadnetwerk (Fighters of Allah: Radical Muslim Women and the Hofstad Network). Philadelphia: University of Pennsylvania Press. 2010.

Guha, Ranajit
1983   *Elementary Aspects of Peasant Insurgency in Colonial India.* Delhi: Oxford University Press.
1989   Dominance Without Hegemony and Its Historiography. *Subaltern Studies: Writings on South Asian History and Society* 6: 210–309. Delhi: Oxford University Press.

Gupta, Akhil
1995   Blurred Boundaries: The Discourse of Corruption, the Culture of Politics, and the Imagined State. *American Ethnologist* 22 (2): 375–402.
1998   *Postcolonial Developments: Agriculture in the Making of Modern India.* Durham, N.C.: Duke University Press.
2001   Governing Population: The Integrated Child Development Services Program in India. In *States of Imagination: Ethnographic Explorations of the Postcolonial State,* ed. Thomas Blom Hansen and Finn Stepputat. 65–97. Durham, N.C.: Duke University Press.

Gupta, Charu
2002   *Sexuality, Obscenity, and Community: Women, Muslims, and the Hindu Public in Colonial India.* New York: Palgrave Macmillan.

Habermas, Jürgen
1991   *The Structural Transformation of the Public Sphere: An Inquiry into a Category of Bourgeois Society.* Cambridge, Mass.: MIT Press.

Halbwachs, Maurice
1980   *The Collective Memory.* Trans. Francis J. Ditter, Jr., and Vida Yazdi Ditter. New York: Harper & Row.

Hall, Stuart
1980   Encoding/Decoding. In *Culture, Media, Language: Working Papers in Cultural Studies, 1972–79*, ed. Stuart Hall et al. London: Routledge with Centre for Contemporary Cultural Studies, University of Birmingham.
1985   Signification, Representation, Ideology: Althusser and the Post-Structuralist Debates. *Critical Studies in Mass Communication* 2 (2): 91–115.
Hancock, Mary
1999   *Womanhood in the Making: Domestic Ritual and Public Culture in Urban South India.* Boulder, Colo.: Westview Press.
Handler, Richard
1988   *Nationalism and the Politics of Culture in Quebec.* Madison: University of Wisconsin Press.
Hansen, Thomas Blom
1999   *The Saffron Wave: Democracy and Hindu Nationalism in Modern India.* New Delhi: Oxford University Press.
2001   *Wages of Violence: Naming and Identity in Postcolonial Bombay.* Princeton, N.J.: Princeton University Press.
2005   Sovereigns Beyond the State: On Legality and Authority in Urban India. In *Sovereign Bodies: Citizens, Migrants, and States in the Postcolonial World*, ed. Thomas Blom Hansen and Finn Stepputat. 169–91. Princeton, N.J.: Princeton University Press.
Harlan, Lindsey
1995   Abandoning Shame: Mira and the Margins of Marriage. In *From the Margins of Hindu Marriage: Essays on Gender, Religion, and Culture*, ed. Lindsey Harlan and Paul B. Courtright. 204–27. New York: Oxford University Press.
Hasan, Zoya
1993   Communalism, State Policy, and the Question of Women's Rights in Contemporary India. *Bulletin of Concerned Asian Scholars* 25 (4): 5–15.
1994   *Forging Identities: Gender, Communities and the State.* New Delhi: Kali for Women.
1996   Communal Mobilization and Changing Majority in Uttar Pradesh. In *Contesting the Nation: Religion, Community, and the Politics of Democracy in India*, ed. David Ludden. 81–97. Philadelphia: University of Pennsylvania Press.
Hawley, John Stratton
1994   Hinduism: Sati and Its Defenders. *In Fundamentalism and Gender*, ed. John Stratton Hawley. 79–110. New York: Oxford University Press.
Hawley, John Stratton and Mark Juergensmeyer
2004   *Songs of the Saints of India.* New Delhi: Oxford University Press.
Hefner, Robert W.
1993   Introduction: World Building and the Rationality of Conversion. In *Conversion to Christianity: Historical and Anthropological Perspectives on a Great Transformation*, ed. Robert W. Hefner. 3–46. Berkeley: University of California Press.
1998   Multiple Modernities: Christianity, Islam, and Hinduism in a Globalizing Age. *Annual Review of Anthropology* 27: 83–104.
2004   Introduction: Modernity and the Remaking of Muslim Politics. In *Remaking Muslim Politics: Pluralism, Contestation, Democratization*, ed. Robert W. Hefner. 1–36. Princeton, N.J.: Princeton University Press.
2005   Discussant Comments, panel "The Cultural Politics of Religion and

Modernity," organized by Kalyani Devaki Menon and Lisa Knight, Society for the Anthropology of Religion, April 8–11, Vancouver, British Columbia.

Hobsbawm, Eric J.
1983   Introduction: Inventing Traditions. In *The Invention of Tradition*, ed. Eric J. Hobsbawm and Terence O. Ranger. 1–15. New York: Cambridge University Press.

Jaffrelot, Christophe
1999   *The Hindu Nationalist Movement and Indian Politics: 1925 to the 1990s*. New Delhi: Penguin.
2007   The 2002 Pogrom in Gujarat: The Post-9/11 Face of Hindu Nationalist Anti-Muslim Violence. In *Religion and Violence in South Asia: Theory and Practice*, ed. John R. Hinnells and Richard King. 173–92. London: Routledge.

Jamison, Stephanie
1996   *Sacrificed Wife/Sacrificer's Wife: Women, Ritual, and Hospitality in Ancient India*. New York: Oxford University Press.

Jeffery, Patricia and Amrita Basu, eds.
1998   *Appropriating Gender: Women's Activism and Politicized Religion in South Asia*. New York: Routledge.

Jeffery, Patricia and Roger Jeffery
1998   Gender, Community, and the Local State in Bijnor, India. In *Appropriating Gender: Women's Activism and Politicized Religion in South Asia*, ed. Patricia Jeffery and Amrita Basu. 123–42. New York: Routledge.

Juergensmeyer, Mark
2000   *Terror in the Mind of God: The Global Rise of Religious Violence*. New Delhi: Oxford University Press.

Kakar, Sudhir
1996   *The Colours of Violence*. New Delhi: Penguin.

Kampwirth, Karen
2001   Women in the Armed Struggles in Nicaragua: Sandanistas and Contras Compared. In *Radical Women in Latin America: Left and Right*, ed. Victoria Gonzalez and Karen Kampwirth. 79–109. University Park: Pennsylvania State University Press.

Katju, Majari
2003   *Vishva Hindu Parishad and Indian Politics*. New Delhi: Orient Longman.

Keesing, Roger
1983   *Elota's Story: The Life and Times of a Solomon Island's Big Man*. New York: St. Martin's.

Khandelwal, Meena
2004   *Women in Ochre Robes: Gendering Hindu Renunciation*. SUNY Series in Hindu Studies. Albany: State University of New York Press.

Khanna, Sunil K.
2001   Shahri Jat and Dehati Jatni: The Indian Peasant Community in Transition. *Contemporary South Asia* 10 (1): 37–53.

Kim, Sebastian C. H.
2005   *In Search of Identity: Debates on Religious Conversion in India*. New Delhi: Oxford University Press.

Kinsley, David
1981   Devotion as an Alternative to Marriage in the Lives of Some Hindu Women Devotees. In *Tradition and Modernity in Bhakti Movements*, ed. Jayant Lele. Leiden: Brill.

Kumar, Amrita and Prashun Bhaumik, eds.
2002   *Lest We Forget: Gujarat 2002.* New Delhi: World Report with Rupa & Co.
Laclau, Ernesto and Chantal Mouffe
1982   Recasting Marxism: Hegemony and New Political Movements. *Socialist Review* 66 (12:6): 91–113.
1985   *Hegemony and Socialist Strategy: Towards a Radical Democratic Politics.* London: Verso.
Lamb, Sarah
2000   *White Saris and Sweet Mangoes: Gender, Aging and the Body in North India.* Berkeley: University of California Press.
2001   Being a Widow and Other Life Stories: The Interplay Between Lives and Words. *Anthropology and Humanism* 26 (1): 16–34.
Lass, Andrew
1997   The Role of Europe in the Study of Anthropology. *American Anthropologist* 99 (4): 721–23.
Madan, T. N.
1997   *Modern Myths, Locked Minds: Secularism and Fundamentalism in India.* New Delhi: Oxford University Press.
Mahmood, Cynthia Keppley
1996   *Fighting for Faith and Nation: Dialogues with Sikh Militants.* Series in Contemporary Ethnography. Philadelphia: University of Pennsylvania Press.
Mahmood, Saba
2005   *The Politics of Piety: The Islamic Revival and the Feminist Subject.* Princeton, N.J.: Princeton University Press.
Malkki, Liisa H.
1995   *Purity and Exile: Violence, Memory, and National Cosmology Among Hutu Refugees in Tanzania.* Chicago: University of Chicago Press.
Mamdani, Mahmood
2001   *When Victims Become Killers: Colonialism, Nativism, and the Genocide in Rwanda.* Princeton, N.J.: Princeton University Press.
Mander, Harsh
2002   Cry, The Beloved Country: Reflections on the Gujarat Massacre by a Serving IAS Officer. *Outlook Magazine,* March 19, 2002.
Mankekar, Purnima
1999   *Screening Culture, Viewing Politics: An Ethnography of Television, Womanhood and Nation in Postcolonial India.* Durham, N.C.: Duke University Press.
Mascia-Lees, Frances E. and Patricia Sharpe
2000   *Taking a Stand in a Postfeminist World: Toward an Engaged Cultural Criticism.* Albany: State University of New York Press.
Mazumdar, Suchitra
1994   Moving Away from a Secular Vision? Women, Nation and the Construction of Hindu India. In *Identity Politics and Women: Cultural Reassertions and Feminisms in International Perspective,* ed. Valentine M. Mogadham. 243–73. Boulder, Colo.: Westview Press.
McGee, Mary
2004   Samskara. In *The Hindu World,* ed. Sushil Mittal and Gene R. Thursby. 332–56. New York: Routledge.
McKean, Lise
1996   *Divine Enterprise: Gurus and the Hindu Nationalist Movement.* Chicago: University of Chicago Press.
McMahon, Felicia R. and Brian Sutton-Smith
1995   The Past in the Present: Theoretical Directions for Children's Folklore.

In *Children's Folklore: A Source Book*, ed. Brian Sutton-Smith, Jay Mechling, Thomas W. Johnson, and Felicia R. McMahon. New York: Garland.

Menon, Kalyani D.
2002   Dissonant Subjects: Women in the Hindu Nationalist Movement in India. Ph.D. dissertation, Department of Anthropology, Syracuse University.

Menon, Ritu and Kamla Bhasin
1998   *Borders and Boundaries: Women in India's Partition.* New Brunswick, N.J.: Rutgers University Press.

Mill, James
1972 [1817]   *The History of British India.* New Delhi: Associated Publishing.

Miller, Barbara Stoler
1977   *Love Song of the Dark Lord: Jayadeva's Gitagovinda.* New York: Columbia University Press.
1986   *The Bhagavad Gita: Krishna's Counsel in Time of War.* New York: Columbia University Press.

Ministry of Home Affairs
2001   Profiles by Main Religion, Christians. Census of India 2001, Census Data Online. http: //www.censusindia.net/religiondata/Summary%20Christians.pdf, vol. 2007.

Minor, Robert N.
1986   *Modern Indian Interpreters of the Bhagavagita.* Albany: State University of New York Press.

Mosse, George
1985   *Nationalism and Sexuality: Respectability and Abnormal Sexuality in Modern Europe.* New York: Fertig.

Narayan, Kirin
1989   *Storytellers, Saints, and Scoundrels: Folk Narrative in Hindu Religious Teaching.* Philadelphia: University of Pennsylvania Press.
1993   How Native Is a "Native" Anthropologist? *American Anthropologist* 95 (3): 671–86.

Narula, Smita
1999   India. Politics by Other Means: Attacks Against Christians in India. *Human Rights Watch* 11 (6): 1–37.

Nash, June and Juan Rojas
1992   *I Spent My Life in the Mines: The Story of Juan Rojas, Bolivian Tin Miner.* Ed. June Nash. New York: Columbia University Press.

Natarajan, Nalini
1994   Woman, Nation, and Narration in Midnight's Children. In *Scattered Hegemonies: Postmodernity and Transnational Feminist Practices*, ed. Inderpal Grewal and Caren Kaplan. Minneapolis: University of Minnesota Press.

Noorani, A. G.
2006   BJP's Second Childhood. *Frontline Magazine* 23 (8) (April 22–May 5), online edition.

Nordstrom, Carolyn
2004   *Shadows of War: Violence, Power, and International Profiteering in the Twenty-First Century.* Berkeley: University of California Press.

Nussbaum, Martha
2003   Genocide in Gujarat: The International Community Looks Away. *Dissent* 50 (3): 15–23.
2007   *The Clash Within: Democracy, Religious Violence, and India's Future.* Cambridge, Mass.: Belknap Press of Harvard University Press.

O'Hanlon, Rosalind
1985   *Caste, Conflict, and Ideology: Mahatma Jotirao Phule and Low Caste Protest in Nineteenth-Century Western India.* London: Cambridge University Press.
Oberoi, Harjot Singh
1992   *Construction of Religious Boundaries: Culture, Identity, and Diversity in the Sikh Tradition.* Chicago: University of Chicago Press.
Olivelle, Patrick, trans.
1998   *Upanishads.* New York: Oxford University Press.
Ong, Aihwa
2006   *Neoliberalism as Exception: Mutations in Citizenship and Sovereignty.* Durham, N.C.: Duke University Press.
Orme, Robert
1974 [1782]   *Historical Fragements of the Mogul Empire, of the Morattoes, and of the English Concerns in Indostan, from the Year M.DC.LIX.* New Delhi: Associated Publishing.
Pandey, Gyanendra
1990   *The Construction of Communalism in Colonial North India.* New Delhi: Oxford University Press.
1992   In Defence of the Fragment: Writing About Hindu-Muslim Riots in India Today. *Representations* 37 (Winter): 27–55.
Philip, A. J.
1999   The Missionary and the Paranoid: Who's Afraid of Conversion. *Indian Express*, New Delhi, 8.
Puri, Rajinder
2002   Bulls Eye. *Outlook Magazine*, August 26. http://www.outlookindia.com/bullseye.asp?fodname=20020826.
Radner, Joan Newton
1993   *Feminist Messages: Coding in Women's Folk Culture.* Urbana: University of Illinois Press.
Raheja, Gloria Goodwin
1994   Introduction: Gender Representation and the Problem of Language and Resistance in India. In *Listen to the Heron's Words: Reimagining Gender and Kinship in North India,* ed. Gloria Goodwin Raheja and Ann Grodzins Gold. 1–29. Berkeley: University of California Press.
Raheja, Gloria Goodwin and Ann Grodzins Gold, eds.
1994   *Listen to the Heron's Words: Reimagining Gender and Kinship in North India.* Berkeley: University of California Press.
Rajagopal, Arvind
2001   *Politics After Television: Hindu Nationalism and the Shaping of the Public in India.* Cambridge: Cambridge University Press.
Ranade, Mahadeo Govind
1900   *Rise of the Maratha Power.* Classics of Indian History and Economics. New Delhi: Publications Division, Ministry of Information and Broadcasting.
Ranganathananda, Swami
2001   *Universal Message of the Bhagavad Gita: An Exposition of the Gita in the Light of Modern Thought and Modern Needs.* Kolkata: Advaita Ashrama.
Rashtra Sevika Samiti
1999a   Matritva ka Aadarsh Jijamata. (The Model of Motherhood Jijamata). *Boudhik Pustak* (January, February, March 1999): 7–9. Uttaranchal: Rashtra Sevika Samiti.
1999b   Jijabai—Ek Vir Patni. (Jijabai—One Brave Wife). *Boudhik Pustak*: 13–14. Uttaranchal: Rashtra Sevika Samiti.

Rashtriya Swayamsevak Sangh
1999   *Sangh Utsav* (Sangh Festivals). New Delhi: Suruchi Prakashan.
Rithambara, Sadhvi
1999   'Ma' Shabd ka Ucharan se hi Hriday Main Vatsalya Umad Padti Hain"
        (Love Fills the Heart Just by Uttering the Word Mother). *Hindu Chetna*
        (September 1–15).
Robben, Antonius C. G. M
1995   The Politics of Truth and Emotion Among Victims and Perpetrators of
        Violence. In *Fieldwork Under Fire: Contemporary Studies of Violence and Sur-
        vival*, ed. Antonius C. G. M. Robben and Carolyn Nordstrom. 81–103.
        Berkeley: University of California Press.
Robben, Antonius C. G. M and Carolyn Nordstrom
1995   Introduction: The Anthropology and Ethnography of Violence and
        Sociopolitical Conflict. In *Fieldwork Under Fire: Contemporary Studies of Vio-
        lence and Survival*, ed. Antonius C. G. M. Robben and Carolyn Nord-
        strom. 1–23. Berkeley: University of California Press.
Rogers, Joann and Jacquelyn S. Litt
2004   Normalizing Racism: A Case Study of Motherhood in White Supremacy.
        In *Home-Grown Hate: Gender and Organized Racism*, ed. Abby L. Ferber.
        97–112. New York: Routledge.
Rosemblatt, Karin Alexandra
2000   *Gendered Compromises: Political Cultures and the State in Chile, 1920–1950.*
        Chapel Hill: University of North Carolina Press.
Sarkar, Jadunath
1955   *House of Shivaji.* Calcutta: Sarkar and Sons.
Sarkar, Tanika
1993   Women's Agency Within Authoritarian Communalism: The Rashtrasev-
        ika Samiti and Ramjanmabhoomi. In *Hindus and Others: The Question of
        Identity in India Today*, ed. Gyandendra Pandey. 24–45. New York:
        Viking.
1995   Heroic Women, Mother Goddesses: Family and Organisation in Hin-
        dutva Politics. In *Women and the Hindu Right: A Collection of Essays*, ed.
        Tanika Sarkar and Urvashi Butalia. 181–215. New Delhi: Kali for
        Women.
1998   Woman, Community, and Nation: A Historical Trajectory for Hindu
        Identity Politics. In *Resisting the Sacred and the Secular: Women's Activism
        and Politicized Religion in South Asia*, ed. Patricia Jeffery and Amrita Basu.
        89–104. New Delhi: Kali for Women.
2001   *Hindu Wife, Hindu Nation: Community, Religion and Cultural Nationalism.*
        New Delhi: Permanent Black.
2002   Semiotics of Terror: Muslim Children and Women in Hindu Rashtra.
        Economic and Political Weekly 37 (28), July 13, 2002.
Sarkar, Sumit
1999   Conversions and Politics of the Hindu Right. *Economic and Political Weekly*
        34 (26), June 26, 1999.
2002   *Beyond Nationalist Frames: Postmodernism, Hindu Fundamentalism, History.*
        Bloomington: Indiana University Press.
Savarkar, Vinayak Damodar
1971   *Six Glorious Epochs of Indian History.* New Delhi: Rajdhani Granthagar.
Scheper-Hughes, Nancy
1995   The Primacy of the Ethical: Propositions for a Militant Anthropology.
        Current Anthropology 36 (3): 409–20.

Schwartzman, Helen B.
1995   Representing Children's Play: Anthropologists at Work. In *The Future of Play Theory: A Multidisciplinary Inquiry into the Contributions of Brian Sutton-Smith*, ed. Anthony D. Pellegrini. 242–56. Albany: State University of New York Press.

Scott, James
1990   *Domination and the Arts of Resistance: Hidden Transcripts*. New Haven, Conn.: Yale University Press.

Sen, Sudipta
n.d.   On the Autonomy of History: Imperial and Early National Histories in British-India and the Struggle for an Indian Past. Manuscript.

Shourie, Arun
1994   *Missionaries in India: Continuities, Changes, Dilemmas*. New Delhi: ASA.

Sinclair-Brull, Wendy
1997   *Female Ascetics: Hierarchy and Purity in an Indian Religious Movement*. Richmond, Surrey: Curzon Press.

Singer, Milton B.
1966   The Radha-Krishna Bhajanas of Madras City. In *Krishna: Myths, Rites, and Attitudes*, ed. Milton B. Singer. Honolulu: East-West Center Press.

Singh, Andrea M.
1976   *Neighbourhood and Social Networks in Urban India*. New Delhi: Marwah Press.

Singh, Rajendra
1993   *Ayodhya Episode: A Turning Point*. New Delhi: Suruchi Prakashan.

Sluka, Jeffrey A.
1999   Introduction: State Terror and Anthropology. In *Death Squad: The Anthropology of State Terror*, ed. Jeffrey A. Sluka. 1–45. Ethnography of Political Violence. Philadelphia: University of Pennsylvania Press.

Smith, Vincent
1919   *Oxford History of India*. Oxford: Oxford University Press.

Snow, David A, E. Burke Rochford, Jr., Steven K. Worden, and Robert D. Benford
1986   Frame Alignment Processes, Micromobilization, and Movement Participation. *American Sociological Review* 51 (August): 464–81.

Spear, Percival
1978   *A History of India*. 2 vols. London: Penguin.

Srinivas, Mysore Narasimhachar
1952   *Religion and Society Among the Coorgs of South India*. London: Asia Publishing House.

Staal, Frits
1983   *Agni: The Vedic Ritual of the Fire Altar*. Berkeley, Calif.: Asian Humanities Press.

Starn, Orin
1994   Rethinking the Politics of Anthropology: The Case of the Andes. *Current Anthropology* 35 (1): 13–38.

Stern, Jessica
2003   *Terror in the Name of God: Why Religious Militants Kill*. New York, N.Y.: Ecco.

Stoller, Paul
1994   Embodying Colonial Memories. *American Anthropologist* 96 (3): 634–48.

Sturken, Marita

1997   *Tangled Memories: The Vietnam War, the AIDS Epidemic, and the Politics of Remembering.* Berkeley: University of California Press.

Sunder Rajan, Rajeswari
2003   *The Scandal of the State: Women, Law, and Citizenship in Postcolonial India.* Durham, N.C.: Duke University Press.

Sutton-Smith, Brian
1995   Conclusion: The Persuasive Rhetorics of Play. In *The Future of Play Theory: A Multidisciplinary Inquiry into the Contributions of Brian Sutton-Smith,* ed. Anthony D. Pellegrini. 275–96. Albany: State University of New York Press.
1997   *The Ambiguity of Play.* Cambridge, Mass.: Harvard University Press.
2001   Emotional Breaches in Play and Narrative. In *Children in Play, Story, and School,* ed. Artin Goncu and Elisa L. Klein. 161–76. New York: Guildford.

Swedenberg, Ted
1995   *Memories of Revolt: The 1936–1939 Rebellion and the Palestinian National Past.* Minneapolis: University of Minnesota Press.

Taussig, Michael
1987   *Shamanism, Colonialism, and the Wild Man: A Study of Terror and Healing.* Chicago: University of Chicago Press.
1992   Violence and Resistance in the Americas: The Legacy of Conquest. In Michael Taussig, *The Nervous System.* 37–52. New York: Routledge.

Tharu, Susie and Tejaswini Niranjana
1999   Problems for a Contemporary Theory of Gender. In *Gender and Politics in India,* ed. Nivedita Menon. New Delhi: Oxford University Press.

Tod, James
1971   *Annals and Antiquities of Rajashtan or the Central and Western States of India.* New Delhi: KMN.

Turner, Victor
1969   *The Ritual Process: Structure and Anti-Structure.* Chicago: Aldine.
1975   Ritual as Communication and Potency: An Ndembu Case Study. In *Symbols and Society: Essays on Belief Systems in Action,* ed. Carole E. Hill. Southern Anthropological Society 9. Athens: University of Georgia Press.
1982   *From Ritual to Theatre: The Human Seriousness of Play.* New York: Performing Arts Journals Publications.

Vajpayee, Atal Behari
2002   Who Are These People Accusing Us, India Was Secular Even Before Muslims and Christians. English translation of speech delivered in Goa on April 12, 2002. *Indian Express,* New Delhi.

van der Veer, Peter
1994   *Religious Nationalism: Hindus and Muslims in India.* Berkeley: University of California Press.
1995   Introduction. In *Conversion to Modernities: The Globalization of Christianity,* ed. Peter van der Veer. 1–21. New York: Routledge.
1999   Monumental Texts: The Critical Edition of India's National Heritage. In *Invoking the Past: The Uses of History in South Asia,* ed. Daud Ali. 34–55. New Delhi: Oxford University Press.
2002   Religion in South Asia. *Annual Review of Anthropology* 31: 173–87.

Vanaik, Achin
1990   *The Painful Transition: Bourgeouis Democracy in India.* London: Verso.

Varshney, Ashutosh
2003   *Ethnic Conflict and Civic Life: Hindus and Muslims in India.* New Haven, Conn.: Yale University Press.

Viswanathan, Gauri
1996   *Outside the Fold: Conversion, Modernity, and Belief.* Princeton, N.J.:
        Princeton University Press.
Visweswaran, Kamala
1994   *Fictions of Feminist Ethnography.* Minneapolis: University of Minnesota
        Press.
Von Herder, Johann Gottfried
1995   Reflections on the Philosophy of the History of Mankind. In *The Nation-
        alism Reader,* ed. Omar Dahbour and Micheline Ishay. 48–59. Atlantic
        Highlands, N.J.: Humanity Books.
Wadhwa, Justice D. P.
1999   *Justice D. P. Wadhwa Commission of Inquiry: Report.* New Delhi: Justice Wad-
        hwa Commission of Inquiry.
Wadley, Susan S.
n.d.   A Woman's Balua and a Men's Kirtan: Enacting Honor, Community,
        and Gender in Cultural Performances in Rural North India. Manuscript.
1991   Why Does Ram Swarup Sing? Song and Speech in the North Indian Epic
        Dhola. In *Gender, Genre, and Power in South Asian Expressive Traditions,* ed.
        Arjun Appadurai, Frank J. Koram, and Margaret A. Mills. 201–23. Phila-
        delphia: University of Pennsylvania Press.
1994   *Struggling with Destiny in Karimpur, 1925–1984.* Berkeley: University of
        California Press.
1995   No Longer a Wife: Widows in Rural North India. In *From the Margins of
        Hindu Marriage: Essays on Gender, Religion, and Culture,* ed. Lindsey Har-
        lan and Paul B. Courtright. New York: Oxford University Press.
2005   *Raja Nal and the Goddess: The North Indian Epic Dhola in Performance.*
        Bloomington: Indiana University Press.
Warren, Kay B.
1999   Death Squads and Wider Complicities: Dilemmas for the Anthropology
        of Violence. In *Death Squad: The Anthropology of State Terror,* ed. Jeffrey A.
        Sluka. 226–47. Ethnography of Political Violence. Philadelphia: Univer-
        sity of Pennsylvania Press.
Werbner, Pnina
1999   Political Motherhood and the Feminisation of Citizenship: Women's
        Activisms and the Transformation of the Public Sphere. In *Women, Citi-
        zenship and Difference,* ed. Nira Yuval-Davis and Pnina Werbner. Pp. 221–
        45. London: Zed Books.
Wikan, Unni
1990   *Managing Turbulent Hearts: A Balinese Formula for Living.* Chicago: Univer-
        sity of Chicago Press.
Williams, Raymond
1977   *Marxism and Literature.* Oxford: Oxford University Press.
Williams, Brackette F.
1991   *Stains on my Name, War in my Veins: Guyana and the Politics of Cultural Strug-
        gle.* Durham, N.C.: Duke University Press.
1996   Introduction: Mannish Women and Gender After the Act. In *Women Out
        of Place: The Gender of Agency and the Race of Nationality,* ed. Brackette F.
        Williams. 1–33. New York: Routledge.
Yuval-Davis, Nira
1997   *Gender and Nation.* London: Sage.
Yuval-Davis, Nira and Floya Anthias
1989   *Woman-Nation-State.* New York: Macmillan.

Yuval-Davis, Nira and Pnina Werbner, eds.
1999   *Women, Citizenship and Difference.* London: Zed Books.

Newspaper Articles

Times of India
1998   Central Team to Submit Report on Dangs Today. *Times of India*, December 31, 1998.
1998   Attacks on Christians signals VHP-BJP Rift. *Times of India*, December 30, 1998.
1998   Dangs Tribals Snared in communal Tussle. *Times of India*, December 31, 1998.
1998   More Attacks of Churches, Schools in Gujarat. *Times of India*, December 28, 1998.
1998   Attack on 4 More Churches in Gujarat. *Times of India*, December 29, 1998.
1999   Four Missionaries attacked in Allahabad. *Times of India*, January 26, 1999.
1999   Killings a Monumental Aberration: Narayanan. *Times of India*, January 25, 1999.
1999   Archbishop condemns missionary's murder. *Times of India*, January 25, 1999.
Indian Express
1998   Staines, Son's were shot First. *Indian Express*, February 28, 1999.
1999   Newsline. Indian Express, November 5, 1999.
1999   Sangh's reconversion mela fizzes out. *Indian Express*, February 15, 1999.
Hindustan Times
1999   Neo-Christians to resist re-conversion. *Hindustan Times*, January 16, 1999.
British Broadcasting Company News
2002   Doubts over Gujarat Train Attack. South Asia: BBC News.

Films

Ram ke Nam. Director Anand Patwardhan. New York: First Run Icarus Films. 1992.
Final Solution. Director: Rakesh Sharma. India: Rakesh Sharma Films. 2004.
Altar of Fire. Directors: Robert Gardner and Fritz Staal. Film Study Center, Harvard University. 1976.
Fire. Director: Deepa Mehta. New York: New Yorker Video. 2000.

Index

Abu-Lughod, Lila, 184, 192
Adivasi, 59, 66, 76; conversion of, 65, 70; schools for, 63. *See also* Tribal
Advani, Lal Krishna, 100, 101; visit to Pakistan, 18–120
Akbar, 40–42, 44, 145–46, 186–87
Akhand Bharat, 92–93, 185
Alter, Joseph, 143, 148
Anderson, Benedict, 15, 33
Appadurai, Arjun: on cricket, 149; on violence, 13, 55, 78
Arya Samaj, 57, 65
Asad, Talal, 24; inseparability of religion and politics, 93, 102, 124
Ayodhya, 99–100, 190. *See also* Babri Masjid

Babri Masjid, 2, 18, 58, 70; idols in, 190; renouncers and, 83, 99–101. *See also* Ramjanmabhumi
Babur, 2
Bacchetta, Paola, 38, 41, 171; on divergent perspectives in movement, 164; on right-wing movements, 10
Bajrang Dal, 54, 66
Balvadi, 116–17. *See also* Schools
Bangladesh, 93
Basu, Amrita, 91, 163; on diverging tendencies in BJP, 15; on recruiting tactics, 98; on renouncers, 52, 99; on Roop Kanwar, 140
Baudhik, 131, 137–41, 154. See also *Shakha*
Bhagavad Gita, 86–88, 127–28, 189; Rithambara's use of, 92, 96–97; Sadhvi Shiva Saraswati's use of, 94–96; and *stri dharma*, 120
Bhagwa Dhwaj, 30–31, 185
Bhajan, 56; *mandali*, 119–21, 143
Bhakti, 119–20; to Ram, 59, 175. *See also* Devotion
Bharat Mata, 10–11, 58, 88–89, 124–25; defense of, 89–90, 145; narratives of violence against, 68, 83, 84; widows and, 127; women as daughters of, 166, 167
Bharati, Kamlesh, 88–89, 189
Bharati, Uma, 83
Bharatiya Janata Party, 3, 6; Advani and, 18–19; and cooperation with Samiti, 32; and Dara Singh, 54; diverging perspectives in, 15; and elections, 84, 128, 177, 191; and Gujarat violence, 66, 130; as leader of coalition government, 103, 129, 139; and reservations, 165, 178, 192; and VHP events, 123. *See also* Mahila Morcha
Bhavani, goddess 49, 152. *See also* Goddess
Bollywood, 159; depictions of Christian women, 71; male actors in, 135; songs from, 143–44
Brahman, 85, 188
Brahmins, 23; and fire sacrifice, 124; Maharashtrian, 49; protection of, 34, 46; RSS and, 175; thread ceremony, 115. *See also* Caste
British, 12; and cricket, 149; imaging of India, 11; missionaries, 57; and Queen of Jhansi, 163. *See also* Orientalism
Buddhists, 124
Butler, Judith, 18, 73–74, 124–25, 132, 169; on dissonance, 158–59

Caste: appeals to members of lower, 33; attempts to transcend, 11, 15, 110, 115, 124; and *bhakti* movements, 120; critique of, 64, 139; and democratic politics, 75; discrimination, 58, 177–78; groups dominant in Hindu nationalism, 2; marrying within, 173–74; of my interlocutors, 23, 168; Rajput, 42, 146; transgressing Hindu nationalist prescriptions on, 175–78; violence of upper, 76
Chati, Usha, 29–30, 185. *See also* Rashtra Sevika Samiti

Class, 8, 160; class-based attitudes to poor, 62, 71, 115–18, 149, 192; and consumption, 176–77; and distinction, 116; divisions, 109; and Hindu nationalism, 110, 175; middle, 107, 153, 173; of my interlocutors, 23, 168; and normative Indian subjectivity, 74

China, 77

Christians, 54–79; and collective memory, 70; critique of Hindu nationalist portrayals of, 154; cultural threat of, 137, 140–41; and Goan Inquisition, 69; and morality, 66–73, 161; and national security, 74–77, 138; right-wing, 183; violence against, 3, 13, 54–55, 66, 187–88; and Wadhwa Commission Report, 54; women, 70–73. *See also* Missionaries

Christianity, 54–79; and national security, 77; threat of, 140–41; Mary, 71, 140; Jesus, 63, 71. *See also* Conversion

Chamar, 177–78. *See also* Dalit.

Chatterjee, Partha, 12, 113, 184

Chinmayananda, Swami, 86

Chudala, Queen, 189

Citizenship, 113, 122; motherhood and, 6–7, 46, 164

Colonialism, 11–12; conversion as, 70; and Orientalism, 38; reactions of Hindus to, 37, 41, 57–58; representations of, 88, 112

Comaroff, Jean and John Comaroff, 16, 129

Communal, 37–38; violence, 42, 184

Communitas, 153. *See also* Turner, Victor

Congress Party, 178, 192

Construction of community, 64, 78; patrilineal ideology and, 45; religion and, 115, 124, 143; violence and, 2

Conversion, 54–70, 140; and national security, 74–77, 112; and reconversion, 55, 59, 65–66. *See also* Christians

Culture, 67–68, 100; and class, 192; destruction of, 22, 55, 192; Hindu, 12, 37, 112; national, 77, 78, 114, 124, 138–39, 147; national security and, 137–38; as an open field, 15–16, 158; spatializing of, 60, 74, 93. *See also* Women

Dalit, 32, 64, 185. See also *Chamar*

Das, Veena, 13, 27, 31

Delhi, 20–21; Development Authority

housing, 23, 168; elections in, 177–78, 191; poor in, 105–18

Devotion, 89, 95–97, 128; women and, 119–20, 162. See also *Bhakti*

Devi Mahatmaya, 45, 166

Dharma, 11, 80–104; Kargil War and, 92, 96, 123, 127; Hindu, 139, 147; *stri*, 120, 146, 161–63, 171

Discipline, 30, 106, 109, 118; of dissonant subjects, 18–20, 74, 136, 142–14, 158; *shakhas* and, 148–49, 152

Dissonance, 2–3, 5–6, 17–20; Hindu nationalist women and, 73–74, 102–3, 158–59, 167–82; Samiti and, 141–42; silencing of, 20, 130, 141–42. *See also* Discipline

Diversity, 138, 179; and dissonance, 3, 132, 142, 167–68; of perspectives within movement, 10, 15–17, 50–51, 181; recruiting support amid, 5, 14, 20, 106, 114. *See also* Pluralism

Douglas, Mary, 72

Dowry, 139, 172, 176; and conversion, 65

Durga, goddess, 88–89, 145–46, 187; Jijabai as, 44–45; members of Durga Vahini as, 166–67. *See also* Goddess

Durga Vahini, 4, 9, 64, 65, 154, 157, 166, 191. *See also* Vishwa Hindu Parishad

Electoral politics, 104, 128, 175–78, 191; numbers and, 75

Everyday life, 17, 39, 51, 82, 129; acts in, 3, 5, 31, 175; complexities of, 14, 159, 168; history in, 26–53; nationalism in, 10–14, 23, 29; religion in, 80–104, 119–28, violence in, 13, 27

Expansionary strategies, 5, 19–20, 25, 156, 159, 181; and constructions of history, 26–53; and discourses of national security, 54–79; and gender, 6–9, 12, 50–52, 55, 98, 110, 183; and religion, 80–104; and social work, 105–30

Family, 1, 30, 43–47; and nation, 7, 46–47, 160–63; women's roles in, 9, 95, 120, 171–74

Femininity, 189; and constructions of men, 12

Feminist, 20, 24; anthropology, 102, 185, 192, ethnography, 17, 24; Hindu nationalist views of, 9

Fernandes, Leela, 116, 139, 176

Fieldwork, 20–25, 30
Foucault, Michel, 106, 109, 184

Games, 142–44, 148, 153–55; *antakshri*, 143–44, 191; *Jai* Shivaji, 151–52; *kisan aur lomdi*, 150; *murgi*, 149; number, 151; tanks, 150; *tota aur pinjra*, 150
Gandhi, Indira, 190
Gandhi, Mohandas Karamchand, 87, 160
Gandhi, Rajiv, 183
Gayatri mantra, 114–15, 118, 125. *See also* Veda
Gender, 6–10, 12; and citizenship, 164; constructions of, 83, 90; and history, 12, 27; Judith Butler on, 18; and nation, 12, 27, 42, 50–52, 127; norms, 41, 72–73, 120; renouncers and, 89–91, 189. *See also* Expansionary strategies
Gitagovinda, 96
Gossip, 41, 73, 102, 135, 174, 180
Goddess, 88–89, 187; Bhavani, 46, 49, 151–52; defeat of Mahisasura by, 1, 158; Hindus as children of, 11, 124–25; Hindu nationalist women as, 45, 127, 146, 166. *See also* Bharat Mata
Gold, Ann Grodzins, 185, 190; and Gujar, 185–86; Raheja and, 102, 192
Golwalkar, M. S., 34
Governmentality, 106, 113; transnational, 106, 111
Gujarat, 64, 65, 188; anti-Christian violence, 54, 66, 78, 187; pogrom, 3, 12, 26–27, 42, 51, 130
Gurudakshina utsav, 30–31

Hall, Stuart, 18, 147
Hansen, Thomas Blom, 129–30, 183; on diversification as a strategy, 15; on sanskritization, 66
Hanuman, 65, 101, 190
Health care, 105–6; pre-natal, 107–11; and Seva Bharati, 112, 119
Hefner, Robert, 14; on conversion, 55
Hegdewar, K. B., 29, 34
Hegemony, 15–17, 129, 184; limits of, 73
Hierarchy, 22–23; caste, 66, 176, 177–78; challenge to, 120, 153–54, 191; class, 117–18; and reinforcement of, 107, 109, 119; Samiti and, 30, 144, 148, 155–56
Hinduism, 166–67; contesting constructions of, 141; and conversion, 55, 62–63, 65; defense of, 83, 100; denigration of,

68; forcible conversions to, 37, 66; nationalist, 57, 61, 66–67, 82, 97, 103, 107, 114, 121, 123, 140; orthodox, 47, 59, 81, 85, 146; as primordial essence, 58, 55, 59, 67; reform of, 57–58; Vedic, 57, 112, 188
Hindutva, 140, 183
History, 12, 26–53; of Christians, 59, 69, 78; and folklore, 43, 93, 145, 186; and memory, 38, 43, 70, 186, 188; personalization of, 43. *See also* Partition
Holkar, Ahilyabai, 35

Identity, 55; communitas and, 153; construction of pan-Hindu, 15, 115, 124–25, 175–78; national subjectivity and religious, 74, 127
Ideology, 14–20, 73–74, 132; of Hindu womanhood, 157–69; *pativrata*, 120; and pluralism, 15–17, 51, 179. *See also* Dissonance
India: as a Hindu nation, 3, 11, 15, 56–61; pluralism in urban, 175, 181; undivided, 92. *See also* Bharat Mata
Islam, 3; conversions to, 26. 57, 140; as a foreign religion, 58, 60, 141; radical, 185

Jainism, 80, 124
Jijabai, 26–53. *See also* Shivaji
Jinnah, Mohammad Ali, 91, 189
Juergensmeyer, Mark, 78, 84, 93

Kali, 88–89, 187. *See also* Goddess
Kanwar, Roop, 139–40. See also *Sati*
Kargil War, 83–84; as a battle against immorality, 84, 92; capitalizing on, 122–28, 191; Rithambara on, 90–92, 96–98. *See also* Martyrs
Kashmir, 84, 91; militancy in, 3, 26, 56
Kelkar, Lakshmibai, 29–31, 36. *See also* Rashtra Sevika Samiti
Khalistan, 75. *See also* Sikh
Khan, Afzal, 47–49
Khilji, Ala-ud-din, 43
Kinship, 7, 45, 161, 187. *See also* Family
Krishna, 96; counsel in the Bhagavad Gita, 87–88, 92, 120, 189; use of imagery of, 126–28. *See also* Bhagavad Gita

Laclau, Ernesto and Chantal Mouffe, 17–18, 132, 169

Lamb, Sarah, 100, 169
Lectures, 116, 119; religious, 82, 98; at Samiti training camp, 35, 137–41, 145. *See also* Speech
Liberation. *See* Moksha
Liberation Tigers of Tamil Eelam (LTTE), 183

Mahabharatha, 86, 92, 93; Jijabai and, 46; Shivaji and, 187; story of Madri in, 140. *See also* Bhagavad Gita
Maharashtra, 48–49, 185. *See also* Shivaji
Maratha, 34–35, 44–45, 187; nationalism, 49. *See also* Shivaji
Mahila Morcha, 5, 9, 126, 165. *See also* Bharatiya Janata Party
Mahmood, Cynthia Keppley, 93, 185
Martyrs, 84, 92, 97, 124, 126–27. *See also* Sacrifice
Masculinity, 37, 125, 184; Muslim, 41; and violence, 12–13, 37. *See also* Gender
Matri Shakti, 9, 43, 62, 157, 161, 191. *See also* Vishwa Hindu Parishad
Menon, Ritu and Kamala Bhasin, 42, 111
Militancy, 3, 26, 93
Missionaries, 54–79, 138, 140, 187. *See also* Christians
Modernity, 14; and Hindu reform, 59; Indian, 15, 18, 159, 181–82; technologies, 57
Moksha, 81, 85, 87, 96
Morality, 102, 145–47; of Christians, 70–73; and cosmic war, 84, 93; goddess and, 187; and immorality, 45, 123; of Muslims, 2, 41; women and, 160–61, 181
Motherhood: and agency, 27, 52, 163; and citizenship, 7, 164; enlightened, 35, 45–47; and forgiveness, 146; and sacrifice, 90; and women's roles in Hindu nationalism, 6, 17, 166, 171
Musharraf, Pervez, 189. *See also* Pakistan
Muslims: and despotism, 38, 186; divided loyalties of, 74; Hindu nationalist histories of, 36–53, 145; as originally Hindu, 66–67; as "other," 10, 11, 38, 52, 85; and veiling, 28, 39, 41; vilification of, 137–40, 166; violence against, 3, 12, 26–27; and women, 28–29, 35

Nation, 15, 58–60, 93; construction of, 16, 113, 122–25, 143, 175; and culture, 77, 78, 138–39; gender and, 6–10, 12, 27, 42, 50–52, 89–90, 127, 164; and invented traditions, 113, 124, 139; self-other discourses of, 10–12, use of religion to construct, 11, 16, 58, 60, 85, 88–89, 114–15, 123–25, 129. *See also* Culture
Nehru, Jawaharlal, 106, 186
Neoliberalism, 105, 111, 129
Nizam of Hyderabad, 40, 186
Norms, 2–3, 72–74, 135, 136, 138, 144, 147, 169; history and, 26–53; and normative constructions, 5, 6–8, 14–20, 78, 102, 127, 141–42, 157–64. *See also* Transgression
Northeast India, 75–78, 188

Orientalism, 11–12, 37–38, 186

Pakistan, 163; Advani's visit to, 18; movement to create, 74–75; war with, 30, 56, 83–84, 91–93, 123. *See also* Jinnah
Partition, 43–44, 74, 91, 163
Pativrata, 120, 127; Rani Padmini as, 43; Sita as, 62, 158, 171; Savitri as, 146
Patriotism, 27; and duty, 89–91, 137–38; Jijabai and, 47; of RSS, 1; violence and, 54, 56
Performative, 18, 73, 125
Play, 142–55
Poverty: 129; Christians capitalizing on, 62–64; and Sewa Bharati, 5, 111–22; VHP and, 105–11
Power, 66; disciplinary, 106, 109; disparities in, 22–23; hegemonic, 16, 18, 129; inseparability of religion and, 101–2; play and, 143, 153; regulatory, 18, 106, 109, 169; of renouncers, 83, 99; women's, 7, 9, 46–47, 160, 166
Prayers, 58, 89, 123; as ways to construct community, 114–15, 124; as ways to renew hegemony, 16, 147
Pluralism, 76, 179; within Hindu nationalism, 5, 15–17, 51, 130
Pracharak, 133, 136; and conversions to Christianity, 75
Pracharika, 13, 63, 133; lectures of, 35, 139

Race, 68; and citizenship, 164; and nationalism, 184; and territory, 60, 67
Rajputs, 34, 40–43, 146

Rani Padmini, 42–43

Rama, 1, 61–62, 147; *rajya*, 95; and Shabari, 58–59; wife Sita, 146. *See also* Ramjanmabhumi

Ramakrishna Mission, 86

Ramayana, 62, 123; dressing up as characters from, 121; Durga and, 187; Jijabai and, 46; and Sita, 146, 171

Ramjanmabhumi, 2, 83; temple, 1, 2, 83, 100–101, 183. *See also* Babri Masjid

Ranade, M. G., 49, 187

Ranganathananda, Swami, 86

Rani of Jhansi, 35, 163

Rashtra Sevika Samiti, 4, 112; camp, 131–56; constructions of history, 26–53; handbook, 162–63, 192; *pracharikas* in, 13, 63–64, 67; *pramukh sanchalika* of, 29, 185; prayers, 58, 124; and RSS, 15, 28; training in 13, 185–86; on women, 164, 166, 171. See also *Shakha*

Rashtriya Swayamsevak Sangh, 1, 4. 175, 183; Advani and, 18–19; and conversion, 63, 75; and diversification, 15; *ekal vidyalayas*, 8; flag, 30–31, 185; on Hinduism, 67; on politics, 101; and Samiti, 13, 28–29, 52; *sarsangchalak* of, 34, 67, 186; and Sewa Bharati, 112; *shakhas*, 148; and Shivaji, 34, 47–49. *See also* Sangh Parivar

Rath yatra, 68, 69, 175

Recruitment. *See* Expansionary strategies

Religion, 5; and conflict with Christians, 54–78; construction of Hindu unity, 112–15, 124–25, 147; and pluralism, 40; and politics, 24, 80–103; Shivaji and, 34, 37, 48; and territory, 3, 11

Renouncers, 80–104; lectures of, 82, 85, 92, 97–98, 102–3; passionate, 90–91, 103; as religious authorities, 82, 83, 97–99, 101–3; as women, 82, 83, 91, 189. *See also* Sadhvi Shakti Parishad

Renunciation, 80–88; classical theories of, 81, 85; modern, 81, 82, 86. *See also* Rithambara

Representation, 22, 169, 173

Reservations, 115, 175, 178; Mandal commission, 175; for women, 164–65, 167, 192

Right-wing movements, 10, 98; women in, 7, 183, 185

Riot, 13, 56. *See also* Violence

Rithambara, Sadhvi, 80–83; on Kargil 90–93, 96–97; at Kargil event, 125; orphans and, 110; power of, 98–99, 101; on women, 166–67. *See also* Renouncers

Ritual, 11, 16, 58, 89; *arti*, 60; of conversion, 65; fire sacrifice, 85, 123–25; and hegemony, 129; Muslim, 74; *rakhi*, 191; and the subject, 18, 113–14; symbols, 154; women's, 127. See also *Yajna*.

Romance, 73, 102, 174; unacceptable, 180

Sacrifice, 125–28; action as, 87; female, 43, 90, 120, 146, 162; and Indian independence, 96; male, 90; of soldiers, 92–93; Vedic, 85, 188. See also *Yajna*

Sadhvi Shakti Parishad, 80, 83; head of, 88; goal of, 92, 100

Samsara, 85, 99; liberation from, 81, 87, 96

Sangh Parivar, 3, 15, 69, 112. *See also* Rashtriya Swayamsevak Sangh

Sanskrit, 97, 123

Sanskritization, 66

Saraswati, Sadhvi Shiva, 94–97

Saraswati, Swami Dayanand, 71

Sarkar, Sumit, 64, 66

Sarkar, Tanika, 46, 89, 162; on Rithambara, 90, 100

Sati, 57, 139–40, 141. *See also* Kanwar, Roop

Savarkar, V. D., 12, 37, 186; definition of Hindu, 67

Schools, 111–23; women teachers in, 8–9; and hegemony, 129

Secularism, 31, 40, 99; and BJP government, 103, 128

Seva, 86, 138

Sewa Bharati, 5, 111–22, 183; and Christian conversion, 56, 63, 65, 70, 75. *See also* Sewing class

Sewing class, 29, 119. *See also* Sewa Bharati

Sex, 90, 174; Hinduism and, 140, 174

Sexuality, 17, 90, 135, 159–61; and Christian women, 72–74, 141; of Muslim men, 12, 37–38; and self-other discourses, 12; violating norms of, 174, 180

Shabari, 58–59; kumbh mela, 59. *See also* Ramayana

Shakha, 4, 29, 30–33; and ideological training, 6, 13, 67, 185; at training camp, 131–34, 140–42, 148–54. See also *Shivir*

Shakti, 9; of the goddess, 45, 166; of women, 88–89

Sharif, Nawaz, 84, 92, 189. *See also* Pakistan

Sharirik, 131, 148–55. See also *Shakha*
Shivaji, 27–28, 32–37, 42–50; game, 151–52; and Hindu epics, 187; and RSS flag, 185. *See also* Jijabai
Shivir, 35, 131–56. See also *Shakha*
Shuddhi. See Arya Samaj
Sikhs, 57; as part of Hindu nation, 113, 123–25; militancy 75, 93
Singh, Rajendra, 34, 67, 186. *See also* Rashtriya Swayamsevak Sangh
Sita, 123, 145–46, 158, 171; dressing up as, 121; story about, 61–62
Slums, 111–12, 119; dwellers, 105, 126, 190; schools in, 1, 63; 115–17; *shakha* in, 32; missionaries in, 70–71
Social work, 95, 105–30; views of Christian, 63–64, 140. *See also* Expansionary Strategies
Songs, 126, 131, 137, 143; as ways to reiterate ideology, 132, 146–47, 155. See also *Bhajan*
Speech, 10; Advani's, 184; anti-Christian, 57, 68; of religious renouncers, 80–103; Vajpayee's, 26; vilification of Muslims in, 28–29; as ways to renew hegemony, 16. *See also* Lectures
Staines, Graham, 54, 75, 187. *See also* Christians
Stories, 67, 101; constructions of the past in, 27–53, 145–46; Mahabharata, 86, 140; Rama, 58–59, 61–62. *See also* History
State, 76, 113; blurred boundaries of, 66, 103–4, 106–7, 111, 128–30; founding of Hindu, 49; hierarchy of, 109, 119; welfare, 105–6
Subjectivity, 2–3, 14–20, 72–74, 157–82; and governmentality, 106–7, 109; history and, 27–28, 34–53; reconversion and, 61; religion and, 122–25, 127–28; of renouncers, 91, 102–3; of researcher, 31; Samiti training camps and, 143, 146–49, 155–56; schools and, 112–17. *See also* Dissonance

Terrorism, 183; and terrorists, 75, 77
Training, 13, 110, 131–32; camps (see *Shivir*); values, 113; violent women, 149, 153; vocational, 5, 8, 106, 111, 119, 121. See also *Shakha*

Transgression, 2, 17, 135; Advani's, 19–20; and transgressive practices, 73, 157–82
Tribal, 55, 59, 66, 76; and Goan Inquisition, 68–69; women, 8. See also *Adivasi*
Turner, Victor, 124, 153–54; on play, 143

Untouchable, 177, 185. *See also* Dalit
Upanishad, 81, 85–86, 188; and Hindu reform, 57
Urban: *bhajan mandalis*, 120; context, 8, 30, 192; fieldwork 20; pluralism, 168, 175; poor (see Poverty); slums (see Slums). *See also* Delhi

Vajpayee, Atal Behari, 36, 84, 92, 98; on Gujarat pogrom, 26–27; on conversions, 54
Vanavasi, 59, 64. See also *Adivasi*
Varna, 23, 176. *See also* Caste
Veda, 85, 114–15, 123–24, 188; and Hindu reform, 57; and Vedic culture, 112. *See also* Hinduism
Violence, 12–13; anti-Christian, 54–55, 66, 69–70, 78, 187; anti-Muslim, 12, 26–27, 38, 51–52; and creation of community, 2, 78; and dharma, 90, 93, 148; in Gujarat pogrom, 26–27, 130; Hutu, 183; in northeast, 76–77; sexual, 12, 26, 27, 42, 54 88–89, 188; women and, 9, 36, 83–84, 155
Vishwa Hindu Parishad, 3–5, 7–9, 15; on caste, 177–79; on Christians, 54, 61–62, 71; constructions of history, 40, 43; and Kargil, 84, 122–26; and Ramjanmabhumi campaign, 2, 100–101; on reconversion, 59, 65–66; recruiting tactics, 98; and renouncers, 83, 86, 95; on *sati*, 139; and social work, 105–11; and training domestic servants, 8; women, 161–67, 170–74
Visweswaran, Kamala, 24, 160
Vivekananda, Swami, 86
Vocational Training. *See* Training; Sewing class

Wadley, Susan, 127, 187; on *bhajan mandalis*, 120–21
West, 22, 68–69; and national security, 77; and origin of RSS games, 148, 152; and separation of religion and politics, 24, 93

Westernization, 145, 161, 171; cultural threat of, 2, 61, 70–72, 137–39

Widows, 90; events to honor, 98, 106, 122–27; immolation of, 139; social work and, 111, 119. *See also* Sacrifice

Women, 6–10; as agents, 6, 16, 27, 28, 35, 36–37, 44, 46–47, 50–52, 83, 184, 189; and culture, 6, 15, 46, 50, 138–39, 165–66; and honor, 7, 41–42, 83, 89, 140, 160, 166–67, 173; as symbols, 7, 42, 72, 89, 162, 167; as victims, 13, 27, 35, 89; violence against, 12, 26–27, 36, 42–43, 54, 188

Yajna, 122–24. *See also* Sacrifice

Youth, 12, 54; training of, 4, 131–56

Yuval-Davis, Nira, 7, 122, 180; and Werbner, 164

Acknowledgments

My greatest debt is to the women and men in the various wings of the Hindu nationalist movement who were willing to share their busy lives with me and generously responded to my intrusive presence and constant questioning. It is with the realization that I would not have been as magnanimous in similar circumstances that I gratefully acknowledge their patience and generosity. There are several women who deserve more personal thanks; however, in the interest of protecting their identities, I will not mention them by name. I will simply say that this research would not have been possible without them.

I would like to thank the American Institute for Indian Studies (AIIS) for funding a year of fieldwork in Delhi with women in the Hindu nationalist movement. I would particularly like to thank Ms. Elyse Auerbach, Dr. Pradeep Mehendiratta, and Mrs. Purnima Mehta of AIIS for facilitating my research in Delhi. I would also like to thank the Mount Holyoke College Alumnae Association for providing funding for a preliminary research trip in 1997 through an Alumnae fellowship. I am also grateful to the Graduate School of Syracuse University for awarding me a Spring Research Grant in 1998, as well as the Maxwell School of Syracuse University for awarding two Roscoe Martin Grants. All these sources of support greatly eased the financial burden of conducting ethnographic research.

I have to acknowledge the generous contributions of several people to shaping this project over the years. Colleagues, editors, and friends have contributed ideas, given feedback, and shaped this project in ways too numerous to recount in these few pages. That said the errors and problems that remain are my own responsibility.

I am particularly grateful to mentors at Syracuse University for their guidance, support, and critique. I am very indebted to Susan Snow Wadley who is an amazing teacher and mentor. I cannot thank her enough for her astute comments, careful criticism, and unwavering support of my project over the years. Ann Grodzins Gold has also been unfailingly supportive of my work, and I am very grateful to her for her insightful, but always gently worded, criticism and the generosity with which she has given me her time and critical reflections at various stages of this project. I am very indebted to John Burdick for his close engagement with my work and his valuable suggestions for broadening its reach. Arlene Davila was a wonderful resource on nationalism and memory, and I am very grateful for her generous comments, support, and enthusiasm for this project. Sudipta Sen was an incredible resource on the history of modern India, who helped me situate some of the themes I examine here within broader historical frameworks. I would also like to thank Monisha Das Gupta and Christopher DeCorse for their insightful comments on my work.

The Five College Women's Studies Research Center at Mount Holyoke College provided generous financial support for writing through a Ford Associateship in 2003 as well as a venue to present pieces of this manuscript to a community of scholars. I am particularly grateful to Amrita Basu, who was the Director of the Center and read the entire manuscript while I was there. I am deeply indebted to her for comments on an early version of the manuscript, the generosity with which she shared her expertise on Hindu nationalist women, and her support of my project. Fellows at the Five College Women's Studies Research Center, faculty from the Five Colleges, and other scholars in the area also provided invaluable feedback during two presentations I delivered there. I am very grateful to them for their serious engagement with my work. I would particularly like to thank Srirupa Roy, Lalit Vachani, Sangeeta Kamat, Biju Matthew, Isis Nusair, and Andrew Lass for their feedback on the parts of this manuscript that they heard. I would also like to thank EB at the Five College Women's Studies Research Center for facilitating my time there with great efficiency and tremendous good cheer.

Many other scholars, colleagues, and friends have helped shape this project in various ways. Several scholars made time in their busy schedules to talk to me during research trips to Delhi in 1997 and in 1999. They listened to early formulations of my research with great patience and provided extremely useful feedback. I would particularly like to thank Ritu Menon, Kumkum Sangari, Vijay Prasad, and Mushirul Hasan for making time to meet me in Delhi. I am grateful to Srirupa Roy for introducing me to two individuals I spoke to in the early days of fieldwork. Other colleagues and friends have generously responded to queries and commented extensively on various versions of this manuscript. I would particularly like to thank Keri Olsen, Lisa Knight, Chaise LaDousa, Gayatri Reddy, John Karam, Amor Kohli, Shailja Sharma, Christopher Mount, Awanti Seth Rabenhoej, and Aditi Joshi for their helpful comments and for their support and friendship over the years. I am grateful to Aliya Latif for help with some of the pseudonyms and for instant email translations when I was stuck on a word or a phrase. I am